# HENRY'S TRIALS

# Henry's Trials

The Extraordinary History
of the Reverend Henry John Hatch

## Peter Maggs

Mirli Books

Published in the UK in 2009 by
Mirli Books Ltd,
PO Box 10528
Chelmsford CM1 9NP
www. mirlibooks.com

ISBN 978-0-9562870-0-7

A catalogue record for this book is available from the British Library

Cover Design by Gill England
Design and typesetting by Michael Shaw

Text set digitally in Sabon

Printed in Great Britain by the MPG Books Group, Bodmin and King's Lynn
via MBC Print Consultancy

This book is dedicated to the memory of Henry John Hatch, in the hope that he will at last have achieved some measure of the justice due to him by the telling of his story.

*Right cannot be where justice is not*

Cicero

# Acknowledgements

It is a pleasure to acknowledge the help and assistance of staff at the various archive and record offices consulted, particularly the British Library at King's Cross, the Newspaper Library at Colindale, the Surrey History Centre at Woking, and the Essex Record Office at Chelmsford. I am grateful to Claire Robey and Nicholas Maggs for finding details of Hatch v Hatch (1804) and the Hatch v Lewis actions in the legal archives, to staff at the Inner Temple Library for the Old Bailey record of Henry Hatch's trial, and to Roger Vaughan who supplied details of Henry John Hatch's time at Eton. Many thanks are due to Nicky Clarke for managing the production of the book, Michael Shaw for the layout and Gill England for the cover design. Diane Hardy did an excellent and most comprehensive job in proof reading, and Paul Robertson provided encouragement and made a number of very helpful contributions.

Lastly, I have to thank my long-suffering wife Jacky, who has not only done much proof reading and made many suggestions regarding style, content, and format, but has also endured a ménage à trois with the Reverend Henry John Hatch for the last three years.

# Contents

| | | |
|---|---|---|
| Introduction | | 9 |
| Dramatis Personae | | 14 |
| Chapter 1 | Hatchings | 19 |
| Chapter 2 | The Philanthropist | 51 |
| Chapter 3 | The Old Bailey | 85 |
| Chapter 4 | Newgate | 146 |
| Chapter 5 | Some Justice | 200 |
| Chapter 6 | Lewis, Lewis, Lewis… | 275 |
| Chapter 7 | The Essex Marshes | 337 |
| Epilogue | | 357 |
| Appendix 1 | Courts of Law in mid nineteenth century Britain | 373 |
| Appendix 2 | Pounds, Shillings and Pence | 376 |
| Appendix 3 | Family Trees | 377 |
| Sources | | 379 |
| Index | | 383 |

# Introduction

In the late spring of 1860, a trial took place in the Central Criminal Court in London that was described by *The Times* newspaper as, '...by common consent one of the most extraordinary that had ever been seen'. The defendant, a female child of twelve, was charged with wilful and corrupt perjury against a Church of England clergyman. The clergyman had brought the case against her from his prison cell in Newgate, where he had been serving a term of four years' hard labour. Henry John Hatch, late chaplain of Wandsworth Prison, had been convicted in the previous December of indecent assault against Mary Eugenia Plummer. Henry was found guilty of a similar offence against her seven year old sister Stephana Augusta Plummer. The prosecution case rested entirely on the verbal evidence of the two girls, partially corroborated by their mother. Even though there were several witnesses in court capable of refuting at least some of these charges, none were called, and the law as it stood forbade the defendant or his wife to give evidence. The defence case relied on character witnesses only. Henry John Hatch was found guilty. In the absence of a Court of Criminal Appeal, his only option for release was to gain a Royal Pardon. This, the Home Secretary decided, would only be granted following a successful action for perjury against his principal accuser.

I came upon this case entirely by accident. During the course of studies into the genealogy of my family, I was investigating the life of my great-great-great grandmother Ann Hatch. Ann was born in 1807 in Sutton in Surrey, and lived there for most of her life. Before she married my great-great-great grandfather, James Chilman, she had given birth to five illegitimate children – of whom some, all or none, may have been fathered by James. The parish records of Sutton state that Henry Hatch, rector of Sutton, christened the second of these children. Naturally, I was fascinated to know whether my Ann Hatch was related to rector Henry Hatch, since if she was, the circumstances would have been quite delicious. And it got better. Henry's brother, Thomas Hatch, was Lord of Sutton Manor.

Extensive investigation has, so far, shown that there is no family connection between my Ann Hatch and Henry Hatch. However in the course of the work, I uncovered a press report of the trial of Henry John Hatch, the nephew of the rector. I also came across some decidedly unsavoury doings among his relatives. Rector Henry Hatch was a scoundrel, and his father and uncle were swindlers. But Henry John Hatch was, in my estimation, a good and caring man, almost destroyed by a combination of circumstances and the British legal system. There is much of the Dickensian tragic hero about him, and something of the comic villain about Caroline Plummer, Mary Eugenia Plummer's mother. There are also parallels with *Bleak House* and the interminable Chancery case of Jarndyce v Jarndyce in Henry Hatch's life – published the year before he too brought an action in Chancery over a disputed will. There is the noble eight year old Lucy, an orphan whose surgeon-father died in the Crimea. Lucy, adopted by Henry and his wife, was described while giving evidence on Henry's behalf at the Old Bailey as, 'a remarkably interesting pretty child [who] gave her evidence in a very clear and straightforward manner'. Unlike most of the literature of Charles Dickens though, the heroes in this tale did not live particularly happily ever after, and the villains prospered and went largely unpunished. In particular, members of the legal profession and government who failed to get Henry justice got off scot-free.

There is much circumstantial evidence to suggest that Henry was well regarded by his many friends. Several of these were ready to put that friendship to the severest test in acting as character witnesses for him at his trial. Given the awful nature of the charges, a lot of people might have been chary of associating themselves with such matters. The fact that several clergymen and magistrates, a solicitor, an MP, and an army officer and his wife were willing, nevertheless, to vouch for Henry's character, speaks volumes for the trust they had in him.

This account is very much a personal view, and while I have tried to be balanced, it has been difficult not to take sides. It should also be understood that I have had no legal training. Quite possibly, my interpretation of some of Henry's legal entanglements is ill-informed, or simply incorrect. However, I take comfort from the proposition that Justice must be *seen* to be done, by which I understand that it must be seen to be 'Justice' by the informed man in the street. The reader must come to his or her own conclusion having read this account, but in my view Henry John Hatch received no real Justice at all.

Although not directly relevant to Henry's story, I have included an account of the Separate System of imprisonment which was implemented in full at the new Surrey House of Correction at Wandsworth Common. Henry would have had to embrace the 'Separate' philosophy, in which the prison chaplain played a key role. The Prison Act of 1877 swept it all away, although changes may well have occurred at Wandsworth before that date as the increase in the prison population forced cells to be shared once more. However, the extraordinary details of the Separate Prison System are worthy of record.

The narrative is factual, based where possible on primary sources. Information about Henry's life and family was built up from genealogical material in the public domain. Details of the trials and other legal actions have been taken from newspaper accounts, legal records, and material held in the British Library and the National Archives. Other material was gleaned from the county record offices of Surrey, Essex and Hampshire, and the Lambeth Palace Library. Reference books consulted for background material are listed. The Oxford Dictionary of National Biography (ODNB) has been used extensively for information on the more notable personalities who appear in these pages, and the Oxford English Dictionary (OED) has provided the meanings of some of the more obscure words. However, it should be noted that this story of Henry John Hatch and his trials and tribulations is not a rigorous *academic* study; rather, it is hoped, it is an accessible journalistic account of an extraordinary series of events. Therefore in the interests of an uninterrupted narrative, I have refrained from referencing material in the text with the exception of that required by copyright.

Of the court hearings detailed in these pages, three of them were reconstructed entirely from press reports – the magistrates' hearing, the case against Walters Freake Pratt and the trial of Eugenia Plummer. The accounts of the proceedings of Hatch v Lewis and the subsequent case for costs in Hatch v Lewis used contemporary legal notes as well as reports in the newspapers. The report of Henry John Hatch's trial occupied barely one column of newsprint, and most of the prosecution evidence was unprintable. However, a transcript of the court reporter's shorthand notes does exist in the British Library, and this has been reproduced – largely unedited – in the chapter on Henry's trial. The notes also provide an unedited copy of the letter sent by Thomas Plummer to the Bishop of Winchester. A number of the press reports reproduce, verbatim, what was said in court, while some reduce the remarks to the third person. In the interests of dramatic style, I have reconverted some of the third-person speeches back into the first person. There is a note in the text to indicate where this has been done. With the exception of the magistrates' hearing, the press reports do not indicate how Henry and Eugenia pleaded in their respective trials; it is assumed that they both pleaded Not Guilty.

Some of the evidence, particularly from Eugenia Plummer, does make uncomfortable reading. However, it is appropriate to reproduce it in order to illustrate the fact that at the height of Victorian prudery, when even piano legs could be supplied with frilly 'pantaloons', such explicit and disturbing details were, nevertheless, being discussed in open court. Further, it was suggested that the inability of the press to report more than the vaguest innuendo in respect of the alleged charges, contributed directly to the lack of public debate on the matter; a debate which could have led to Henry John Hatch being released far sooner than actually happened.

Any piece of writing involving even the simplest genealogy becomes difficult to follow, as the reader struggles to remember who is whose father, cousin, uncle etc, and how the various protagonists are related. I have sought to minimize this difficulty by providing family trees of both the Hatches and the Cliffes. In addition, there is a *Dramatis Personae* listing and identifying the main characters. Where there is an ambiguity in the narrative – between Henry John Hatch and his uncle Henry, or between Henry John's father Thomas Hatch, and his grandfather, also called Thomas Hatch – Henry John's uncle will be called 'Uncle Henry', and his grandfather will be called 'Thomas Hatch Senior'. The names of the two children who made accusations against Henry Hatch were Mary Eugenia Plummer and Stephana Augusta Plummer. Mary Eugenia was generally known as *Eugenia* but sometimes referred to as *Eugenie*; her sister was known as *Stephana*, sometimes called *Stephanie*. Unless quoting verbatim, their names in the text will be *Eugenia* and *Stephana*.

Wandsworth Prison was initially a 'House of Correction', used for custodial punishment and reform. The establishment at Horsemonger Lane, was known as the Surrey County Gaol or Prison. It was a holding area and place of execution. In practice, Houses of Correction were referred to, interchangeably, as either Gaols or Prisons, and that practice will be followed in this narrative. A brief account of the Victorian legal system, together with a description of pre-decimalization British currency and a list of references consulted are included in appendices.

Peter Maggs, August 2009

# Dramatis Personae of the Main Characters

### Henry John Hatch, his Family, Friends and Colleagues

| | |
|---|---|
| Henry John Hatch | HJH, First chaplain of Wandsworth Prison |
| Susannah Arnold/Cliffe | Mother of Cassandra Arnold and Margaretta Eleanora Cliffe |
| Mrs Esther Dillon | Mother of Essie Hatch |
| Ellen Farr | The Hatches' cook |
| Joseph Gegg | Deputy Chaplain of Wandsworth Prison |
| Anna Marie Ellen Hatch, née Birch | Mother of HJH |
| Cassandra Hatch, née Arnold | Wife of Giles Hatch, half-sister of Margaretta Eleanora Cliffe |
| Charles Hatch | Uncle Charles, uncle of HJH, Vicar of Fordingbridge, 1839 - 1878 |
| Essie Lucy Hatch, née Dillon | Wife of HJH |
| Giles Hatch | Great-Uncle of HJH, Rector of Sutton 1767 - 1800, husband of Cassandra Arnold |
| Henry Hatch | Uncle Henry, uncle of HJH, Rector of Sutton 1831 - 1858 |
| Lucy Harriet Hatch, née Buckler | Adopted daughter of HJH and Essie Hatch |
| Margaretta Eleanora Hatch, née Cliffe | Wife of Thomas Hatch senior, grandmother of HJH, half-sister of Cassandra Arnold |
| Thomas Hatch | Father of HJH, Vicar of Walton on Thames, 1816 - 1851 |

| | |
|---|---|
| Thomas Hatch, Senior | Father of Thomas, Charles and Henry Hatch, husband of Margaretta Eleanora Cliffe, grandfather of HJH; attorney at Windsor |
| Martha Howe | Lucy Hatch's governess |
| Richard Onslow | Governor of Wandsworth Prison |
| Mary Ann Reed | Servant of the Hatches |
| Edward Wise | Friend of HJH and Essie Hatch |

## Judges, Barristers and Solicitors

| | |
|---|---|
| Mr Gordon Allen | Prosecution barrister at Eugenia Plummer's trial |
| Baron Bramwell | Trial judge at HJH's trial and Hatch v Lewis hearings |
| Serjeant Ballantine | Main defence barrister at HJH's trial, and barrister at Walters Freake Pratt hearings |
| Sir Alexander Cockburn | Lord Chief Justice, presided at the hearings on Walters Freake Pratt |
| Baron Channell | Trial judge at Eugenia Plummer's trial and Hatch v Lewis hearings |
| Sir Charles Crompton | Judge at the Walters Freake Pratt hearings |
| Montague Chambers, QC | Prosecution barrister in Hatch v Lewis |
| Mr W Cooper | Prosecution barrister at HJH's trial; defence barrister at the Walters Freake Pratt hearings |
| Mr Gifford | Prosecution barrister at Eugenia Plummer's trial |
| Mr Richard Garth | Prosecution barrister at the Walters Freake Pratt hearings and Hatch v Lewis |

| | |
|---|---|
| Sir Hugh Hill | Judge at the Walters Freake Pratt hearings |
| Mr Holt | HJH's second solicitor |
| William Hitchcock | Agent of Walters Freake Pratt |
| Mr Humphries | London solicitor consulted on behalf of the Plummers |
| Edwin James, QC | HJH's senior prosecution barrister at the Walters Freake Pratt hearings and Eugenia Plummer's trial |
| Mr Justice Keating | Trial judge at Eugenia Plummer's trial |
| Frederick Henry Lewis | James Lewis' son, defence barrister at HJH's trial |
| George Lewis | Junior partner in Lewis & Lewis; James Lewis' son |
| George Lewis, Senior | Uncle George; Senior partner in Lewis & Lewis |
| James Lewis | Senior partner in Lewis & Lewis; HJH's first solicitor |
| Mr Lush, QC | Defence barrister in Hatch v Lewis |
| Mr Metcalfe | Prosecution barrister at HJH's trial |
| Mr Macaulay | Defence barrister at the Walters Freake Pratt hearings |
| Sir Samuel Martin | Judge at the Hatch v Lewis hearings, son-in-law of Sir Frederick Pollock |
| Mr Charles Pollock | Defence barrister in Hatch v Lewis, son of Sir Frederick Pollock |
| Sir Frederick Pollock | Lord Chief Baron, chief judge in the Hatch v Lewis hearings |
| James Pratt | The Plummers' solicitor, father and partner of Walters Freake Pratt |
| Walters Freake Pratt | The Plummers' solicitor |

| | |
|---|---|
| Mr Robinson | Defence barrister at HJH's trial |
| Serjeant Shee | Main defence barrister at Eugenia Plummer's trial and the Hatch v Lewis hearings |
| Sir William Wightman | Judge at the Walters Freake Pratt hearings |

## Others

| | |
|---|---|
| Mary Eugenia Plummer | Principal accuser of HJH, sister to Stephana |
| Stephana Augusta Plummer | Accuser of HJH, sister to Eugenia |
| Caroline Plummer née Taylor | Mother of Eugenia and Stephana, wife of Thomas Plummer |
| Thomas Plummer | Father of Eugenia and Stephana, husband of Caroline Plummer |
| John Thadeus Delane | Editor of The Times newspaper, 1841 – 1877 |
| John Gay | The Plummers' doctor |
| Sir George Cornewall Lewis | Home Secretary, 1859 – 1861 |
| Viscount Palmerston | Henry John Temple, 3rd Viscount Palmerston, Prime Minister, 1855 - 1858 and 1859 – 1865 |
| Thomas Smethurst | Pardoned convicted murderer and bigamist |
| Dr Charles Sumner | The Bishop of Winchester, 1827 – 1869 |

# Hatchings

In 1834, William Crawford, a member of the Society for the Improvement of Prison Discipline, published a survey of two prison systems in use in the USA where the idea of preventing contact between prisoners had found favour. Hardened criminals were unable to 'contaminate' first timers, and by stopping all other social intercourse the reforming influence of the prison chaplain was reinforced. Auburn Prison in New York operated the Silent System. Prisoners were kept in solitary confinement at night, and were allowed to work together during the day but in silence. The slightest communication by word or gesture was punished – the nature and severity of the physical punishment inflicted being at the discretion of the prison governor. The system that evolved at the Eastern State Penitentiary in Philadelphia became known as the Separate System. In the Separate System, solitary confinement at night was followed by daytime work done in the same cells. The inmates were hooded whenever they were outside their cells, the hoods – with eye-slits – preventing any possibility of recognition by other inmates; numbers on their uniforms were the prisoners' only identification.

The Silent System was adopted at the Coldbath Fields Prison in London in the same year as Crawford's report. It was cheaper to implement than the Separate System, but required considerable surveillance to prevent contact between the prisoners – 54 warders and 218 trustee prisoners to supervise 682 inmates. Its main disadvantage though, was that it was found to be virtually impossible to stop intercommunication by prisoners who developed sundry ways of overcoming the rules. It was therefore the Separate System that found favour in Britain. The Separate System was more expensive in the requirement of its buildings – the prisoners were required to work and sleep in their (separate) cells, which needed to be of sufficient size and have certain amenities. But it was much more effective in preventing communication between the inmates, and relied far less on surveillance, instead maximising the influence of the prison chaplain on prisoners otherwise virtually devoid of human contact. In 1835, the Separate System was promoted in the report of a committee of the House of Lords. The same report also recommended the appointment of prison inspectors, and the regularisation of prison rules and diets across all institutions.

Pentonville 'model prison', which opened in 1842, was the first prison purpose-built to the Separate System. Each prisoner was confined in his own cell, allowing no contact with the other prisoners. *The Times* newspaper railed against the idea of the Separate System, citing the real insanity that some prisoners would be driven to by solitary confinement. The prediction, made in 1841, was not idle invective. The statistics of lunacy in all prisons in England and Wales in the years 1842 to 1849, showed an incidence of 5.8 persons per 10,000 prisoners. At Pentonville over the same period, the rate of lunacy was 62 per 10,000, more than a factor of ten higher. The figures had to be viewed in context though. The total prison population included a large number of short confinements where lunacy would hardly have had time to develop. More importantly, in the first six years of its life Pentonville was used for prisoners prior to transportation. The inmates had to endure eighteen months of the Separate System in the certain knowledge that afterwards, they were to be sent to Australia leaving family and friends behind for the duration of their sentences – possibly forever. It is no wonder that some of them went mad. It is also entirely possible that even the prospect of Bedlam – the Bethlehem Hospital for the Insane – was less of a horror than banishment to the other side of the world. And with the state of knowledge of psychoanalysis in the mid nineteenth century, who could say for sure that a 'lunatic' was not shamming, using any excuse to stay in England.

At the general Quarter Sessions held at Reigate in 1845, a committee of Surrey magistrates was formed to consider the new system adopted at Pentonville and its possible application to Surrey. They were called upon to consider whether the Surrey County Gaol at Horsemonger Lane, or one or more of the Houses of Correction – at Guildford, Kingston and Brixton – could be profitably modified to the new system. There were generally two types of prison in use at the time. County gaols existed not for custodial punishment but as temporary holding areas. They held debtors in order to '...secure the debtor until the debt was paid...', prisoners on remand, and those awaiting execution or transportation. This was the function of Horsemonger Lane. Punishment by imprisonment for short terms was provided by the Houses of Correction. These institutions, known as 'Bridewells' in London, were set up initially to deal with vagrancy. The control of vagrants – Vagrant: 'Itinerant beggar, idle loafer or tramp' (OED) – was adjudged a serious problem. During Henry VIII's reign, vagrancy was punished with a whipping. A second offence resulted in cutting off part of the right ear; a third offence earned the death penalty. By the time of Elizabeth I, this was moderated to imprisonment in a House of Correction if the initial whipping, '...until his or her body be bloody', had not effected reform. Labour, subsequently Hard Labour, was required of the prisoners from 1611, in order to '...set the rogues to work...' This, together with some Christian instruction, was intended to reform the malefactors. From 1706, judges were allowed to hand out sentences of up to two years in a House of Correction.

The Surrey magistrates' committee reported in 1846; they concluded that the Separate System could not be introduced into the Surrey prisons without 'their entire reconstruction'. They did comment, however, that those prisons were in an unsatisfactory state; they did not conform to the recommendations of the prisons inspectors, nor even in some cases, to the law. They stated that in the not too distant future, either extensive alteration of the existing prisons would be needed, or a completely new prison based on the Separate principle would have to be built. They concluded by observing,

> ...the current system of discipline neither operates as a punishment nor as a means of reformation, [and] as far as we are able to judge, we are of the opinion that the separate system offers the means of a great improvement on both these points.

Having endorsed the Separate System, they finished by cautioning against the large capital expenditure needed before 'the experiments which are now in progress in other counties, have been more fully tested'.

Six months later, the situation had got worse. In Brixton prison, prisoners were sharing three or four to a cell, with each man having in some cases, no more than fifteen inches width to sleep. Among other things, overcrowding meant that contagious diseases spread uncontrollably. Another committee was hastily formed to address the problem. They reported the following January, estimating that there was a shortage of 440 prison cells in the county. If the Kingston House of Correction was closed, which they recommended, then that figure increased to 500. They concluded that a new house of correction holding 750 prisoners should be built, and the existing three at Guildford, Kingston, and Brixton, be closed.

The New Surrey House of Correction was duly authorized; it was built in just over two years at Wandsworth Common at a cost of £140,000. Henry Mayhew and John Binny were not impressed with the design:

> ...the exterior is...mean and ill proportioned to the last degree...the architecture of the outbuildings exhibits all the bad taste of Cockney-Italian villas, and none of the austere impressiveness that should belong to a building of a penal character...the central mass rising behind the stunted gateway is heavy even to clumsiness, and the whole aspect of the structure uncommanding as a Methodist college.

The final report of the committee of justices appointed to superintend the erection of the new House of Correction at Wandsworth Common was issued in 1852, before Mayhew and Binney's comments were published; much of what follows was extracted from it. The prison was opened in 1851 with accommodation for 708 prisoners, each in a single 'residential' cell, together with 24 reception cells, 22 punishment cells and 14 large rooms for 'misdemeanants of the first class', or 'in other respects improper objects for separate confinement'. Since there would inevitably be prisoners in the reception cells, punishment cells, infirmary, and the 'large rooms', the requirement for an establishment holding 750 prisoners was achieved. The accommodation blocks were built to the ground plan of a St Andrew's cross, with a central hall where the four wings came together. The plan allowed for the prison accommodation to be extended to 1000 prisoners, and a fifth wing was added a few years later. The Separate System was invoked to a fault. Prison uniform was worn, and the prisoners had a number painted on his or her uniform, with their cell number engraved on a brass disk worn in view. When outside their cells, women wore veils and men wore masks or hoods to obviate any communication between them. Exercise was taken with the prisoners – veiled or masked – marching in single file around the circumference of two circles in the prison yard: able-bodied on the outer (longer) path, weaker on the inner path, an appropriate distance being maintained between each prisoner. Contemporary pictures are reminiscent of Escher engravings, where grotesque creatures follow one another through nightmare landscapes.

Accommodation by the standards of the time was extremely good. The buildings were ventilated and heated, and the cells, thirteen feet long, seven feet wide and nine feet high, were each supplied with their own water closet complete with a piped water supply, and gas lighting. These were luxuries unknown in most households of the period. In lieu of a bed, a hammock, complete with sheets and blankets, was slung between hooks in the walls.

If the accommodation was innovative, then so was the realization of hard labour – most prison sentences including that courtesy extra. There were different methods available to the authorities. The treadwheel (or tread*mill* where the power generated was used for grinding material or some other useful purpose) had been in use in some places since the 1820s. It resembled a wide water-wheel. The inmates were required to climb up the paddles of the wheel which then turned beneath them. The work was arduous and very tiring, and treadwheels operated no machinery, being used simply to 'exercise' the prisoners.

The Surrey building committee decided that the treadwheel was not appropriate to the Separate System, since it would be impossible to prevent contact between the prisoners working on adjacent parts of the wheel. However, there was also a financial dimension. New treadwheels at Wandsworth would cost around £18 per head to install. Moving the treadwheels from Brixton, which was to be closed, would cost £13 per head. The committee decided, therefore, to advertise for 'Labour Machines', requesting 'Persons engaged in the manufacture of such, to favor [sic] them with an inspection of their different inventions'. Five different machines were presented to them. In outward design the machines were similar. A horizontal crank-handle just above waist height was connected to a mechanism for varying the amount of labour needed to turn the handle and recording the number of turns executed. The committee considered that two of the machines were unsuitable. The other three were submitted to Charles May, 'an engineer of great eminence', for a comparative analysis and assessment. The first two machines used a friction band running over an iron cylinder to resist turning the handle, this being adjusted by screws or weights. The third machine churned sand to achieve the same effect. Engineer May found that the turning resistance varied with the position of the crank on the machine using sand, and he inspected similar machines in use at the Coldbath Fields prison to assess their effectiveness more accurately. He found that the load changed according to whether the sand was wet or dry, making it impossible to vary accurately the force needed to turn the handle – although this could be varied to some extent by altering the amount of sand in use. Of the machines using the friction band, the one where the load was varied by attaching or detaching weights was adjudged to be the best. Captain Williams, the Inspector of Prisons, agreed with this finding, commenting that some other machines set to a resistance of 12 lbs needed up to 60 lbs to turn the crank from cold. The machine in question would present a constant load. Regarding cost, the unsatisfactory sand based machines cost £4 10s each in quantities of 100. The machines using a friction band regulated by screws cost £6 10s each as an installed fixture, or £7 10s as a moveable unit. The machines of choice, using adjustable weights, cost £8 10s each in quantities of 100. The report says that 150 of them were duly ordered, although this seems later to have been reduced to 100. The prisoner was required to turn the handle between ten and twelve thousand times per day. It was the job of the medical officer to determine the appropriate weight loading for each prisoner.

It is notable that in the 55 page report on the prison, five pages were devoted to a full and detailed account of the provision of the labour machines. The committee had clearly suppressed any appreciation of the irony of their own 'hard labour' in selecting these machines. In the provision of labour machines, they had saved the county between £5 and £10 per prisoner head (compared with the treadwheel), a labour entirely wasted except in the provision of 'reform' to the prisoners.

Useful work was, however, performed elsewhere in the prison. The pump-house had twenty-four stalls, each with a handle connected to machinery, which drew water from the well below the prison. The committee were proud of the well. It was 483 feet deep, including 126 feet bored through water-bearing chalk, and was capable of supplying up to 100,000 gallons per day of certified 'good, wholesome, and well-aerated water'. Upwards of 5000 gallons a day was pumped into a tank providing the prison with its water. The basement of 'A' wing contained the Mill House. Here, there were twenty hand mills – each in a separate stall – for grinding wheat for bread.

Another favourite labour – which occupied more than a quarter of the prison population at Wandsworth – was oakum picking. Oakum was old ship's rope, mostly saturated with hard pine tar, which had to be hand picked to the individual strands of hemp. These were then were used as packing material in the building and marine industries. The work was difficult and dirty, and had to be done without tools. In the survey conducted in 1862 at Wandsworth, nearly 100 prisoners were using the labour machines, while over 200 were occupied with picking oakum.

A major opportunity for reform was attendance at services in the prison chapel, which the prisoners were required to do twice on Sundays. Here, Separation was achieved by the use of a process pioneered at Pentonville Prison that was a wonder of Victorian ingenuity. A large number of the inmates had to be able to attend the service simultaneously, but be incapable of contact with any other attendee. They should, however, remain in full view of the minister conducting the service as well as the prison guards. In order to achieve this, a series of vertical coffin-like structures or stalls were arranged in ranks facing a raised platform. The top and forward parts of the stall were omitted to chest height, enabling the occupant to see forward to whoever was occupying the platform and be seen by them. Sideways visibility was impossible; the neighbour at the back was blocked by the high back of the stall, and the neighbour in front could not be seen because of the high back of his stall. Thus upwards of four hundred persons could be preached to, each one having zero visibility of the other three hundred and ninety-nine. The arrangements for entering and leaving the stalls were complex, access along the ranks being via the adjacent stalls. Thus if a troublemaker at the end of one rank had to be removed, all the occupants of that rank had to be removed first. And in order to maintain anonymity, each person had to be properly hooded or veiled when moving between their cell and the chapel. Contemporary reports talk of about one hour being needed to fill or empty the chapel, which is not surprising. However, in addition to the existing complexity of the process, each stall was numbered and registered to its occupant's cell number. Any 'impropriety during the service', could be traced to the prisoner concerned. One can only marvel at the administrative organisation involved in getting four hundred hooded prisoners into or out of four hundred numbered stalls, whilst preserving the correspondence between both.

There had been some debate among the Wandsworth building committee members regarding the appropriateness of adopting the Pentonville chapel system, and the fitting out of the chapel was delayed as a result. Some prison inspectors objected to it. There were concerns that notes could be passed under the doors of adjacent stalls, and worries concerning the difficulty and confusion attending the removal of single prisoners after 'becoming ill, or pretending to be so'. There was the problem of getting the females and their officers into and out of the chapel without being observed by the males. There was also the fact that some chaplains preferred 'social worship on principle', considering it to be far more effective. On the other hand, open seating would have been entirely contrary to the philosophy of the Separate System. More importantly, there would have been a serious risk of unruly behaviour or worse, among a large number of prisoners assembled together with relatively few prison guards; excluding administrative staff, the prison would contain only 23 warders for male inmates and seven for females. The committee decided that modifications to the design of the stalls would prevent the passing of notes, and the female part of the chapel could be screened off. They felt on balance that even though there were differences of opinion, the Pentonville-type Separate Chapel System should be adopted at Wandsworth.

The reform of prisoners could also be accomplished by the provision of schooling and instruction. When Wandsworth opened for business, some of the prisoners were very young indeed. A contemporary visitor to the prison school reported nineteen juveniles of between *seven* and thirteen years old under instruction – each in their separate stall in a schoolroom. In a later report on the prison, Henry Hatch stated that many of the juveniles thus instructed, were taught to read and write as a result of their lessons whilst in custody. Adult classes were taught in the chapel; instruction of both young and old seemed generally to be in Bible studies. Even Henry though, questioned the effectiveness of reform in the prison, particularly in respect of the young. He reported in October 1855 that in the previous year, of 4,872 prisoners admitted for periods of between fourteen days and two years, 2,244 had been under instruction. Of these, 313 were boys under fourteen years of age, and of these boys 65 had been in prison twice, 33 three times, 24 four times and 13 five times and more. He lamented the fact that the situation would not change until boys could be cleared from the streets and sent to schools.

No record exists of the chaplain's job-description for the Surrey House of Correction, but some idea of what was involved can be gained from a House of Commons committee report of 1835, where the chaplain of Millbank Penitentiary detailed exactly what he did during the day. For an hour in the morning, he received prisoners who wished to see him on various matters. From ten o'clock until one o'clock he delivered lectures in the chapel on scriptural and religious subjects. Then he visited prisoners in the punishment cells, followed by visits to prisoners in the infirmary. He read and signed every prisoner's letter – incoming as well as outgoing – 3,500 in the year in question, around ten per day. He engaged in correspondence with prisoners' friends and relatives and answered enquiries regarding the character of ex-prisoners. He kept a journal of daily events as well as the prisoners' character books – in which were entered their offences and punishments while in prison. He also superintended the prison schools. And on Sunday, he prepared two sermons and held two full services in the chapel.

In September 1851, the Reverend Henry John Hatch, BA Cantab, was appointed the first chaplain of the New Surrey House of Correction. As chaplain, he was second in seniority only to the prison governor.

When Henry John Hatch was born on 2nd January 1818 in Chertsey, his immediate prospects were relatively modest. He was the second son of the Reverend Thomas Hatch and his eighteen year old wife Anna Maria Ellen. Thomas Hatch was vicar of Walton on Thames, and he christened his new son there a few weeks later. The Hatches had their roots in Windsor. Henry's great-grandfather, William Hatch, draper, JP, and sometime mayor of that town, had made his money purveying his wares to the minor royals and officials surrounding the Court in early Georgian times. It was not the most glittering period for Royal Windsor, but business was good enough to allow William to send his eldest son, Giles, to Eton and Cambridge. His youngest son, Thomas, Henry John's grandfather, became an attorney in Windsor. He prospered, and was able to send *three* of his sons to Eton and Cambridge, all of whom became clergymen. Thomas's legal business may have done well, but it was his wife who was the real source of his wealth. When Margaretta Eleanora Cliffe was three years old, her father Henry Cliffe died, and left her the Manor of Sutton in Surrey. Her grandfather, Captain Henry Cliffe of the East India Company, had purchased the manor in 1716 having made his money bringing coffee from the Persian Gulf and tea from China. Thomas Hatch became Lord of the Manor upon his marriage to Margaretta. He died in 1819; Margaretta died three years later, in 1822. Thus their eldest son, the Reverend Thomas Hatch, inherited the title, the land and the income. Henry John's father was no ordinary country vicar.

Henry's mother, Anna Maria Ellen Birch, was born in Calcutta into a distinguished Anglo-Indian family. Her father was Richard Comyns Birch of the Indian Civil Service, master of the first Masonic lodge of Bengal, and grandson of John Zephiniah Holwell, briefly governor of Bengal and author of *A genuine narrative of the deplorable deaths of the English Gentlemen and others, who were suffocated in the Black Hole* (of Calcutta, published in 1756). Her mother was Frances Jane Rider, daughter of William Rider, sheriff of Calcutta. Anna Maria had a number of brothers and sisters, and her younger brother Richard, who was a soldier in India, eventually became Lieutenant General Sir Richard James Holwell Birch KCB, secretary in the military department to the Indian Government during the Indian Mutiny in 1857. These were Henry's antecedents; comfortably establishment, highly respectable and not without money on both sides of the family.

Whatever the rigours were of being brought up a clergyman's son in the lean years following the Napoleonic War, at least Henry would have been adequately clothed and fed. The income from Sutton manor alone would have made Henry's father a reasonably wealthy man. It was just as well, because he and Anna Maria were producing children at a prodigious rate. Anna Maria had had eight children before her thirtieth birthday, and another four by the time she was thirty-seven. And there is evidence to suggest that it was a happy family. After Thomas and Anna Maria died, a memorial was erected in Walton Church by 'sorrowing children to their kind and affectionate parents'. Words other than 'kind and affectionate' would surely have been used of parents who did not have those qualities. Henry John Hatch grew up in a happy household full of children, and by virtue of his father's occupation, life revolved around the church.

The church of St Mary's at Walton on Thames has stood on its present position close to the river since Norman times, and some of the original pillars from that period are still visible in the nave. Also in the nave, extraordinary in what used to be a rural English parish church, is a large memorial to Richard Boyle, Viscount Shannon, an 18th century soldier, politician, and resident of Walton who fought as a youth volunteer at the Battle of the Boyne. Apart from the martial content, this marble extravaganza would not look out of place in a church in renaissance Rome or Florence. It is interesting to speculate on the effect that the Shannon memorial had on Henry John and his growing band of siblings. Young and impressionable boys (and girls) must have been influenced by its realistic diorama of cannon, mortar, flags, and drums, and uniformed central hero mourned by a comely woman swooning at his feet. It might have encouraged Henry's two younger brothers. George and Richard Hatch both went to India and joined the Bengal Infantry, probably assisted by their uncle Richard Birch. Richard Hatch died in India in 1843, but George Cliffe Hatch rose to the rank of general, and was Judge Advocate General for sixteen years, being awarded Companion of the Star of India.

In 1830, the family were devastated by the death of Thomas's eldest son, also called Thomas, who was only fourteen years old. In 1828, Thomas and Anna's fourth daughter, Caroline, had died in infancy, and two years on, Anna Maria was heavily pregnant with daughter Eleanora, born just eight days after Thomas's funeral. It must have been a difficult time for all, but Henry's prospects changed abruptly. Following his brother's death, Henry was now the eldest son and heir to the family fortune, and would have the financial independence to be able to follow whatever career path he chose.

Henry John Hatch was sent to Eton and Cambridge like his father and uncles. Eton College had been established by Henry VI in 1440, in order to provide 70 King's Scholars or 'Collegers' with a free education; this to be continued at King's College Cambridge, which he established the following year. By Henry Hatch's time, the number of pupils at Eton had swelled to nearly 600. The boys who were not one of the Collegers were called 'Oppidans' (town-dwellers), and lodged in town. Oppidans paid for their own accommodation and tuition fees. The records show that Henry, although he came from a wealthy family, was probably a Colleger and must therefore have had sufficient and proven academic merit. He was at Eton during the reign of the famous Dr Keate (headmaster 1809 – 1834), and may have been present at his leaving ceremony. Keate was presented with silverware to the value of £600 and was, for the first time as far as anyone could remember, entirely lost for words. John Keate was small in stature – five feet tall – but within that space was concentrated 'the pluck of ten battalions…' At Eton, Keate had to endure from the pupils smashed windows, garden walls pulled down, fireworks and rotten eggs being thrown in lessons, and on one occasion his desk being smashed to pieces – an event which he elected to ignore, standing among the debris and carrying on the lesson as normal. He was famous for his floggings and once flogged 72 boys five cuts apiece in a single session. Lytton Strachey described the school in Keate's time as 'a system of anarchy tempered by despotism'. Many years later, Henry Hatch included an account of Eton scholars' misdemeanours and the wrath of Dr Keate, in his story *The Heir of Raven's Nest*.

Until the 1860s, King's College took students only from Eton, and Collegers could expect to be accepted there. Henry's father attended Eton and King's, so did uncles Charles and Henry, and Henry's cousin Cliffe Hatch. But by Henry John's time, the Hatch name was somewhat out of favour. In 1836, Cliffe Hatch had been deprived of his fellowship for being a married man, 'according to the college statutes'. Uncle Henry, also a fellow of King's, had been publicly humiliated in the insolvent debtor's court, having run up thousands of pounds of debt, much of it in Cambridge. As it happened, he was also married in contravention of the college rules, but does not appear to have been found out. So Henry John Hatch had to eschew the glories of King's College Chapel – he was an accomplished musician and chorister – and settle instead for Magdalene College, with its modest but comfortably traditional chapel. To this day, it has copies of the Book of Common Prayer in regular use, that were already nearly a hundred years old in Henry's time.

Henry went up to Magdalene in 1837, but before finishing his studies at Cambridge he decided to take a gap. It was to be quite a long gap. His BA was not awarded until 1849; his MA he received in 1852. Starting around 1840, he spent two or three years tutoring. Among his clients were Lawrence Peel, youngest and 'least distinguished' brother of Prime Minister Sir Robert Peel, and Sir Edward Knatchbull, politician and sometime member of Peel's administration (ODNB). Henry was well connected, probably through his contacts at Eton and Cambridge. But then the idea of travel formed in his mind. As heir to Sutton Manor, Henry had the financial resources to have gone almost anywhere. Travel to France and Italy would have been easy; he could even have gone to the USA. But Henry decided to take a radical step. Some time in the early eighteen-forties he took the momentous decision to become a tutor in Australia, established as a penal colony barely fifty years previously.

In 1770, Captain Cook had explored and claimed the eastern part of Terra Australis Incognita for King George, naming it New South Wales. One of the members of his expedition, Sir Joseph Banks, recommended Botany Bay as a suitable place for a convict settlement; somewhere was needed for transported felons following the loss of America, Britain's previous repository for convicts.

The first expedition, consisting of eleven ships, arrived in January 1788 with 736 transportees, 188 of them women. Botany Bay proved to have little fresh water, poor soil and inadequate anchorage. Port Jackson, an inlet to the north, was found to be ideal and a settlement was founded there on 26th January 1788. It was named after the Home Secretary, Thomas Townshend, Viscount Sydney. The town and the state prospered. By 1840, New South Wales had four million sheep. By 1850 it had fifteen million. Over the same period, exports to Britain of Australian Merino wool grew from one quarter to one half of the entire British market. Economic migrants started arriving, subsidized by the British government using revenue from the sale of Crown land in Australia; 30,000 between 1830 and 1840, 80,000 between 1840 and 1850. In 1840, after nearly 80,000 men and women convicts had been sent to 'Botany Bay', the transportation of felons to New South Wales ceased (they were sent instead to Van Diemen's Land, Norfolk Island and Port Phillip), and in 1842, Sydney declared itself

Australia's first city, with a population of more than 30,000. There may have been some bravado in this since the colony was going through a severe depression, a consequence of the depression in Britain, its main export market and provider of investment capital.

Just what Henry John Hatch found in Sydney when he arrived, and the nature of his journey, can be judged from the account of a barrister, Charles John Baker, who travelled to Melbourne and Sydney in 1841. Baker published an account of his experiences, ostensibly as a guide to prospective emigrants. The trip out took 103 days, without stops, in a 500-ton sailing ship – three and a half months at sea. Baker advised that before departure, passengers should assure themselves that the ship had a surgeon, and that fresh meat should be available on board for meals twice a day. Also available, should be soft bread, 'not ship's biscuit, which is called bread on board ship', beer, wine and spirits, a cow for fresh milk, and a good water filter. A horn drinking cup, wineglass, and teaspoon should be brought along, together with a supply of lemons and apples. A personal source of brandy should also be secured. He advised against carpet on the cabin floor, and suggested that any trunks should be raised off the deck to avoid damage by the salt water that inevitably came down the hatchways and through portholes. In the interests of tidiness, a dustpan and brush, dusters, and slop-cloths should also be available. On clothes he was quite specific, detailing the number and type of coats – not Mackintosh since 'the salt water destroys the India rubber' – waistcoats, jean-jackets, blouses, slippers, and boots that should be taken, together with 'personal linen according to habit'.

Baker arrived at Port Phillip in 1842. He visited Melbourne, and then travelled by steamboat to Sydney where he rented lodgings. Sydney, he commented, was very English, with streets, houses, shops, churches, carriages, and cabs all as in England. Several of the roads were paved, some were lit by gas, and there were markets with fish, meat, poultry, vegetables, fruit, and butter. The houses all had gardens, and property prices were similar to those found in London; the churches, though, were in a poor state, many without roofs. Baker commented on the economic depression, noting that the price of sheep had fallen by a factor of eight, while cattle prices were half what they were two years previously. He seemed to ignore the effects of the depression in Britain, suggesting instead, that the main problem was a lack of circulating cash, the result of the proceeds of Crown land sales going straight back to Britain. Also, there had been too rapid a growth in the period 1839 to 1841.

So much for the fledgling city, but Charles Baker was a professional man, and was concerned to know where persons like him could relax in the company of their peers. The answer was *The Australian Club*, situated at 165 Macquarie Street, established in 1838 as a Gentleman's Club similar to those in London and elsewhere. The entrance fee was £30 with an annual subscription of £7 10s. In 1842 it had 219 members who were mostly of 'superior breeding and education and unblemished character, active in mind and body and of agreeable and open manners'. However, Baker cautioned that there were also others, 'whom no gentlemen would want to associate with'. There was, he commented, no lack of 'Society' in Sydney but, as elsewhere, it was divided into sets. The company admitted to Government House, 'the steadiest test of station and character', was the only one with whom it was desirable to associate. This company comprised members of the Legislative Council, bishops, archdeacons and other clergy, judges, barristers, solicitors, other government executive officers, magistrates, sheriffs, medical men, merchants, and some students.

This was the Sydney of the early 1840s when Henry John Hatch arrived. The question remains though, what was his motivation for going there? Was his trip just a glorified

Victorian Grand Tour, an 'educational rite of passage'? Did he just want to see the world? His brothers were both in India; perhaps he wanted to go one better. There were two ways of getting to Australia at the time. The direct sea route via the Cape of Good Hope was the quickest, but meant being at sea for months. Alternatively, a good part of Europe and Asia could be seen by taking a mixed land and sea route. Charles Baker detailed the possibilities. When he travelled back to England from Sydney, the journey proceeded by boat to Singapore, thence Bombay, Suez, overland to Cairo and Alexandria, Alexandria to Malta and Naples, and thereafter home via Rome, Pisa, Genoa, Marseilles, Avignon, Lyons, Paris, Rouen, and Le Havre to Southampton.

Henry went to Australia to be a tutor, and he had 'charge of the sons of several influential gentlemen' during his time in the colony. One of the influential gentlemen was the Hon C D Riddell, Colonial Treasurer and later member of the Legislative Council. Henry was also likely to have been employed by members of the legal profession; he certainly moved in legal circles during his time in New South Wales. He was acquainted with George Wise, JP, and his brother Edward Wise, who was a Supreme Court Judge, Sir Alfred Stephen, Chief Justice of New South Wales and Sir William M Manning, the Attorney General of New South Wales. Sir William Manning may have been one of Henry's employers. In 1845, when Manning was Solicitor General, he acquired land in the Illawarra, an area about 70 miles south of Sydney. There is a parish and hundred named 'Southend' in Cumberland County, New South Wales, close to the Illawarra; many years later when Henry Hatch was living in Southend in England, he named his house there *Illawarra Lodge*.

Tutoring, however, was not Henry's only interest. *The Sydney Morning Herald* of 3rd April 1843, announced that 'Thomas Walker, BA, Jesus College Cambridge, and Henry John Hatch, Magdalen College Oxford [sic]', were now the proprietors and editors of *The New South Wales Magazine*. The magazine had been started in January 1843 by Thomas Henry Braim, a schoolmaster and clergyman originally from Yorkshire. Published monthly, it was a journal of 'General Politics, Literature, Science, and The Arts.' The Rev Braim had started it in order to provide 'a community boasting so much intelligence as New South Wales [with some] Periodical Literature'.

The first edition of *The New South Wales Magazine* under the editorial control of Henry and his colleague, published in April 1843, contained among other things, a thinly-veiled attack on Phrenology as being un-scientific, poems, stories, part II of a tragedy in the style of a Shakespeare play set in Venice, an essay on education, and a piece on the politics and economics of South Australia. Later offerings included articles as diverse as a mathematically detailed account of the appearance and trajectory of Halley's Comet, and the publication of extensive statistics of the commerce of New South Wales. Contributions were sprinkled with quotations from Virgil, Plato, Aristotle, Aristophanes, and Plutarch. The journal appeared to be a very competent academic offering, no doubt assuring its readers that even though they were marooned on the other side of the world, they were not divorced from informed and intellectual comment on the arts and sciences.

Ten out of the sixty pages in the April edition were devoted to advertising; by November 1843, this had been reduced to only four pages. Even though the number of subscribers was approaching 400, the recession in Australia and the consequential reduction in advertising revenue, probably meant that the journal could not survive. It was Henry's first disappointment. However, he used the final edition to advertise the opening of a school in Sydney for the education of a 'select number of gentlemen's sons'. It would be run by himself and another Cambridge man – presumably Thomas Walker. Boarders at sixty guineas per annum and day pupils at twenty-five guineas per annum were to be taught classics and mathematics.

Taking the major step of opening a school, suggests that Henry Hatch's voyage to Australia was more than a Grand Tour. It implies that, Sutton Manor notwithstanding, he was there for good. However the time Henry spent in New South Wales was not mentioned in his entries in Crockford's Clerical Directory – which mentions almost everything else that he did. And his trip was expensive; Charles Baker's journey back from Sydney to England cost in excess of £240 (~ £10,600 in today's money). Henry could have travelled steerage, but Thomas Hatch would not have wanted to risk his eldest son and heir in sub-standard accommodation on such a long and arduous journey. A comfortable passage would probably have been provided by his father. The exact date of Henry's departure to Australia is not known, but he was certainly there in early 1843, so he must have left England no later than 1842.

While in Sydney, Henry met Esther Lucy – Essie – Dillon. Essie, born in Dublin, had come to Australia with her parents, John and Esther Dillon, around 1832. Her father was a solicitor in Sydney, and had been a subscriber to *The New South Wales Magazine*. John Dillon had trained as a solicitor in Dublin, and seems to have been a bit of a Jack-the-Lad. It was said of him, that he had not served the necessary period of clerkship in Ireland, but had been admitted early as a solicitor in the interests of clients, following the death of his master. When he arrived in Sydney, he filed a 'bold affidavit' in which he demanded to be admitted to practice, without having given a full term's notice to do so. He did this even though another solicitor, also from Dublin, had been rejected the previous year on the same point of procedure. His application was rejected, but he was admitted to practice in March of the following year having gone through due process. A year into his practice, and he was up before the judges having been accused of grossly overcharging a client. The Chief Justice, Sir

Alfred Stephen, decided to dismiss the case, but warned Dillon against being similarly accused in future. Not long afterwards, Dillon successfully defended a suit to have him struck off for a perceived wrongdoing against a client. This time he was the innocent party, the Chief Justice declaring that there were not the slightest grounds to support his being struck off. In 1846 he was declared insolvent, but appears to have survived because in 1847 he was in trouble again. Dillon was suspended for three months for bringing a frivolous action and then abandoning it, leaving himself open to a charge of extortion. The following year, he was once more in the dock for practising law during his period of suspension.

Whether or not John Dillon's personal life was as unconventional as his professional practice, he evidently approved of Henry. In August 1845, Henry John Hatch and 'Essy Lucy Dillon' were married in St Andrew's church Sydney; Henry was twenty-seven years old, Essie was nineteen. Henry was living in Hereford House, an 'Elegant Regency' residence in the Glebe – a region of central Sydney originally church glebe land. It is clear from the details of their wedding that Henry and Essie moved in exalted circles. There were four witnesses: Isabella Simpson, John Dillon, Eliza Jane Laidley, widow of James Laidley, Deputy Commissary General, and John Hubert Plunkett, Attorney General, sometime Solicitor General and member of the Executive Council, and President between 1857 and 1858. Even Robert Knox Sconce, the parish priest who performed the ceremony, was out of the ordinary. Three years later, following John Henry Newman and the Oxford Movement, he renounced Anglicanism in favour of the Catholic Church. John Dillon and Essie were likely to have been Catholics, John Plunkett was one of the colony's most notable Catholics and Robert Sconce must, by then, have been courting Catholicism. Thus they would seem to have been a curious group to have presided over what Henry Hatch must surely have wanted – judging by his later ordination into the

Anglican Communion – a completely orthodox Anglican wedding ceremony.

Intriguingly, there is a Margaretta Cottage in Leichhardt Street in the Glebe, dating from the 1830s. The name Margaretta is sufficiently unusual to pose the question whether Henry and Essie occupied the cottage following their marriage, naming it after Henry's grandmother (and the source of his wealth) Margaretta Eleanora Cliffe…

In England, Henry's parents had to endure another family tragedy. In the December of 1843, the news came through from India that their youngest son Lieutenant Richard Charles Hatch had died there at the age of twenty-two. With two sons dead, George in India in the army and Henry John in Australia, Thomas Hatch must have felt bereft. He was now fifty-five years old, and as well as his church duties, he had the management of Sutton Manor to be attended to, and six unmarried daughters to worry about. Thomas decided that the manor had to go, and in September 1845, he sold it to a local man, Thomas Alcock.

All that is known for certain regarding what happened next, is that sometime in 1846 or 1847 Henry was back in England with Essie, staying with Thomas and Anna Maria at Walton. Having returned home, Henry finally made up his mind what he wanted to do with his life, and in 1848 he was ordained first deacon, and then, after taking his BA at Cambridge in 1849, priest at Lichfield. Once again, he had chosen a more complex way of furthering his career than might have been necessary. His father had been ordained in London, Uncle Charles at Ely, and Uncle Henry at Winchester. But Henry, having travelled half-way around the world to live in sub-tropical Sydney for several years, then chose the bleak industrialized Midlands, and was ordained in Lichfield. He became a curate at Talke (known as Talk 'o the Hill) in Staffordshire, near Newcastle under Lyme, and later was appointed perpetual curate to nearby Chapel Chorlton. This was an area of pottery making and coal mining, a lifestyle quite unknown to a clergyman from a well-off family in rural Surrey. Henry may have been motivated by a Christian wish to help his fellow man in an area of deprivation, but his personal situation was not uncomfortable. The 1851 census finds him and Essie living in Chapel Chorlton with three servants and a resident pupil. Seemingly though, Henry was still not satisfied, and he and Essie were soon on the move again.

Thomas Hatch had received around £13,000 when he sold Sutton Manor, and he probably had other assets inherited from his father and mother. His will designated settlements on his six daughters, and although his younger son George did not figure in the will, he was likely to have been made a separate settlement. Apart from that, the lion's share of the balance would come to Henry John Hatch; perhaps not a fortune, but in excess of five or six thousand pounds – equivalent to £0.5M today. It was enough to allow Henry and Essie to live very comfortably as country parson and wife if they had wished to do so. But Henry was not satisfied with that, and decided that he needed to increase his prospects on his own account, regardless of what he might inherit. The gross income of Chapel Chorlton was barely £100 per annum; Henry's salary would have been less than that, so when the new Surrey House of Correction was to be opened at Wandsworth Common, he applied for the job of chaplain. During Henry's time in Australia, even though transportation to the Sydney area had ceased, he must have come into contact with many convicts and ex-convicts. It is quite possible, therefore, that he was motivated by a wish to help with the education and rehabilitation of prisoners.

*The Times* of 22nd April 1851 carried the advertisement for the '...appointment to the several offices of...' Chaplain, annual salary £250, Surgeon (£220), Matron (£125), Chief Warder (£120), Governor's Clerk, and Chief Storekeeper (both £100). All positions to include accommodation. The responsibility for the spiritual health of the prisoners was deemed to be the most valuable requirement, their physical wellbeing slightly less so, but both were valued twice as much as that of ensuring that the inmates stayed inside the prison.

The chaplain was to be married, and be between thirty and fifty-five years of age (Henry was thirty-three). Competition was fierce. The desirability of the position, and the level of Henry's success in winning, can be gauged from the fact that there were twenty-three candidates. Eleven were eliminated because they did not meet the qualification requirements, but the balance of twelve were subjected to a selection board on Monday, 2nd June 1851. This consisted of over sixty persons, including Surrey magistrates and other worthies. A vote was taken. George Allan, the incumbent chaplain to the Brixton House of Correction, polled the most votes at 19. Henry polled 18 votes, and William Cooper polled 13 votes. Two other candidates, Lewis Page who polled 9 votes, and W S Rowe, chaplain at Horsemonger Lane gaol who polled 4 votes, were eliminated, along with the seven other candidates who received no votes at all. For Henry to have scored as well as he did against the obvious local favourite, as well as out-performing one other of the local prison chaplains, meant that he must have made a very good impression. No doubt his Surrey family background weighed in his favour.

It might also have been expected that the new prison governor had more than a little influence on the voting. Richard Onslow was a barrister of Middle Temple, who had been Deputy Clerk of the Peace for Surrey until 1849. He was appointed governor of the new prison at Wandsworth, at a salary of £600 a year. His grandfather, George Onslow, was first cousin to the first Earl of Onslow (another George Onslow), MP for Guildford. The parallels between the lives of Henry Hatch and Richard Onslow were remarkable. Notwithstanding Onslow's noble relatives (although Henry too had some noble antecedents, his great-great-great grandmother had been the Countess of Donegal), both grew up in rectories with at least one uncle also a clergyman, and Richard Onslow, like Henry Hatch, had family links in Australia and the civil and military service in India.

Whatever the views of the prison governor, and Richard Onslow was certainly well regarded among the Surrey magistrates, it was a free vote and the board now had to exercise it over the remaining three candidates. This time Henry scored a clear victory polling 31 votes, against 20 votes for George Allan, and 10 votes for William Cooper. Henry John Hatch was duly elected as chaplain of the new Surrey House of Correction; a post that he took up on 25th September 1851, entering what was to be the most momentous decade of his life.

There were other reasons for Henry wanting to come back to Surrey. His father was in poor health, and he needed Henry to be close by to assist him. Henry, as his father's executor, would be responsible for his five unmarried sisters (Mary-Jane had married in 1847), and the conduct of his father's estate, after Thomas's death. There was also the issue of his inheritance. Thomas Hatch's will had no legacy for Henry, other than that he should be presented to the Sutton living, if he wished, when it became vacant. It was not unusual for a financial settlement to be made to the main legatee beforehand, so exactly what his father gave Henry, and when, cannot be known. But as observed above, it must have been in excess of £5000 – twenty times his annual salary at Wandsworth.

However, of more importance to Henry was the 'family' living of Sutton. When his father sold Sutton Manor in 1845, he did not sell the advowson of Sutton. The advowson of a parish living or benefice bestows on the owner the right to present a suitable candidate to the diocesan bishop for appointment to that benefice. The bishop is not obliged to accept the candidate offered, and unless the living is vacant, either by the death or resignation of the previous incumbent, the possessor of the advowson can take no action. Nevertheless, advowsons were regularly being advertised for sale or wanted, and could change hands for several thousand pounds. Parish advowsons frequently formed part of The Manor, having their origin in pre-Norman times. The Lord of the Manor having built the parish church at his own expense, tended to acquire the right to choose the priest.

There were two tangible benefits to the owner of an advowson. Firstly, it provided that person with the gift to someone of their choice – sometimes themselves – of a good, regular and safe income for life, in return for not a particularly daunting amount of effort. Secondly, advowsons had a good resale value. In 1855, the Sutton living returned a net annual income to the rector of £330. Ten years later, the Sutton advowson was sold for £5,500, an annual return of 6% at a time when 3% was the norm. It was not even necessary to sell the advowson in order to glean financial benefit. Just the 'next presentation' could be sold; in exchange for a financial consideration, the owner of the advowson could agree to present a particular candidate to the bishop. For example, in 1799, Henry's great uncle, Giles Hatch, agreed to sell the next presentation to the parish of Sutton for £2,100.

The duties of the rector included Sunday services and sermons (although written sermons could be purchased), christenings, marriages, and funerals (for a fee), visiting parishioners, and exuding a general air of sanctity. It was even better than that. In the case of Sutton, the annual income of £330 was paid to the rector, but the parish accounts had already set aside the annual salary of £150 for a curate, and the curate could carry out the more tedious work. Thus the rector could cherry-pick what, if any, of the parish duties he had to perform. It could be a very desirable occupation, and this explains the enduring financial attractiveness of advowsons.

The Sutton advowson, and its access to the Sutton parish living, was the jewel in the crown of Thomas Hatch's estate and Henry's principal legacy. He was to be presented to the living on the death or resignation of the current incumbent – his Uncle Henry. But Henry John Hatch was concerned about the conduct of Sutton parish affairs, because Uncle Henry was a very dubious character.

Uncle Henry had gained his MA at King's in 1821, although he waited another nine years before taking Holy Orders. He finally did so, conveniently close to the death of the then rector of Sutton. In 1831, The Reverend Thomas Hatch, owner of the advowson of Sutton, presented his younger brother to the Bishop of Winchester as the next rector. Uncle Henry, like his cousin Cliffe Hatch, had been married while being a fellow of King's College, but that was not a hanging offence. What was questionable though, was the fact that on the same day in 1832, in Sutton, four of Uncle Henry's children were received into the Church in private baptisms, and they were not infants at the time. Thus, an ordained clergyman of the Church of England had not had his children baptized into that church upon their birth. Of course, Uncle Henry might have been a member of another church, or no church at all, and then suddenly had an epiphany, whereupon his whole family were received into the Anglican Communion. But he had been ordained in 1830, why did he wait another two years before baptizing his children? Uncle Henry's motives for becoming a priest and the purity of his Christian belief start to look decidedly suspect. A mere six weeks after becoming installed as rector, he mortgaged the glebe lands (lands owned directly by the parish living) for £600, adding to the £1,400 mortgage he had already taken out with a Samuel Wexford of Devon. Then in 1832, the Reverend Henry Hatch, rector of Sutton, was declared an insolvent debtor, and the Sutton parish income from tithes and fees was sequestered by court order. He was left with an annual stipend of £120, paid directly to him by the bishop of Winchester, and charged to the costs of sequestration.

The totality of Uncle Henry's insolvency was clarified the following April. He appeared in the Insolvent Debtor's Court with debts of £7,700 (and the £2000 mortgage with Samuel Wexford may not have been included in that sum). This was an incredible amount, being equivalent to around £750,000 today. He had eighty-four debtors, including his brother Charles for more than £1000, thirteen tailors, including a Mr Bishop of Cambridge to whom he owed £500, a Mr Morris, of the Strand, who had supplied furniture for the Sutton rectory to the value of £400, and a Mr Webb who had supplied robes and palls to the value of £40. In addition, Henry owed money to eight tavern-keepers and wine-merchants and sundry other persons in trade including a gun maker, and a coal merchant in Mitcham. Worse still the poor rates, the highway rates, and the salary of the curate, were 'among the claims unliquidated'. In other words, not only had Henry been obtaining from tradesmen goods he had no means to pay for, he had also pinched some of the parish revenue and owed his curate wages. And what must have been worst of all for the family, the details of his profligacy were published in *The Times* for all to see.

Uncle Henry may well have tried to turn over a new leaf, but in 1844 he received a letter from the Bishop upbraiding him for mainly financial misdemeanours. He had increased the 'fees for the burial of the poor...to an amount which must be most oppressive to them.' This was 'not legal and cannot be permitted.' The churchwardens were to be instructed to draw up a table of 'what appear to have been the customary fees in the time of the Revd. Giles Hatch', this table to be submitted to the bishop for signing, after which it was to be hung in the vestry for all to see. There were the proceeds of five charitable bequests, left in trust to be disposed of by the rector and churchwardens, which had not been paid. The bishop instructed, 'the sums due on these respective accounts are to be paid immediately.' In future an account book was to be kept, together with receipts, signed by the rector and churchwardens, and made up every Easter. The collection for the National

Society made under the Queen's letter on the 1st Sunday in July (The National Society for Promoting the Education of the Poor into the Principles of the Established Church), had still not been received at the office in London on 30th August, and, the bishop continued, 'I must desire that this remittance may be made immediately.' Henry was even suspected of having been at the alms (money for the poor), and was instructed to divide these into three parts, to be distributed by himself and the two churchwardens, and was advised to keep 'an account of the mode in which you disburse your share, to be exhibited when occasion requires'. There were also delinquencies in visiting the sick and poor, and failure to make arrangements with his colleagues to cover the parish during his absences.

Uncle Henry's character left a lot to be desired. It was one thing to take goods off greedy tradesmen only too ready to extend the brother of the Lord of Sutton Manor as much credit as he could muster. It was quite another to pocket the income from charitable trusts and alms for the poor, not to mention overcharging them for burying their dead. And failing to remit a collection for the religious education of the poor made under the direct command of Queen Victoria, was just beyond the pale. Since Uncle Henry was also neglecting his parochial duties, the bishop would have been entirely justified in dismissing him. The fact that he did not do so is a matter to ponder.

In 1857, during the *seventh* consecutive sequestration of the Sutton living to liquidate Uncle Henry's debts, the case appeared once more in the debtor's court. A dispute had arisen from the fact that Henry's annual stipend – which had been increased to £150 in 1837 – was paid to him in the years 1851, 1852 and 1853, in spite of the fact that the Reverend Mr Vernon performed the duties of Henry's cure in Sutton during those years. Rev Vernon had been appointed curate of Sutton in 1845, possibly to keep an eye on things following the bishop's letter. In addition to his curate's salary, Mr Vernon received surplice fees of around £12 per year and the use of the rectory house (with or without the use of Henry's furniture one wonders?). The sequestrator, quite rightly as the court decided, had set aside the charge to the accounts of £448 by the bishop of Winchester, covering Henry's stipend for the three years in question. The bishop's attorney pointed out that under ecclesiastical law 'the bishop had power to assign to an incumbent a certain allowance for his maintenance'. To which the judge, Mr Commissioner Phillips, commented that he 'apprehended that the law did not contemplate a payment for doing nothing'. Quite so.

What happened next is not clear. It may be that the Bishop of Winchester, following this incident, decided that he had had enough of being made a fool of by Rector Henry Hatch, and finally had him dismissed. Perhaps Henry resigned. If so, it was under pressure. In the 1861 census, he was living in the East End of London, still signing himself as Rector of Sutton. In any event, his term of office at Sutton is recorded in Crockford's as 1831 to 1858. As a footnote to his career, *The Times* of 19th June 1861, had a notice to the effect that Henry Hatch 'late of Sutton in Surrey', would effectively be declared debt-free if no other debtors came forward by 1st July 1861. It had taken twenty-nine years to pay off his debts. Uncle Henry died in 1866.

Fifteen years earlier as he contemplated his new situation at Wandsworth, Henry John Hatch would have been well aware of his uncle's financial situation and the fact that the Sutton living had been under sequestration for a generation. He would also have been concerned about the possibility of his uncle asset-stripping the parish. The glebe had already been mortgaged. If the mortgage payments were in default, then the glebe lands would have been forfeit. Now that Henry John was living within an easy train journey to Sutton he could keep an eye on his uncle, although how much influence he could have had over events is doubtful.

These were the complex issues facing Henry, as he and Essie took up residence in the substantial chaplain's house built next to the main entrance of the new prison at Wandsworth. But they were too late to provide Henry's father with any material assistance. Thomas Hatch had died in July, and within a month, Anna Maria too was dead. Thus within the space of a few weeks, Henry John Hatch had to bury his parents and move from Staffordshire back to Surrey. He had to start a new and very responsible job in a brand-new prison operating a radical new prison system. And as head of his family and sole executor, he had to manage his father's estate and look after the welfare of his five unmarried sisters. If he had not done so before, Henry John Hatch definitely grew up in 1851.

# The Philanthropist

Having become established as the chaplain at Wandsworth, Henry found himself invited on to a number of committees for good works. In May 1853, he was appealing for funds for a reformatory home in Stepney for boys aged between 10 and 16 recently released from prison. Two years later, he was a committee member for the National Orphan Home. He was seeking support particularly for orphans of the 'war and pestilence' in the Crimea, where far more of the soldiers died from disease than in battle. He was also on the committee of The Playground Society, patroness Lady Byron, fundraising to provide playgrounds for 'poor children in populous places'. In the same year, he presented a lecture on 'Criminal Reformation' in aid of the Preventative and Reformatory Institution. Henry started to attend conferences, and in 1857, he read a paper on the Reformatory and Refuge Union to a meeting of the National Association for the Advancement of Social Science in Birmingham. In 1858, he spoke at length at a meeting of the Royal Benevolent Society. Henry was also vice-president of the London Sacred Harmonic Society, an amateur choral group founded in 1832. Since he also composed music, he may well have written material for them to perform.

In the prison, Henry was able to introduce a minor easing of the Separate System rules of non-communication in the chapel. He got permission from the Surrey magistrates for the prisoners to make responses during the services, and was actively seeking to extend this to the singing of hymns and psalms, believing this to add to the solemnity and devotion of the services.

Henry John Hatch was a cultured and educated man, and with his reformist outlook it is impossible that he was not an avid reader of Charles Dickens. Between 1852 and 1853 Dickens published *Bleak House*. The story centred on a case in Chancery over a disputed will. Jarndyce v Jarndyce had dragged on longer than anyone could remember, causing at least one member of the Jarndyce family to commit suicide in despair. In the end the case was 'won', but the costs were such that the entire legacy was consumed by legal fees. In *Bleak House*, Dickens chided the iniquities of the Court of Chancery, a so-called court of equity, in the same way that he had earlier castigated the injustices of the Poor Law Amendment Act in *Oliver Twist*. It is therefore ironic, and the parallels cannot have been lost on Henry, that in the following year, he too brought a suit in Chancery against his Uncle Charles over a disputed will.

In order to understand what he did and why he did it, it is necessary to consider again the circumstances of the Sutton advowson. The advowson, it may be remembered, was the right to present a candidate to the diocesan Bishop for consideration as rector of the parish of Sutton. It was acquired by Henry Cliffe when he purchased Sutton Manor in 1716. Henry John's father, Thomas Hatch, used it to present his brother, 'Uncle Henry', as rector of Sutton in 1831. But when Thomas Hatch sold the Manor in 1845, he held on to the advowson. The Sutton advowson had exercised several generations of Hatches, and in order to understand the background to Henry's action in Chancery, it is necessary to follow its progress through his family.

When Thomas Hatch senior, Henry John's grandfather, married Margaretta Eleanora Cliffe, he should have taken control of the advowson since it had been left to Margaretta, together with Sutton Manor, by her father. In fact she had already sold it, but as it transpired the sale was made under circumstances that amounted to theft. Giles Hatch was the elder brother of Thomas Hatch senior, and Giles had introduced the Cliffe family to the Hatches. He became acquainted with Susannah Cliffe, a widow, and her two daughters, Cassandra Arnold and Margaretta Eleanora Cliffe. Cassandra was Susannah's daughter by George Arnold, her first husband; Margaretta was her daughter by her second husband, Henry Cliffe. Giles, evidently, made a good impression on the whole family, because on 1st January 1767, he married Cassandra Arnold, aged seventeen, 'by consent of her guardian, Susanna Cliffe'. Seven days later, he was installed as rector of Sutton under the patronage of 'Margaret Eleanor Cliffe [aged nine] by advice of Susanna Cliffe, widow, her guardian'.

Susannah directed in her will that William Stead of 'Ryegate', clerk, and Richard Barnes also of Ryegate, gentleman, should become her trustees and guardians of the young and unmarried Margaretta. However, it was Giles Hatch, Margaretta's brother-in-law, who became her guardian following Susannah's death. This arrangement continued until Margaretta's subsequent marriage at the age of twenty-seven. Recognising an opportunity, Giles Hatch married the heiress to his brother Thomas, literally, performing the ceremony in Sutton in 1785. Sutton Manor was valued at around £15,000 at the time, which in modern money is in excess of £1.5M. Margaretta Eleanora Cliffe was thus in possession of an extremely valuable piece of real estate, and a bride to be sought after, a circumstance recognized and exploited by Giles and his brother.

Giles Hatch died in 1800, and in his will of June 1799, he bequeathed the Sutton advowson to his son Cliffe Hatch. But then in a codicil dated 4th November, later in the same year, he declared that he had sold the next presentation

to William Chapman of King Street Cheapside in the City of London stationer for the sum of two thousand one hundred pounds, [and] whereas a dispute has arose [sic] as to the validity of my Title to the said next presentation and to obviate and decide it a suit is now pending and undetermined in the High Court of Chancery wherein I am plaintiff and the said William Chapman defendant...

And so on.

What happened to the case in Chancery is not known. The next rector commenced his duties in March 1800, four months after the Chancery case was initiated. But the question arises, how did Giles come to *own* the advowson in the first place, since it had belonged to Margaretta along with Sutton Manor? All was revealed a few months later. With Giles safely dead, Thomas Hatch and his wife, Margaretta, filed a suit in Chancery claiming fraud by Giles on the young Margaretta while he was her guardian.

As mentioned previously, Margaretta had gone to live with Giles and Cassandra, her half-sister, after the death of Susannah Cliffe in 1772. Giles had become her guardian, being responsible for her upkeep and education. This was not exactly a philanthropic act, since he collected an annual allowance of £130 from Margaretta's estate for the privilege. In addition, as Margaretta's guardian, Giles had day-to-day responsibility for the management of Sutton Manor and no doubt reaped some financial benefit from that. His position provided him with considerable opportunities to influence the young heiress, made far more significant by the fact that she had a serious disability. She was profoundly deaf.

In October 1779, Margaretta came of age, and on 20th January 1780 she sold the advowson of Sutton to Giles Hatch, '...in consideration...of her great friendship, kindness and regard for him, the care taken of her by him, love and affection, and 10s.' Ten shillings! Of course, it was a nominal sum; Margaretta was effectively giving the advowson to Giles. The fact that just the next presentation to Sutton was potentially saleable twenty years later for over two thousand pounds, illustrates either her generosity, or the extent of the fraud.

The alleged illegality of the transaction was the issue of the Chancery case, Hatch v Hatch, which finally came to judgement in 1804. Thomas and Margaretta were claiming fraud by Giles, in that he was the beneficiary of the transaction, while at the same time having responsibility as Margaretta's guardian for her estate; effectively, he gave the advowson to himself. They claimed that Margaretta had only intended to sell the next presentation to the Sutton benefice, which would probably have been to the benefit of Giles' son Cliffe Hatch if he had taken holy orders. However the culpability did not stop with Giles. The attorney who drew up the deed of transfer and witnessed the document, was none other than Thomas Hatch, Giles' brother, the same Thomas Hatch who was now claiming fraud on his wife!

Thomas's quite breathtaking duplicity is to be wondered at, and it was not lost on the Lord Chancellor when the case came to judgement. It took four years to conclude, and much of the judgement was concerned with the fact that although Margaretta was in her majority when the sale was transacted, Giles remained her de facto guardian for another five years – probably on account of her deafness – until she married. During this time, Giles had effective control and management of her estate including the sale of assets, of which the advowson was one.

In his judgement, the Lord Chancellor, Lord Eldon, was suitably damning, 'The circumstances of this case are to be lamented.' Since Margaretta could only be conversed with by the use of sign language, there was 'a duty…upon her guardian and her attorney to give her full information'. Further, Giles as the rector of Sutton, would have known the annual income generated from the parish, and thus the concomitant value of the advowson. This he had a clear duty to declare, and this he clearly failed to do. In 1780, the annual income from the parish was around two hundred pounds, '… capable of improvement…', as indeed it was. By the middle of the nineteenth century the gross income was well in excess of six hundred pounds, more than twice what would have been expected from inflation in the intervening period.

On Thomas Hatch, the attorney in the 'illegal' transaction and the current plaintiff, Lord Eldon was unrelenting in his condemnation:

> Upon her attorney also there was a duty, which he most grossly violated…if ever there was a married woman, whose case was likely to be entangled in difficulty by the blameable conduct of the person, who becomes her husband, this is that case…I am very sorry to give the husband any relief. But I know of no instance… where the objection, that a party not deserving of the relief, will get it, deriving it through the other, has prevailed.

In a final coup de grâce, Lord Eldon finished,

> If the bill had been filed by her [Margaretta, had Thomas died], I should have directed the deed to be cancelled, with costs to be paid by the defendant [The estate of Giles Hatch]. On account of the conduct of the husband, I shall direct it without costs.

So Thomas and Margaretta won the four-year suit, having to pay their own costs, but the Sutton advowson came back to Margaretta. No doubt a considerable dent was made in their finances as a result. It is interesting to note, that appearing for the plaintiffs and winning the case for Thomas and Margaretta was the Attorney General, Spencer Perceval. This was the same Spencer Perceval who was to become Prime Minister a few years later, only to be murdered in the lobby of the House of Commons. He was shot down by John Bellingham on 11th May 1812; the only Prime Minister of Britain to have been assassinated.

Although Margaretta did get back the advowson, it remained fallow until well after both she and Thomas were dead. When Giles Hatch died in 1800, his son Cliffe was not in Holy Orders and Charles Gardiner became rector of Sutton, a position he held for the next thirty-one years.

But it was Margaretta's will, like a ticking time bomb, that was to cause her grandson Henry John Hatch grief when he launched his own Hatch v Hatch more than fifty years later. Three of Margaretta's sons were clergymen: Thomas, Henry and Charles. Thomas, the eldest, Henry John's father, inherited Sutton Manor and also the *ownership* of the advowson. But Margaretta directed in her will that should the living of Sutton fall vacant, and if her son Henry was in holy orders, he should be presented. The will then appeared to say, that should Henry not wish to be presented to the living, or in the event that he did, but then subsequently died while Charles was still alive, then Charles should be presented. Nine years after Margaretta's death in 1822, her son Henry Hatch was duly presented to the living of Sutton; now as it appears, not because of the generosity of his brother Thomas, who owned the advowson, but consequent on their mother's will.

This was the situation in 1854 when Henry John Hatch launched his own Hatch v Hatch. Uncle Charles was still very much alive, and vicar of Fordingbridge in Hampshire. In the event of his brother Henry's death, their mother's will directed that Charles should be presented to the living of Sutton. Three years earlier, in 1851, Thomas Hatch, the owner of the advowson, died and *his* will determined how the Sutton advowson and the proceeds of the sale of Sutton Manor should be distributed. Unfortunately, the will was poorly drafted, and was in contradiction to that of his mother. Thomas directed that his son Henry John Hatch should enjoy the next presentation to the Sutton living. It was to resolve this conundrum that Henry John Hatch entered a writ in Chancery with himself as plaintiff, and Uncle Charles as defendant; Henry's wife and his sisters, their husbands and children were also defendants since they all had an interest in Thomas's will. The claim was filed in December 1854 and fortunately for Henry's bank balance, judgement was handed down just four months later. The question was simple: was Margaretta's will satisfied by *either* of her sons – Henry and Charles – being presented to the Sutton living or *both*, Charles following Henry after the latter had died or resigned.

Henry John Hatch had been chaplain of the Surrey House of Correction for just over three years. The work was undoubtedly hard, and brought him into contact with a variety of criminals, many of whom must have been depressingly beyond redemption. It is likely, therefore, that in looking to the future he wanted to ensure a safe and comfortable environment in which to live as he got older and less able to meet the rigours of the prison system. It was not an unreasonable aspiration since his father had left him stewardship of the family living in his will. It must have been a bitter disappointment for Henry to discover the conflict with his grandmother's will.

The judgement was made against Henry; his Uncle Charles's claim to the living was upheld. If Uncle Henry died or resigned, Uncle Charles should be presented as the rector of Sutton. Nothing daunted, Henry John Hatch picked himself up, and soon found another project in which to sink his energy and his enthusiasm.

It was the reform and rehabilitation of offenders that was to become Henry's mission in life following the disappointment of Sutton. The outstanding calls on his father's estate having been largely settled by 1855 when the last of his sisters was safely married, he felt able to invest what was left of his legacy after the Hatch v Hatch reversal in a venture now closest to his heart.

A new periodical, *The Philanthropist, a Record of Social Amelioration, Journal of the Charitable Institutions and Prison and Reformatory Gazette*, had been launched in January 1855. *The Philanthropist* was a twenty-four-page journal of three-column newsprint. Reformatory establishments were invited to contribute material to the journal, while being warned that any such institutions seeking charity would be subjected to rigorous scrutiny to ensure financial rectitude. *The Philanthropist* declared itself ready to investigate any and all misuses of public charity. The first edition contained articles covering reform institutions and schools, public nurseries (crèches), the condition of Christ's Hospital, and an appeal for poor needlewomen making greatcoats for use in The Crimea. There was a substantial piece on Florence Nightingale at the Scutari hospital. There were also reports from various societies, an article on prison discipline, and stories on false begging. *The Philanthropist* strongly supported reform, (note, of prisoners, not the prison system), but the misappropriation of charitable contributions was to be investigated ruthlessly. Subsequent editions included more stories about false begging, the use of photography in the aid of justice, sanitary reform, and appeals for wounded soldiers and soldiers' widows. The Reverend J Davis, the Ordinary (chaplain) of Newgate Prison, wrote an article on the causes of crime in the metropolis. Several years later, Henry was to encounter Rev Davis under quite distressing circumstances. There were articles about an asylum for orphans of the Crimean war, and a new hospital for sick children at Great Ormond Street. In edition number three of *The Philanthropist*, an editorial stated that the journal 'had secured the cooperation of Rev. J Hatch and Rev. W Edwards chaplains of Wandsworth House of Correction'. Henry's name started to appear regularly from this date. In edition four, it was reported that the secretary of the Surrey Society for the Employment and Reformation of Discharged Prisoners, Rev Henry J Hatch, had preached at Walton on Thames, collecting £11 9s 11d in donations, and £6 5s in annual subscriptions. Edition six, reported a lecture on Criminal Reformation by Henry J Hatch. He commented on the relentless quantity of legislation, and its apparent minimal effect on the criminal population; the towns were teeming with vice and misery, at least half of which was due to drunkenness (plus ça change...) He recorded that in one year, nearly thirteen thousand juveniles were sent to prison.

The first edition of *The Philanthropist* had stated that unsolicited copies would be distributed. This was an attempt to build up a readership willing to pay sixpence for a fortnightly journal on prisoner reform. Unfortunately, by the time that the seventh edition was printed in April 1855, the initial investment had been exhausted and the journal ceased publication. An editorial in the final issue complained that although it had published the proceedings of eighty 'benevolent institutions' so far, none of the more than five hundred such societies in the metropolis, had taken out a subscription to *The Philanthropist*. It is conjecture, but it seems likely that Henry decided to invest some of his capital in a re-launch of *The Philanthropist*, which duly appeared as a new series on 1st June 1855. Perhaps he hoped that his experiences on the *New South Wales Magazine* would help him to run the journal more efficiently. By November 1855, Henry was definitely the editor of *The Philanthropist*, and his entry in Crockford's listed him as proprietor also.

As if to underline the importance of its mission, the editorial in the first edition of the new *Philanthropist* contained a quotation from a distinguished (but anonymous) foreigner, who was asked for the best evidence of England's greatness. He said it amounted to three things: social freedom, the provision of asylum to the refugees of Europe, and its benevolent institutions. Henry was redoubling his efforts in aiming what was now his journal, at the advancement of the benevolent institutions. He explained (it is assumed that Henry was writing the editorials) that philanthropy, embodied as it was in the public charities and institutions, was one of the facts of the age, but possessed no 'organ' through which it could make appeals, offer suggestions or record progress. *The Philanthropist* was to supply this deficiency. He proposed to

> present and popularise useful and cheery facts, tell the world what England is doing, what it ought to be doing and what it may do, and to elevate and bless Mankind.

The columns of *The Philanthropist* would be open to all who had useful information to communicate, or suggestions to propose, 'appertaining to benevolent thought and action'. Mindful of economic realities, Henry appealed to the friends of *The Philanthropist* for support; he also started to accept more advertising. Thus along with articles on *The Ladies Institution for Female Idiots* and *Homes for Motherless Girls*, started to appear advertisements for toilet cream and hair dye. Pieces about the *Ladies Association for the Diffusion of Sanitary Knowledge* and *The Society for the Rescue of Young Women*, rubbed shoulders with advertisements for 'Glanville's Hydrosulphate of Iron Mixture, a Certain and Expeditious Cure for Cholera, Diarrhoea, Dysentery and Sundry Bowel Complaints etc', 'Croggon's Patent Asphalt Roofing Felt... Efficient, Light and Cheap', 'Glenfield's Patent Starch', and 'Condy's Patent Concentrated Pure Malt Vinegar'.

Creditable ideas started coming thick and fast. Number three of the new series contained a piece approving the idea of a 'missionary' to accompany newly released prisoners to their homes, and help them to buy food and clothes. Number four, had four pages of advertisements together with the news that *The Philanthropist* now had its own reporter to attend and report meetings. Number five had an editorial suggesting that the National Gallery and the British Museum should open on Saturdays to allow working people to visit them. It also suggested that London Zoo and The Crystal Palace should make Saturday a sixpence entry day – Crystal Palace normally cost five shillings on Saturdays. And so on.

If Henry's duties in the prison were half as onerous – or as conscientiously executed – as those of the chaplain of Millbank, then together with his work on *The Philanthropist*, he would have had very little leisure time. It was left to Essie, his loving and devoted wife, to organize their home and preside over the many social gatherings and parties held at their house. But one of the main constituents of happy family life was missing. Their marriage had not been blessed with children. By 1856 when Henry and Essie had been married for eleven years, they decided to adopt a child. Lucy Harriet Buckler was the youngest of five children orphaned by the Crimean War. Her mother, Anne, had died of peritonitis in early 1855. Her father, Cass Buckler, was a military surgeon on active service who died – probably from disease – in the Crimea at around the same time. Cass and Anne – who lived on the Isle of Wight – left five children: two sons, Cass aged nine and John aged seven, a pair of twin girls, Martha and Mary aged six, and Lucy aged four. The orphans were known to Edward Wise, who was the executor of their grandfather's will, and he became a sort of guardian for them. Edward Wise had made his money in the brewing industry. His two sons and a daughter lived in New South Wales; his sons Edward and George were a judge and JP respectively, and his daughter Emily was married to the Solicitor General, William Manning. These were the eminent legal people that Henry and Essie were acquainted with when they were living in Sydney, and in this way came to know Edward Wise. Lucy, the Buckler's youngest child, was duly adopted by Henry and Essie, and became known as Lucy Harriet Hatch.

Henry's financial resources were becoming strained. Although Hatch v Hatch had been settled quickly, it had not been without cost, and he was also supporting the publishing and printing of *The Philanthropist*. Then, just as the journal was starting to pay its way and generate some income, the Surrey magistrates decided that Henry's proprietorial and editorial duties were incompatible with those of his prison chaplainship, and he was forced to give it up. Unfortunately, Henry quite likely brought this decision upon himself. He had become carried away with his editorial muscle, and had criticized the Surrey magistrates in print. In the edition of *The Philanthropist* published in November 1858, the editorial complained that the magistrates were not disposed to listen to the advice of the Rev Mr Jessop, a prison chaplain at Kingston. In his annual report, Rev Jessop had told the magistrates that they had 'misapplied their powers' under the Criminal Justice Act in a 'very culpable manner', by allowing persistent offenders early release from custody. Henry's article named two of the magistrates, Colonel Challoner and Captain Best, and having reported a complaint from them about their time being wasted listening to the Rev Jessop, he commented, 'we trust it was not near dinner hour'. It was most unwise considering that the Surrey magistrates were effectively Henry's employers at Wandsworth. No doubt Colonel Challoner and Captain Best were furious. In the following edition of the journal, Henry was once more critical of the magistrates. This time, the issue was a failed employment opportunity at Wandsworth Prison, where the prisoners could have been paid for rag picking. It was not surprising that the Surrey magistrates acted as they did.

Losing *The Philanthropist* was a bitter blow with a serious impact on Henry's finances. So he must have been very seriously upset shortly afterwards, to receive a communication from John Cochrane, a court official from British India. In 1853, Henry had performed the marriage ceremony between his sister Eleanora Wingfield Hatch and Alexander Hamilton Earle Durnford at St Anne's church in Wandsworth. Alexander Durnford, educated at St John's College, Cambridge, son of Colonel Durnford of the Royal Artillery, nephew of General Durnford of the Royal Engineers, was vice-principal of St Thomas's College in Colombo, the capital of Ceylon (Sri Lanka). He appeared, therefore, to be a suitable husband for Eleanora and brother-in-law to Henry. Two years later, however, Alexander Durnford was bankrupt, and John Cochrane had been appointed to acquire whatever assets were available to defray the insolvency. Since Eleanora was Alexander's wife, it was open season on her also, and her assets were vested in the residue of her father's estate, which was administered by Henry John Hatch.

John Cochrane demanded that Henry, as the sole executor of his father's will, render to him that portion of the will remaining as Eleanora's legacy, viz a share of the proceeds of the sale of the Sutton advowson! Suddenly, Henry realized that his plan to eventually succeed to the Sutton living – Uncles Henry and Charles notwithstanding – was in jeopardy. The residue of Thomas Hatch's will was to be shared equally between his six daughters. But the fateful advowson of Sutton could be sold if Henry did not want to become rector, with two-thirds of the proceeds to be shared between the daughters; the other third was to provide an income to Essie. Henry declined. Naturally it could not end there, and John Cochrane filed a writ in Chancery against Henry John Hatch for the value of the legacy due to Eleanora. For Henry it was a wretched situation. He had lost the potential income from *The Philanthropist*, and had had to sell the journal at a loss. The settlement made on him by his father was, by now, significantly depleted. He could have offered Cochrane cash if he had had the money, although Cochrane may have been insisting that the advowson be sold in order to maximize the revenue generated. Henry had no alternative other than to fight the case. If the court decision went against him, the advowson could be sold by court order and he would lose forever any right to be presented to the Sutton living. John Cochrane filed his claim in March 1859; Henry could only hope that the painfully slow process of Chancery would put off a decision as long as possible. His only chance for the Sutton rectory was to outlive both of his uncles. The snail-like pace of the Court of Chancery might work in his favour.

However, Chancery and his sister Eleanora were not finished with Henry. Three months later the family solicitor, George Annesley, brought another action against Eleanora, her husband, their children, her husband's brother and Henry; this time for £434. Annesley had advanced £800 to Eleanora for the purchase of a house in 1852, and £434 was still owed. Henry had been a signatory of the agreement and, as such, was implicated in the debt.

Henry cannot have been a happy man at this time, and in the summer of 1859, he and Essie made a fateful decision, one that would change their lives forever. Lucy, aged seven and a half, was in need of some formal education. The Hatches decided to employ a governess and advertise for extra pupils to be educated along with Lucy, not only to defray the costs of the governess, but also to improve the family revenue in the light of the legal expenses of the Cochrane and Annesley claims.

Henry placed the following advertisement in *The Times* of 24th June 1859:

> Home education. A clergyman and his wife are anxious to meet with a CHILD to EDUCATE, with their only daughter, age seven and a half, under a superior governess. References given and required.
>
> Address, Rev. M.A. post-office, Wandsworth.

The 'M.A.' was a nom-de-plume for the purposes of confidentiality.

The advertisement was answered by Thomas Plummer of Great Blunsdon in Wiltshire, a landed proprietor with a private income. Following some further correspondence and a preliminary visit, Mr Plummer, his wife Caroline, and their eleven year old daughter Mary Eugenia Plummer came to the Hatches' house in Wandsworth on Thursday, 11th August, 1859, having travelled up from Swindon by rail. On the same day, Martha Howe the new resident governess previously in the employ of another clergyman, also arrived. Henry was to receive £50 per year from the Plummers for educating Eugenia along with Lucy. His study was to be turned into a schoolroom, the hours of school being between nine and twelve in the morning and two and four in the afternoon.

The house was quite full on that fateful Thursday. Essie's mother, Esther Dillon, was staying there on an extended visit from Australia, together with two French ladies, Leonie and Valerie Raffiel, friends of Essie's, who were paying guests. During luncheon, Mrs Plummer said that Eugenia was used to being 'petted' and to come into her bed in the morning. She (Eugenia) had done so at a previous school – with the Rev Mr Brighton – and Mrs Plummer wanted the Hatches to promise to do the same, which they did, even though Lucy had not previously been allowed the same privilege. Mrs Plummer told the Hatches, in the presence of Mrs Dillon and Martha Howe, that her daughter Eugenia was untruthful, deceitful, and 'reserved and unconfiding' since her return from her last school. Caroline Plummer expressed an interest to go upstairs and see Eugenia's bedroom. Her demeanour had an unsettling effect on Essie, and she whispered to Henry to accompany her upstairs as she was a little afraid of her. While upstairs, Mrs Plummer asked for some brandy and water which was duly supplied by the servant Mary. Mrs Plummer desired that the doors of Eugenia's bedroom should always be wide open – even to the extent that they should be removed.

The Plummers had to decline tea in order to catch the train back to Swindon, and on departure Mrs Plummer behaved in a quite intemperate manner; she 'cried and screamed in a loud and violent tone – threw her arms about, and behaved as a person out of her mind', before getting into the cab which was to take them back to Paddington. No doubt it was the effect of maternal grief on parting from her daughter, assisted by the brandy and water. Henry and the two children followed the cab a short way down the road, and then returned to the house. Seeing that Eugenia was in low spirits on her mother's departure, Henry invited her and Lucy to run after him in the garden for a few minutes until tea was ready. His wife, mother-in-law, the two French ladies and Miss Howe watched them from the living room window.

Eugenia's bedroom was next to that of Henry and Essie. It had two doors, one into the passage and one adjoining their room. In deference to Mrs Plummer's wishes, both doors were kept wide open, and a large screen was placed between the adjoining door and the Hatches' bed in order to afford them some privacy. The doors were only closed when the servant Mary was bathing Eugenia. This followed a morning ritual of Eugenia and Lucy joining the Hatches in their bed for a few minutes. Henry had expressed some unease at this arrangement, but acquiesced because he and Essie had promised Mrs Plummer. Since Eugenia was allowed in the bed Lucy came also, both children being allowed only under the counterpane (bedspread), Lucy on the side of Henry, and Eugenia on Essie's side. They spent the time there spelling the names of articles in the room.

Shortly afterwards, Henry received another letter from the Plummers following which they came again to Wandsworth, bringing with them their youngest child Stephana Augusta Plummer who was a similar age to Lucy. Stephana was to be educated along with Eugenia and Lucy. Naturally, since this meant another £50 per year, the Hatches were keen to have her, notwithstanding her mother's strange behaviour. If anything, Mrs Plummer was even more eccentric than before, once more demanding brandy and water upstairs, and complaining that since her daughter was an heiress to £15,000, she should have calico sheets on her bed. Later at dinner, Mrs Plummer told them that Eugenia was 'betrothed' to their medical man – a Mr Gay – to which Eugenia added, 'Yes, and when I am seventeen, I intend to marry him.'

No doubt Henry and Essie discussed the strange behaviour of Mrs Plummer and Eugenia and her betrothal late into the night. No doubt also, Henry reflected on the forty per cent improvement to their income. And it is likely that there was plenty of discussion, since they were kept awake by a severe thunderstorm. Before they went to bed, Essie and Martha Howe went up several times to check that the children were not disturbed by the thunder and lightning. Mary, the maid, was required to sleep on their floor for the night to comfort them in case they woke up. The following day, the Hatches were surprised, yet again, to find the Plummers at their door. They were even more surprised, when Caroline Plummer announced that the storm on the previous night was a 'judgement of God against her for separating herself from her daughters', in addition to which she had promised her mother to return home with them. One can have some sympathy for Caroline Plummer. Travelling back to Swindon the previous night, hurtling along the Great Western Railway at high speed during a severe thunderstorm, with the noise of the train, the steam and smoke, the sparks from the engine and the thunder and lightning must have seemed like God's wrathful judgement indeed. Some sympathy perhaps; but a balanced person does not act in the way she did, no matter the state of the elements.

Upon leaving, Mrs Plummer gave Lucy some money and a toy, and told Henry that he was to write to her to let her know if he would receive the children again if she changed her mind. They shook hands 'in a very cordial manner', and the two children kissed Henry, Eugenia promising that she would write. No doubt Essie breathed a sigh of relief when they were gone, and it may be that Henry too was not greatly sorry given the quite unstable behaviour of Caroline Plummer. If he considered the state of his finances, he probably thought that at least what had been accomplished once could be done again.

And there matters stood until 3rd of October, when Henry received a letter from the Bishop of Winchester stating that the Plummers were accusing him of having molested their daughters whilst they were under his care. A few days later, on 8th of October, he was sent a copy of the Plummers' letter with the charges explicitly stated, and his world started to crumble:

To the RIGHT REVEREND FATHER IN GOD - The Lord Bishop of WINCHESTER.

My Lord Bishop.

I have the painful duty of placing before your Lordship a most serious complaint against a Clergyman of the Church of England resident in Your Lordship's Diocese, viz.: the Reverend Henry J. Hatch, Chaplain to the Wandsworth Prison, Wandsworth Common.

The complaint is as follows:

I am the father of two children, both girls; the eldest is named Mary Eugenia Plummer, and was eleven years of age on the 29th of March last, and the youngest is named Stephana Augusta Plummer, and will be eight years of age on the 3rd of October next.

I was desirous of placing my children with a Clergyman of the Established Church to be educated, as was also my wife, and in consequence of seeing in the Times newspaper, of the 24th of June last, an advertisement, of which I have the honour to enclose a copy (No. 1.) I wrote to the address therein given, requesting to know if there was any objection to the two children being sent, to which I received a reply, dated the 29th of June, of which I also enclose a copy (No. 2.)

Shortly after the receipt of this letter I wrote to Mr. Hatch, informing him that Mrs. Plummer and myself would call upon him, which was answered by a letter dated July 13th, a copy of which I also enclose (No. 3.)

Soon after the receipt of this letter we went to Wandsworth, taking our eldest child with us, and arranged with Mr. and Mrs. Hatch to place the children there.

I next received a letter dated July 28th, a copy of which I also enclose (No. 4.), and, in consequence, my wife and I went to Mrs. Hatch's house with our eldest daughter, who we left there, and arranged to take our youngest child within a fortnight from that time.

Before the expiration of the fortnight, my wife received a letter from Mrs. Hatch, dated 13th August, a copy of which I also enclose (No. 5), and at the expiration of the fortnight my wife took our youngest child to Mrs. Hatch's house, and left her there with Mr. and Mrs. Hatch, and returned home the same evening.

As if through the interposition of Providence, Mrs. Plummer felt very uncomfortable all night, and in the morning went off again to Mrs. Hatch's with the determination of taking away the children, and told Mrs. Hatch she had come to take the children away, and then, for the first time, discovered she could not speak to her child (Mary) alone, as in every attempt to take her into a room to speak to her, Mrs. Hatch followed, and at length seeing no alternative she took the child into the water-closet, knowing no person could follow her there.

The interview there lasted but a few minutes, Mrs. Plummer merely asking Mary in general terms, and ordinary questions, how she liked the School, &c. &c. The child in reply told her mother 'She was very glad they were going to take her away, for she did not like Mr. Hatch, he was a disgusting man, for he had got such a curious penny.' Mrs. Plummer then said 'Child! what do you mean?' The child again made reply, 'Well, he has mamma, for I have seen it.' Upon Mrs. Plummer requiring a further explanation she stated that the very first night she was left at Mrs. Hatch's house she was walking in the garden with Mr. Hatch and his adopted child, when Mr. Hatch placed her (my daughter Mary's) hand in one of his trouser's pockets, and the hand of the adopted child in the other pocket; but the pockets were not sewn up, and that her (the child's) hand touched his private parts. That nearly every night she (my daughter Mary) was at his house, Mr. Hatch used to come into her bed-room and pull the bed clothes off, and then lay himself across her, and take indecent liberties with her in handling her person, and making her handle his.

My daughter further states that on one occasion when there was company, Mr. Hatch while the company was assembling was with my daughter and his own adopted child in a bed-room, and he took my child on one knee and his adopted child on the other, and unbuttoned his trousers and made them take his person in their hands.

Upon Mrs. Plummer speaking to my youngest child, not yet eight years of age, it appears that, although she was there only one night, yet Mr. Hatch was wicked enough to treat her partly in the same disgusting way that he had done her sister.

My Lord, my children have been carefully and properly brought up from their birth, and are children of truth, and have always been taught to reverence their God, and to do right and eschew wrong; and both Mrs. Plummer and I thought, in placing our children with a Clergyman, their morals, as well as their education, would be carefully attended to, and that they would be properly protected. Guess, my Lord what my wife's and my own feelings must have been, and how great our misery was on hearing such details from the innocent childish lips of our own children.

In my distress of mind I found a great difficulty in determining the course I should pursue. While I felt grateful to Providence, that the persons of my children had not received absolute injury, yet I feared that the mind might be contaminated by what had occurred, and that if I allowed the matter to rest without complaint, I should be guilty of neglect towards other children who might be entrusted to the same hands and become utterly ruined. I therefore determined to address your Lordship, in the hope that your Lordship would institute an ecclesiastical inquiry, by issuing your Commission to investigate the circumstances, and with that view I lay the above statement before you, – which, though it does not go into the full details as my poor children could, it is substantially an account of that which took place.

I have the honour to be, My Lord,
Your Lordship's most obedient humble Servant,

(Signed) THOMAS PLUMMER,

Holcroft House, Great Blumsden [sic], Highworth, Wiltshire.
16th September, 1859

Henry must have thought that he was going mad. Of all crimes, the sexual molestation of children is reviled and (almost) universally condemned. Only child murder is worse. But against Henry the charges were even more serious. He was, after all, not only a Church of England clergyman and guardian of morals, but in pastoral care of several hundred prisoners, male and female – including young girls – at Wandsworth Prison.

Essie was shown the original letter from the Bishop so she was aware that the Plummers had made some sort of charge against Henry, but the nature of it was not specified. The second letter with the copy of the Plummers' letter he did not show her because as he said later, Lucy was named in it, effectively as an accomplice, and he did not want his wife to talk to her about it. No doubt also, he found the charges so monstrous and disgusting, that he could not bring himself to discuss them even with his trusting wife.

On 11th October, the visiting magistrates at Wandsworth were informed of the charges against Henry. He was granted leave of absence until 28th October, when a formal hearing would be held with witnesses for both sides present. On 24th

October, Henry had an interview with Richard Onslow, the governor of the prison. If Henry's first error of judgement had been to allow Eugenia into his bed in the morning – although that, of itself, would not have precluded the majority of the charges that followed – arguably his major mistake was what he did after he had spoken to the governor. Mr Onslow suggested that even if the charges against Henry were without foundation, his position afterwards would be 'rendered so distressing', that he could 'scarcely with comfort' retain his appointment as prison chaplain. He pointed out that the enquiry in front of the visiting magistrates would not be on oath, so things might be said that would otherwise not be said. If it was found that Henry had a case to answer, he would be suspended and subsequently dismissed. And of course, and here was the crux, the enquiry would be in public so everyone would know the details. If Henry resigned his post the enquiry would stop, since he would cease to be a public servant. On 26th October 1859, Henry John Hatch formally resigned his position as chaplain of Wandsworth Prison.

Was it a mistake to resign? Did he really think that the serious accusation that had been made against him would be withdrawn by the Plummers simply because he had resigned his position? On the other hand, if he had elected to answer the charges in the magistrates' hearing, no amount of evidence from defence witnesses and a finding in his favour, would have prevented some of the mud from sticking. How could he possibly have retained his position in the prison in such circumstances? In the event it made no difference whether he resigned or not – except that it could be read subsequently as an admission of guilt. On day the magistrate's hearing was due to have taken place, 28th October, Thomas Plummer instituted a formal prosecution against Henry John Hatch. This made a court appearance unavoidable. The next day, a warrant was issued for Henry's arrest.

Meanwhile Henry, whose world was rapidly collapsing about him, found – as he maintained in his subsequent petition to the Queen – that on the same day, and having just lost his sole source of income, he was threatened with another debt. It was a claim against him from yet another case in Chancery. The General Indemnity Insurance Company was in the process of being wound up. Henry was a director and shareholder, and was liable for the sum of £200 against his shares.

The General Indemnity Insurance Company had been set up in 1853 with a capital of £200,000. The aims of the company were to indemnify persons against criminal offences, to insure against fire, to guarantee rents, dividends, tithes, rates and taxes, to act as debt collectors and estate agents, to make loans, to grant and sell endowments and annuities, and to act as agents of other companies. The company seemed to be very broad-based in its business model. By February 1854, its capital stood at £132,000, and it decided to raise another £500,000 by the issue of £5 shares as well as £250,000 by loans. Henry was appointed a director, and acquired 100 shares at £2 each. By late 1859, the company was bust and in the process of being wound up. As a director, Henry was financially liable. He was concerned that as soon as it became known that he had lost his only source of income, the claim would be immediately enforced. This would have put him in even deeper distress with visions of bailiffs carting off the furniture or worse. He thus decided *before* he knew that Thomas Plummer had preferred charges against him, to remove to a place where the debt-collectors could not find him in order to try and work out his finances. This he did on Friday, 28th October. He chose Poplar in east London, and only Essie, subsequently, knew his whereabouts. His leaving, the day before the warrant was issued for his arrest, was to seem later as though he had absconded. His departure was made under the most distressing circumstances, to the extent that Essie was afraid that he would take his own life. She immediately wrote to the Plummers, throwing herself and Henry on their mercy:

Dear Mrs. Plummer,

I write almost distracted to ask and pray of you not to press matters further towards my poor husband. He has gone away, I know not where, distracted, and here am I a delicate and helpless wife, without a farthing, and with a poor mother subject to epileptic fits, and a helpless little child. I appeal to you as you would to your God to have pity on me. I know not what has occurred, but something that has driven my husband distracted away from home. He has given up his situation, and we have therefore now nothing in this world, if he is taken from us. I hope you will have mercy on us, and write to me to say you will forgive him. We have nothing now left us in this world. When he heard from the bishop he at once gave up his situation, and now we shall be starving. If I was not so helpless, and my poor mother and little child, I could work. Whatever has been done, surely my husband and myself are sufficiently punished. I cannot believe you will press matters more. You would not have kissed me in the affectionate way you did, and spoken to me in the friendly way you did when bidding me good bye, if you had not had a heart to have pity on me in my forlorn state. I have lost my husband, and am almost distracted. Write to me by return post.

I am, &c

E Hatch, 28th October

Of course whether or not Mrs Plummer would have been moved by this heart-rending appeal – and one suspects not – the charge against Henry had already been filed.

A warrant for the arrest of Henry John Hatch was issued on Saturday, 29th October 1859, to Constable William Taylor; he went to the Hatches' residence to serve it, finding that Henry was not there. On Monday, 31st October, Essie told Henry by post that the warrant had been issued. Henry must have sent her his address as soon as he found lodgings. Subsequently, Henry said that as soon as he received this information, he fully intended to give himself up – but this he failed to do for another twelve days.

On 11th November, Essie was visited by a young lawyer, the unlikely named Walters Freake Pratt, one of the solicitors engaged by the Plummers. He asked to see Essie alone, and told her that if she gave him Henry's address and put down in writing that she thought he was guilty of the charges, the matter would be dropped. Essie declined on both counts, pointing out that she still had no idea of the detail of the charges so she could hardly declare whether Henry was guilty or not. She also said that she could not divulge his address without his prior agreement. She then sent for Mr Onslow to provide her with some guidance in the matter. Pratt was against involving another party, but Mr Onslow came nevertheless, and had a private conference with the solicitor. Mr Onslow then told Essie that she had to give up Henry's address and he should acknowledge his guilt, at which point the matter would be dropped. If Henry did not surrender at once, his name would be advertised in *Hue and Cry* with a £100 reward offered for his apprehension. Walters Freake Pratt returned the following day. Essie, having had contact with her husband, told him that Henry maintained his innocence but that he would surrender to Pratt at Ridler's Hotel, where he (Pratt) was staying, at 7:30 that evening. Essie became quite emotional at this point asking Pratt whether it was money he was after, since they had none, and crying out aloud that she did not know what to do. Pratt, apparently pitying her – or just fishing for further information – offered her his private services, which she declined to take.

Henry surrendered to Walters Freake Pratt at Ridler's Hotel, Holborn, on Saturday, 12th November, and was handed over to Constable Taylor. Once more the offer was made, by Pratt, to withdraw the charge in exchange for an admission of guilt; this time it was Henry himself who declined to do so. He did, however, say something like, 'deal with me as leniently as you can', and according to Pratt, although Henry subsequently denied it, he said, 'I am mad', or, 'I was mad'. In the cab to the police station, Henry asked Constable Taylor the nature of the charges against him, and the likely punishment if found guilty. Taylor told him that he thought that there were two charges of common assault, for which the magistrate could sentence six months hard labour for each. Henry did not have to wait very long to find out what was going to happen, spending the weekend in custody at the police station before the first hearing.

The case was heard at the Wandsworth magistrates' court on Monday, 14th November 1859, when the evidence was presented in all its awfulness, and the proceedings – less the more graphic details – were reported in the newspapers. *The Morning Chronicle* confirmed the regard in which the residents of Wandsworth held Henry:

> From the well-known popularity of the reverend gentleman, numbers of the inhabitants of Wandsworth flocked to the court at an early hour, for the purpose of procuring a place...but a great many were disappointed...consequently, the yard and the front of the court were thronged with persons during the whole investigation.

The prosecution witnesses were a tearful Eugenia, followed by Stephana and their mother. In response to questions from the prosecution barrister, Mr Cooper, Eugenia described how Henry had forced her to 'place her hand upon his person' saying that it had happened in the garden, in her bed, in his bed, and also while sitting on his knee. Essie had retained the services of Mr George Lewis of Lewis and Lewis for the defence, and he now questioned Eugenia. He asked her whether she had complained of Henry's behaviour to any of the five ladies living in the house and how much she had told her mother when she had arrived with Stephana. She replied that she had told no-one, and had only asked her mother to take her away. His questioning became quite brutal:

| | |
|---|---|
| *Mr. Lewis:* | Have you been in any other person's bed? |
| *Eugenia:* | None, with the exception of theirs [The Hatches'] and my papa's |
| *Mr. Lewis:* | Are you not under an engagement to be married? |
| *Eugenia:* | I don't know what you mean. |
| *Mr. Lewis:* | Do you know a doctor? Have you ever been in his bed? |
| *Eugenia:* | (still crying): No, never. |
| *Mr. Lewis:* | Are you not under an engagement to him to be married? |
| *Eugenia:* | I never told him of it. |

This was a reference to Eugenia's supposed betrothal to the family doctor, Mr Gay, which had been mentioned both by Eugenia and her mother when they were at the Hatches'...

| | |
|---|---|
| *Mr. Lewis:* | Don't you know what marriage means? |
| *Eugenia:* | Yes. |
| *Mr. Lewis:* | Have you not promised to be married to him? |

| | |
|---|---|
| *Eugenia*: | I don't know who you mean. Do you mean the doctor at Mr. Hatch's? |
| *Mr. Lewis*: | I would rather not mention names. |
| *Eugenia*: | At home do you mean? |
| *Mr. Lewis*: | Yes. |
| *Eugenia*: | I only said it in fun sometimes. I have never been in his bed. |
| *Mr. Lewis*: | Quite sure of that? |
| *Eugenia*: | (Crying) Yes, I am. |
| *Mr. Lewis*: | Did you not hear your mother tell Mr. Hatch to take great care of you as you were very forward and untruthful? |
| *Eugenia*: | I did not hear her say so. |
| *Mr. Lewis*: | Were you kindly treated at Mr. Hatch's? |
| *Eugenia*: | I did not like them. |
| *Mr. Lewis*: | Then you told all this tale to get away? |
| *Eugenia*: | I wanted to go away. I saw my mother again when she brought my little sister…I did not tell her what had taken place…I only cried to go home… |

Mr Lewis asked Eugenia whether an indecent word she had used to describe Henry's behaviour had been used by her before going to the Hatches'. She said that she might have done so, but did not remember it. He then asked her about the bedroom doors…

| | |
|---|---|
| *Mr. Lewis*: | Were your bedroom doors kept open? |
| *Eugenia*: | Mother said they were to be kept open. They [The Hatches] did not do it. |

Then, in response to a further question, Eugenia said, 'I know a Mr. Brighton. I was never in his bed.' Mr Lewis was to come in for some criticism, subsequently, for his failure to examine the *defence* witnesses before the magistrates' hearing, and prepare an adequate defence. He could certainly not be faulted on his probing questioning of Eugenia…

Stephana was now called. Responding to various questions from Mr Cooper: '…He came into my room…He laid across me…He had his night-shirt on, and no trousers…' In response to Mr Lewis, she denied that she had used the indecent word Eugenia had admitted using, although she had heard it used before they went to the Hatches'. Then,

When we went up to bed, Mrs Hatch was in her bedroom…[their] bedroom opened into mine. I knew she was there as I saw her. He left Mrs. Hatch to come to me. He remained between a quarter of an hour and half an hour. I did not scream. I was afraid to do so…

On the subject of going into people's beds: 'I know Mr. Brighton. I have seen him once. I don't know whether she [Eugenia] has been in his bed. She has never told me so.' And regarding Eugenia's alleged betrothal to their doctor…'She has told me she was going to marry him. I do not know that it is settled…' Mr Ingham, the magistrate, intervened with Mr Lewis asking him what it was he was trying to prove, commenting that when he was six, he was engaged to marry his two aunts. Mr

Cooper commented that the doctor was 'an old man' [he was thirty-seven or thirty-eight at the time], implying presumably, that the union was, in any case, somewhat unlikely as a serious undertaking.

The last prosecution witness was Caroline Plummer, the girls' mother. In response to questions from Mr Cooper, she claimed that when she visited the Hatches' bringing Stephana, she was unable to talk to Eugenia alone except in the water closet, because of the constant presence of the Hatches. Mr Cooper asked her whether she had described Eugenia to the Hatches as, '…forward, and given to tell untruths.' She responded emphatically that she had not. Mr Lewis now questioned her for the defence. He established that following the Plummers' departure from Wandsworth on 26th August, nothing was done regarding a complaint until the end of September when a letter was written to the bishop. This closed the prosecution case.

Mr Lewis made a 'formidable address' to the magistrate on behalf of Henry, pointing out that the prisoner had voluntarily surrendered to meet the charge. He then called his witnesses for the defence.

The first of these was the governess, Martha Howe. She confirmed that when Mrs Plummer had first brought Eugenia to the Hatches', she had said that since Eugenia's last school she had not been so open in her manner, and had become reserved and not truthful. She [Martha Howe] had Eugenia 'under her eye' from the moment she was dressed until she went to bed at night, and she [Eugenia] made no complaint. From her knowledge [Miss Howe's], the bedroom doors were kept wide open. Mr Hatch was a perfect gentleman and 'modest and correct'.

Essie's mother, Mrs Dillon, was called. She too recalled Mrs Plummer saying that her daughter was untruthful and deceitful. She also repeated Mrs Plummer's claim that Eugenia was to marry their medical man. Ever since Henry had been married to her daughter [fourteen years], he had been a decent and modest man.

Ellen Farr, the cook, was called and declared Henry to be a 'very good man'. The housemaid, Mary Ann Reed, was called. She confirmed that the bedroom doors were always open and that Mr Hatch's conduct was always proper. She said that Eugenia had told her in the hall that she was sorry to be leaving. Mr Cooper then questioned Mary Ann. Eugenia never went to bed until after prayers at nine o'clock. Mrs Hatch went up to see her in bed, followed by Henry after he had had supper. They were the last up. She also added that 'the [bedroom] doors were open when I went to bed, and they were open when I came down in the morning.'

Lastly, Mr Lewis called Lucy. She described 'walking' in the garden, with her on one side of Henry and Eugenia on the other. Mr Ingham, the magistrate, took up the questioning:

| | |
|---|---|
| *Mr. Ingham*: | Did anything happen? |
| *Lucy*: | No. |
| *Mr. Ingham*: | Did you hear him ask Miss Plummer to put her hand in his pocket? |
| *Lucy*: | No. |
| *Mr. Ingham*: | Did you put your hand in his pocket? |
| *Lucy*: | No. |

Lucy then described to Mr Cooper how she ran about the garden, and Eugenia was left with Henry once or twice.

The governor, Richard Onslow, was called and said that he had known Henry for eight years since the prison opened, and he had never had a suspicion about him; never a single complaint regarding his immorality or indecency. Charles Wilkinson, the resident surgeon at Wandsworth Prison, said he had known Henry for eight years and had never heard anything 'detrimental to his character'. If he had a child of his own, he said, he should have placed it in Henry's care with complete confidence. Lastly Joseph Gegg, Henry's assistant chaplain, was called, and confirmed Henry's 'very high character'. This completed the case for the defence.

The magistrate said that a case of this importance should be 'investigated by another tribunal', and committed Henry for trial on two charges – one each for assaulting Eugenia and Stephana – at the next session of the Central Criminal Court at the Old Bailey. Henry was unable to produce bail of £500, together with two sureties of £250 each, and neither his sisters and their families, nor his cousins, nor even his Uncle Charles were able, or willing, between them to raise the £1000 necessary to maintain his liberty. He was sent to prison to await trial. There was one very small consolation. They did not send him to Wandsworth but to the Surrey County Gaol at Horsemonger Lane. Having spent eight years as a prison chaplain, Henry John Hatch found out for the first time what it was like to be issued prison uniform, and locked up with the other prisoners. At least he was spared the indignity of this being done by his former colleagues.

# The Old Bailey

nother small consolation, given what must have been the state of Henry's mind at this time, was that he had to endure only two weeks at Horsemonger Lane before his appearance at the Old Bailey. The trial took place on Thursday, 1st December 1859. The proceedings of the case were reported in the press, although the precise details of the evidence were not. The case was heard before (Judge) Baron Bramwell, with Mr Cooper and Mr Metcalfe conducting the prosecution and Serjeant Ballantine, Mr Robinson and Mr F H Lewis for the defence.

Baron George William Wilsher Bramwell was 52 years old at the time of the trial. He had been admitted to Lincoln's Inn in 1830, and was called to the bar in 1838. He was appointed a 'Judge as Baron of the Exchequer' in 1856. Bramwell was described as 'domineering, entertaining, and consciously concerned to mould the law to ends which he favoured' (ODNB). Serjeant Ballantine had been retained by Henry's solicitor, Mr Lewis, as his defence counsel. Since his actions were critical to the conduct of the case, it is appropriate to consider his background in more detail. Serjeant-at-Law William Ballantine was called to the bar in 1834 and received the Serjeant's coif in 1856. Thus he had 25 years experience when he was retained for the Hatch defence. Ballantine moved in exalted circles; he was a member of the Garrick Club, and rubbed shoulders with Dickens, Thackeray, and Trollope. He was entertained at Farnham Castle by Dr Sumner, the Bishop of Winchester, who had written to Henry John Hatch with the Plummers' accusations (and also to Uncle Henry over his misappropriation of Church funds). Ballantine was subsequently involved in a number of notable actions, not least of which was the Mordaunt divorce case of 1870, when he was 'distinguished by the tact which he displayed...when the Prince of Wales was subpoenaed by the court' (ODNB). Less well known though, was his unsuccessful defence of Mrs Manning on a charge of murder. Marie de Roux, born in Switzerland, had come to England and married an Englishman, Frederick George Manning, while maintaining a friendship with Patrick O'Connor who was a moneylender. Mrs Manning had been in domestic service before her marriage, and at different times had been a lady's maid to Lady Palk and Lady Blantyre (ODNB). Marie Manning and her husband shot and battered O'Connor to death at their house and buried his body under the floor, after which they went to his lodging and stole cash and share certificates to a value of more than £4000. They were caught and tried, each blaming the other for the murder. In Marie's defence, Ballantine tried to claim that as a foreigner, she was not subject to British jurisdiction. This move was rejected by the court, since she had acquired citizenship by virtue of her marriage to a British subject. The deputy governor of Newgate described Mrs Manning as 'a very resolute woman...the most callous of females', while Mr Manning was 'a very imbecile character...dragged into crime through the strong mind of his wife'. The Mannings were found guilty, sentenced to death, and hanged together on the roof of the entrance of Horsemonger Lane gaol in front of a great crowd in November 1849. Charles Dickens was present, and famously wrote to *The Times* deprecating the '...inconceivably awful...wickedness and levity of the immense crowd'. He was not too disgusted though, that he did not pay ten guineas for the rental of a flat roof with a grandstand view of the gallows. The use of a back kitchen was included in the transaction, and considering the time of year and the fact that he had arrived the previous evening in order not to miss anything, one assumes that the kitchen was kept busy supplying him and his party with hot drinks throughout the night. Dickens' character Hortense, Lady Deadlock's maid in Bleak House who murdered Mr Tulkinghorn, was said to have been based on Mrs Manning. It is interesting to speculate that it may well have been Ballantine with his personal knowledge of Marie Manning who gave Dickens the material for the character. It is further interesting to wonder whether Henry Hatch knew that a previous client, unsuccessfully defended by Serjeant Ballantine, had been hanged on the very entrance gate through which he had to pass on his way to the Old Bailey...

Central Criminal Court, Thursday, December 1st 1859.

Before Mr. Baron Bramwell

The Queen v. Henry John Hatch

Indicted for unlawfully and indecently assaulting Mary Eugenia Plummer on divers [sic] days. Other counts for like assaults upon Stephana Augusta Plummer.

Messrs. Cooper and Metcalfe conducted the Prosecution.

Mr. Serjt. Ballantine and Mr. Robinson, appeared for the defence. [Mr F H Lewis, as the junior barrister, was apparently omitted from the court reporter's notes]

Mr Cooper, addressing the jury, said it was his painful duty to bring this most distressing case before them:

The defendant was charged with the most atrocious conduct towards two little girls, the daughters of a gentleman of fortune residing in Wiltshire, who had been placed in his charge at a school kept by him at Wandsworth…The issue of the enquiry must undoubtedly be a most fearful one, the character of the defendant and the future prospects and happiness of these young children being involved in the investigation.

His colleague, Mr Metcalfe, then proceeded to examine Mary Eugenia Plummer. In the prosecution evidence that follows, the exchanges have been reproduced, mostly verbatim, from the court reporter's transcript. However, in its printed form, the transcript grouped together evidence from the different witnesses relating to the same incidents – in the garden, in Eugenia's bedroom, in the Hatches' bedroom etc – presumably to ease consideration of the evidence as a whole for each incident. Since the witnesses were examined sequentially, and separately, by the defence and prosecution barristers, it has been necessary to disentangle these different sections in order to reconstruct the order of events in court. Where the questions and answers seem repetitive, this may be due to an error either of the court reporter in gathering the different strands of the evidence together, or the present author in the reconstruction. However, it is probable that the barristers and the judge deliberately repeated the same questions several times, particularly to Eugenia, in order to probe the truth of the answers. Where the dialogue appears to be a little disjointed, this is due to the court reporter's rendering of exactly what was said without any editing. No similar record of the defence case exists, and the details of this, and the rest of the court proceedings, have been assembled from the newspaper reports.

The first part of Eugenia's evidence relates to what happened in the garden on the day she arrived at the Hatches' on 11th August 1859, immediately after her mother and father had left…

Mary Eugenia Plummer, sworn and examined by Mr. Metcalfe:

| | |
|---|---|
| *Mr. Metcalfe*: | On the first day that you went to the house, after your mother left, did you walk in the garden with Mr. Hatch? |
| *Eugenia*: | Yes. |
| *Mr. Metcalfe*: | Was Lucy with you? |
| *Eugenia*: | Yes. |
| *Baron Bramwell*: | How old is Lucy? |
| *Eugenia*: | I think she is seven. |
| *Mr. Metcalfe*: | Did anything happen while you were in the garden with Mr. Hatch? |
| *Eugenia*: | He put my hand into his pocket, and put his penny into my hand. |
| *Mr. Metcalfe*: | Into his pocket you say – was it a pocket? |
| *Eugenia*: | It was a hole in the pocket. |
| *Mr. Metcalfe*: | Your hand went through the hole you mean? |
| *Eugenia*: | Yes. |
| *Mr. Metcalfe*: | At this time you were walking round the garden with him? |
| *Eugenia*: | Yes. |
| *Mr. Metcalfe*: | Did he do anything else in the garden at all? |

| | |
|---|---|
| *Eugenia*: | He kept it there till he went in, and that was all he did. |
| *Mr. Metcalfe*: | Did you at all try to take it away? |
| *Eugenia*: | Yes I did; I tried to take it away. |
| *Mr. Metcalfe*: | Did he prevent your taking it away? |
| *Eugenia*: | Yes. |
| *Mr. Metcalfe*: | He kept it there till you went in, you say? |
| *Eugenia*: | Yes. |

Eugenia's use of the word 'penny' to indicate Henry's virile member may be baby-talk, contemporary slang or even a euphemism introduced by the court shorthand writer. Thomas Plummer had also used the word in his letter to the bishop. He may have been quoting his daughter, or the court reporter in transcribing that letter may have used the same euphemism. Perhaps the reporter could not (or would not) do 'penis' in shorthand. Confusingly, later in her evidence Eugenia uses the same word in reference to her own genitals. It may have been Eugenia's own word, which the court then proceeded to adopt in order not to embarrass or confuse Eugenia (or itself...)

Henry allegedly made nightly visits to Eugenia's bedroom...

| | |
|---|---|
| *Mr. Metcalfe*: | What took place the next night? |
| *Eugenia*: | When I went to bed, after I had been in my bed, he came into my bed-room and undone [sic] his trowsers [sic], and put his penny in my hand. |

| | |
|---|---|
| *Mr. Metcalfe*: | Were you in bed at the time? |
| *Eugenia*: | Yes. |
| *Mr. Metcalfe*: | When he put his penny, as you say, into your hand, did you feel his flesh? |
| *Eugenia*: | Yes. |
| *Mr. Metcalfe*: | When was the next time? Did he at any time after that do anything to you? |
| *Eugenia*: | Not again that night. |
| *Mr. Metcalfe*: | The next night, did he? |
| *Eugenia*: | He done [sic] the same. |
| *Mr. Metcalfe*: | When you were in bed, in the same way? |
| *Eugenia*: | Yes. |
| *Mr. Metcalfe*: | And how long did he continue the next night? |
| *Eugenia*: | After about a week, he did about the same thing; but he touched my penny. |
| *Mr. Metcalfe*: | But first of all, you say, that on the second night – the night after you have told us of – he did the same thing? |
| *Eugenia*: | Yes. |
| *Mr. Metcalfe*: | And the third night that you were there, do you say he did the same? |
| *Eugenia*: | Yes; the same. |

| | |
|---|---|
| *Mr. Metcalfe*: | That is, he put his penny into your hands? |
| *Eugenia*: | Yes. |
| *Mr. Metcalfe*: | And a week afterwards it was that he put his against yours, you say? |
| *Eugenia*: | His finger, I thought it was. |
| *Mr. Metcalfe*: | Between that time – between the third night you were there and a week afterwards that you speak of – had he been into your bed-room? |
| *Eugenia*: | Yes. |
| *Mr. Metcalfe*: | How often did he come? |
| *Eugenia*: | He came every night into my bed-room. |
| *Mr. Metcalfe*: | When he came, did he do anything? |
| *Eugenia*: | Yes; he done the same thing; he put his, and touched my penny [sic]. |
| *Mr. Metcalfe*: | Every night? |
| *Eugenia*: | Yes. |
| *Mr. Metcalfe*: | Did he do anything else – did he touch you at all with his hand? |
| *Eugenia*: | Yes; after a week. |
| *Mr. Metcalfe*: | Then he touched you with his hands? |
| *Eugenia*: | Under the clothes. |

| | |
|---|---|
| *Mr. Metcalfe*: | And upon you, did he? |
| *Eugenia*: | Yes. |
| *Mr. Metcalfe*: | I think you say that this went on every night except for the first night, every night you were there? |
| *Eugenia*: | Yes. |
| *Mr. Metcalfe*: | Did you ever go into his bedroom? |
| *Eugenia*: | In the morning. |
| *Baron Bramwell*: | Let me understand this. You say he put his finger, as you thought, against you. Did he do that more than one night? |
| *Eugenia*: | Yes. |
| *Mr. Metcalfe*: | How often did he do that? |
| *Eugenia*: | He done it every night after a week. |

He '…done the same thing… he done it…' Clearly, Eugenia's education was somewhat wanting; was she really the daughter of a gentleman? Still, that did not justify the assaults she was alleging…

| | |
|---|---|
| *Mr. Metcalfe*: | About what time did you go to bed? |
| *Eugenia*: | A little past eight. |
| *Mr. Metcalfe*: | How shortly after that did he come into your room? |
| *Eugenia*: | Directly I was in bed. |
| *Mr. Metcalfe*: | How long did he remain? |

| | |
|---|---|
| *Eugenia*: | For rather a long time. |
| *Mr. Metcalfe*: | Could you judge at all how long? |
| *Eugenia*: | About a quarter of an hour I should think. |
| *Mr. Metcalfe*: | Did he continue doing that all the time during that quarter of an hour? |
| *Eugenia*: | Yes. |
| *Mr. Metcalfe*: | Did you try to get your hand away – try to prevent him? |
| *Eugenia*: | Yes; I tried to get it away. |
| *Mr. Metcalfe*: | Then after the quarter of an hour, he went out of the room, did he? |
| *Eugenia*: | Yes; he went out of my room. |
| *Mr. Metcalfe*: | When he went out of your room did you notice anything on your hands at all? |
| *Eugenia*: | Yes, my hands were wet, and I got out of bed and wiped them on the towel. |

This evidence, in its graphic and sickening detail, probably did more to sway the jury in Eugenia's favour than anything else. After all, how could an eleven-year-old child possibly know about 'wet hands' in the context of what was being alleged unless she had actually experienced the event? The questioning was carefully arranged by Mr Metcalfe to generate the strongest revulsion in the jury. No doubt it succeeded.

After some clarification requested by the judge, Mr Metcalfe continued:

| | |
|---|---|
| *Baron Bramwell*: | Did you sleep in the room by yourself? |
| *Eugenia*: | Yes. |
| *Mr. Metcalfe*: | Was that room next to his room? (Hatch's). |
| *Eugenia*: | There were two doors, one opened into a passage, and one into his room. |
| *Mr. Metcalfe*: | When he came into your room, did he come from his own room, or from the passage? |
| *Eugenia*: | From his room. |
| *Mr. Metcalfe*: | Was the door between his room and your room generally kept closed or open? |
| *Eugenia*: | Generally kept open. |
| *Mr. Metcalfe*: | And was the door in the passage opened or closed? |
| *Eugenia*: | Closed. |
| *Mr. Metcalfe*: | Did you always go into your bed-room through his bed-room? |
| *Eugenia*: | Yes; because the other door was locked. |
| *Mr. Metcalfe*: | The other door was kept locked was it? |
| *Eugenia*: | Yes. |

| | |
|---|---|
| *Mr. Metcalfe*: | Was anything placed against the door inside? |
| *Eugenia*: | Yes; a bath. |

This sounds like a strange and unlikely arrangement. Why should the Hatches' privacy be compromised by limiting access to Eugenia's room through theirs? The question was clearly prearranged, Mr Metcalfe leading Eugenia to give a credible reason for the outer door to be locked, with the implication that Eugenia's movements were constrained. Having the door locked was in direct contravention of Mrs Plummer's strict instruction. In any event, the servant Mary would have been able to confirm or otherwise the truth of the arrangement.

Now the questioning turned to the morning visits to the Hatches' bed:

| | |
|---|---|
| *Mr. Metcalfe*: | You say you went into Mr. Hatch's bed every morning, did you? |
| *Eugenia*: | Yes. |
| *Baron Bramwell*: | What did your mamma say to that? |
| *Eugenia*: | Mamma did not think it was right for me to go into their room – into their bed. |
| *Mr. Metcalfe*: | Did your mother say so at all? |
| *Eugenia*: | Yes: when she took me away she did; she said it was not right. |
| *Mr. Metcalfe*: | Do you remember whether it was when you went or when you were taken away? |
| *Eugenia*: | I think it was when I came. |

| | |
|---|---|
| *Mr. Metcalfe*: | And it was then your mother said she did not think it right? |
| *Eugenia*: | Yes. I think it was then. |
| *Mr. Metcalfe*: | Then after your mother had gone were you told to come into the bed-room by anybody? |
| *Eugenia*: | Yes; Mr. Hatch told me. |
| *Mr. Metcalfe*: | Was Lucy there when you went into his bed-room? |
| *Eugenia*: | Yes. |
| *Mr. Metcalfe*: | And was Mrs. Hatch there? |
| *Eugenia*: | Yes. |
| *Mr. Metcalfe*: | When you went into the room? |
| *Eugenia*: | Yes. |
| *Mr. Metcalfe*: | Did Mrs. Hatch, each morning when you went into the room, go out to wash the little girl? |
| *Eugenia*: | In the same room. |
| *Mr. Metcalfe*: | She washed Lucy in the same room did she? |
| *Eugenia*: | In the same room. |
| *Mr. Metcalfe*: | While she was washing Lucy in the same room, where were you? |
| *Eugenia*: | In the bed. |
| *Baron Bramwell*: | In the bed? |
| *Eugenia*: | In the bed, waiting for the servant to come and wash me. |

| | |
|---|---|
| *Baron Bramwell*: | What, in the bed? |
| *Eugenia*: | In Mr. Hatch's bed. |
| *Mr. Metcalfe*: | While you were there, did he do anything? |
| *Baron Bramwell*: | Was he in the bed too? |
| *Eugenia*: | Yes. |

Evidently the judge was having some difficulty believing what he was hearing…

| | |
|---|---|
| *Mr. Metcalfe*: | Did he do anything then to you, while Mrs. Hatch was washing Lucy? |
| *Eugenia*: | Yes. |
| *Mr. Metcalfe*: | What did he do? |
| *Eugenia*: | He put his penny into my hand. |
| *Baron Bramwell*: | Did Mrs. Hatch know that you were in the bed? |
| *Eugenia*: | Yes. |
| *Mr. Metcalfe*: | Did he do anything else besides putting it into your hand? |
| *Eugenia*: | Yes, and touching mine. |
| *Mr. Metcalfe*: | Your what? |
| *Eugenia*: | My penny. |
| *Mr. Metcalfe*: | Anything else? |
| *Eugenia*: | No, he done that all the time. |
| *Mr. Metcalfe*: | Besides touching you in that way, and putting his penny into your hand, did you see him at all? |

| | |
|---|---|
| *Eugenia*: | Yes. |
| *Mr. Metcalfe*: | How came that? |
| *Eugenia*: | I saw his penny. |
| *Mr. Metcalfe*: | How came you to see that? |
| *Eugenia*: | Because the clothes were up. |
| *Mr. Metcalfe*: | Who put them up? |
| *Eugenia*: | Mr. Hatch. |
| *Mr. Metcalfe*: | And that being so, you saw what you call his penny? |
| *Eugenia*: | Yes. |
| *Mr. Metcalfe*: | Who told you to come into that bed? (Mr. Hatch's bed). |
| *Eugenia*: | Mrs. Hatch told mamma that Lucy came into their bed in the morning, and I was to. |
| *Baron Bramwell*: | How old are you? |
| *Eugenia*: | Eleven. |

Eugenia was effectively accusing Essie of complicity in the assault. Essie could hardly have failed to be aware of what was going on if Eugenia's allegations were true. Eugenia also alleges that her mother disapproved of her going into the Hatches' bed.

One evening, the Hatches had a party with some guests:

| | |
|---|---|
| *Mr. Metcalfe*: | Do you remember one day when there was to be a party? |
| *Eugenia*: | Yes. |

| | |
|---|---|
| *Mr. Metcalfe*: | When you were waiting for the people to come, before they came, do you remember anything taking place with Mr. Hatch, you and Lucy? |
| *Eugenia*: | Yes; he took me on his knee. |
| *Mr. Metcalfe*: | What room were you in at that time? |
| *Eugenia*: | In his room. |
| *Mr. Metcalfe*: | His bed-room? |
| *Eugenia*: | Yes; I was passing through his room to go down stairs. |
| *Mr. Metcalfe*: | And was Lucy there also? |
| *Eugenia*: | Yes. |
| *Mr. Metcalfe*: | He took you on his knee, you say, where was Lucy? |
| *Eugenia*: | On his other knee. |
| *Mr. Metcalfe*: | While you were sitting, one on each knee, did he do anything then? |
| *Eugenia*: | Yes; he undone his trowsers, and put his penny in my hand. |
| *Mr. Metcalfe*: | How long did that continue? How long did that last? |
| *Eugenia*: | Not long, that was not. |

So Lucy, also, was complicit in the assault. If she was sitting on Henry's other knee, she could hardly have failed to see what was going on, although in the Plummers' letter to the bishop, it was claimed that Lucy was not just an observer…

Now Eugenia was asked about what happened on 25th August. Eugenia had been at the Hatches for about two weeks when her parents brought Stephana...

| | |
|---|---|
| *Mr. Metcalfe*: | When your mother came, did you see her alone at all? |
| *Eugenia*: | We went into the water closet |
| *Mr. Metcalfe*: | You did – with your mother? |
| *Eugenia*: | Yes. |
| *Mr. Metcalfe*: | Did you make any complaint to your mother at all? |
| *Eugenia*: | No; I only cried and told her to take me home. |
| *Mr. Metcalfe*: | Did you say anything at all about Mr. Hatch then? |
| *Eugenia*: | No. |
| *Mr. Metcalfe*: | Your mother left your little sister there that night, did she? |
| *Eugenia*. | Yes. |
| *Mr. Metcalfe*: | On that night, after your little sister was left, did anything happen? Did Mr. Hatch do anything to you? |
| *Eugenia*: | Yes; he came into me that night. |
| *Mr. Metcalfe*: | Into your bed-room? |
| *Eugenia*: | Yes. |
| *Mr. Metcalfe*: | Did you sleep in the same bed with your sister? |
| *Eugenia*: | No; I did not. My sister slept in |

|  | the room that I did, and I went into the next room. |
| --- | --- |
| *Mr. Metcalfe*: | Then he came into your room did he? |
| *Eugenia*: | Yes. |
| *Mr. Metcalfe*: | How would he get into that room – through your sister's room? |
| *Eugenia*: | No, through a passage; there is only one door to that. |
| *Mr. Metcalfe*: | Did he do anything when he came into your room that night? |
| *Eugenia*: | Yes; he done the same. |

It was now Serjeant Ballantine's opportunity to cross-examine Eugenia for the defence. He decided to ignore the events in the garden and the night of the party, and launched straight into the alleged visits to Eugenia's bedroom. He tried hard to get her to contradict herself, and in endeavouring to do so, the questioning became very searching…

| *Serj Ballantine*: | You have said that Mr. Hatch put your hand to his 'penny', and that on one occasion you found your hands wet afterwards, and went and wiped them on a towel? |
| --- | --- |
| *Eugenia*: | Yes. |
| *Serj Ballantine*: | Did that occur every time? |
| *Eugenia*: | Yes. |
| *Serj Ballantine*: | Do you remember when you |

|  | were examined before the magistrate? |
|---|---|
| *Eugenia*: | Yes. |
| *Serj Ballantine*: | And you swore that you told your mother that your hands had been wet every time? |
| *Eugenia*: | Yes. |
| *Serj Ballantine*: | And that it happened every night? |
| *Eugenia*: | Yes, excepting the first. |
| *Serj Ballantine*: | And did you wipe your hands every time? |
| *Eugenia*: | Yes. |
| *Serj Ballantine*: | Where? |
| *Eugenia*: | On my towel. |
| *Serj Ballantine*: | Every time on your towel, did you? |
| *Eugenia*: | Yes, I got out of bed and wiped it. |
| *Serj Ballantine*: | You got out of bed and wiped it? |
| *Eugenia*: | Yes. |
| *Serj Ballantine*: | How was he lying when he put your hands on his penny? |
| *Eugenia*: | He was sitting on my bed. |
| *Serj Ballantine*: | In his clothes, or in his night-dress merely? |
| *Eugenia*: | In his clothes. |

*Serj Ballantine*:      Sitting on your bed was he?

*Eugenia*:      Yes.

*Serj Ballantine*:      Do you mean with his trowsers unbuttoned?

*Eugenia*:      He unbuttoned his trowsers.

*Serj Ballantine*:      He then sat on your bed.

*Eugenia*:      Yes.

*Serj Ballantine*:      Did you see what he did after you had done this?

*Eugenia*:      I saw that he did put it in my hand.

*Serj Ballantine*:      And after you felt your hand wet, what did he do?

*Eugenia*:      I did not wipe my hand until he went out of the room.

*Serj Ballantine*:      Did he button up his trowsers?

*Eugenia*:      Yes; before he went out of the room.

*Serj Ballantine*:      You remember that?

*Eugenia*:      Yes.

*Serj Ballantine*:      Every time?

*Eugenia*:      Yes.

*Serj Ballantine*:      You have said on some occasions after the first week he put his finger into your person?

*Eugenia*:      I suppose it was his finger. I thought it was.

| | |
|---|---|
| *Serj Ballantine:* | Cannot you tell whether it was his penny or not? |
| *Eugenia:* | No; I don't know which it was. |
| *Serj Ballantine:* | You know he had been behaving in this bad way to you, and you had been obliged to put your hand to his "penny". Do you mean that at the end of the week you could not tell whether it was his finger or his "penny?" |
| *Eugenia:* | I think it was his finger. |
| *Serj Ballantine:* | Do you not know? |
| *Eugenia:* | No; I don't know which it was, but I think it was his finger. |

Serjeant Ballantine was trying to get Eugenia to make conflicting statements. To an adult, given the circumstances, it would be difficult not to know whether it was Henry Hatch's finger or something else that was put 'into [her] person'. Unfortunately, in his cross-examination the Serjeant seemed to have uncovered more lurid and unpleasant detail…

| | |
|---|---|
| *Serj Ballantine:* | How were you lying, or what were you doing, when he did it? |
| *Eugenia:* | I was lying in bed. |
| *Serj Ballantine:* | And how did he do so? |
| *Eugenia:* | He put his hand inside the clothes – he was lying across them. |
| *Serj Ballantine:* | Do you mean he laid upon you? |
| *Eugenia:* | Across the bed. |
| *Serj Ballantine:* | Inside? |

*Eugenia*: No; outside.

*Serj Ballantine*: Outside the bed, did he?

*Eugenia*: Yes.

*Serj Ballantine*: And put his hand inside?

*Eugenia*: Yes.

*Serj Ballantine*: Then you must know it must have been his finger, it could not have been his penny?

*Eugenia*: I said I thought it was his finger.

*Serj Ballantine*: But you know it?

*Eugenia*: No; I am not certain that it was.

*Serj Ballantine*: Why, he was lying outside the bed with his clothes between him and you. Did he hurt you?

*Eugenia*: Yes.

*Serj Ballantine*: Very much?

*Eugenia*: Yes.

*Serj Ballantine*: Then did he put his finger into your person?

*Eugenia*: Yes.

*Serj Ballantine*: And kept it there for any time?

*Eugenia*: Yes.

*Serj Ballantine*: For a long time?

*Eugenia*: Not very long.

*Baron Bramwell*: What part of you did he hurt?

*Eugenia*: My penny.

| | |
|---|---|
| *Serj Ballantine*: | Inside it? |
| *Eugenia*: | Yes. |
| *Serj Ballantine*: | And when was the last time before you were taken away that he did this? |
| *Eugenia*: | When I was in bed with him. |
| *Serj Ballantine*: | About how long before you were taken away? |
| *Eugenia*: | Mamma came in the afternoon. |
| *Serj Ballantine*: | Then it was the very same day? |
| *Eugenia*: | It was in the morning he done it. |
| *Serj Ballantine*: | In the morning of that day? |
| *Eugenia*: | Yes. |
| *Serj Ballantine*: | You say he has hurt you a good deal? |
| *Eugenia*: | Yes. |
| *Serj Ballantine*: | The other thing did not hurt. It was very bad and very wicked and all that, but it did not hurt you. Did you not tell your mother about this hurting when she took you to the water-closet? |
| *Eugenia*: | I told you that he did hurt me. |
| *Serj Ballantine*: | But did not you tell your mamma in the water-closet that he hurt you? |
| *Eugenia*: | Not in the water-closet; I told her going home. |

| | |
|---|---|
| *Serj Ballantine*: | How came you not to tell her then? |
| *Eugenia*: | Because mamma did not stay there long. |
| *Serj Ballantine*: | Did you forget it? |
| *Eugenia*: | No; I did not forget it. |
| *Serj Ballantine*: | But you did not tell it because your mamma did not stay there long? |
| *Eugenia*: | No; because she went away. |
| *Serj Ballantine*: | Did you tell her on your way home? |
| *Eugenia*: | Yes. |
| *Serj Ballantine*: | In the cab? |
| *Eugenia*: | Yes. |
| *Serj Ballantine*: | You told her that Mr. Hatch had put his hand into your penny and hurt you very much? |
| *Eugenia*: | Yes. |
| *Serj Ballantine*: | Did your mamma examine your person? |
| *Eugenia*: | No; mamma did not. |
| *Serj Ballantine*: | Did anybody? |
| *Eugenia*: | Yes, the doctor. |
| *Serj Ballantine*: | What is his name? |
| *Eugenia*: | Mr. Gay. |
| *Serj Ballantine*: | When was that? |

| | |
|---|---|
| *Eugenia:* | The day we came home – the next day. |
| *Serj Ballantine:* | I want to know, during that last day, did he put his hands to your penny in the same way? |
| *Eugenia:* | Yes. |
| *Serj Ballantine:* | When? At the time he was using his hand to put into your person; At the time he was putting his finger into your person? |
| *Eugenia:* | I do not understand you. |
| *Serj Ballantine:* | At the time he was putting his finger into your penny, did he put your hand then to his? |
| *Eugenia:* | No. |
| *Serj Ballantine:* | Never? |
| *Eugenia:* | No. |
| *Serj Ballantine:* | Then when was it that was done? When used he to put your hand to his penny, when used he to do that? |
| *Eugenia:* | He done it every night. |
| *Serj Ballantine:* | He did that every night too? |
| *Eugenia:* | Every night I was there excepting the first night. |
| *Serj Ballantine:* | Then he must have come in twice? |
| *Eugenia:* | I do not know what you mean. |
| *Serj Ballantine:* | Did he come in twice? |

| | |
|---|---|
| *Eugenia*: | Do you mean in one day? |
| *Serj Ballantine*: | One night? |
| *Eugenia*: | No, he did not come in twice of a night. |
| *Serj Ballantine*: | Then how was it it happened that he put his finger into you, was it after that that he put his hand to you? |
| *Eugenia*: | After the first week he put his penny into my hand, and put his hand to my penny; after a week in my body, and in his bed as well. |
| *Serj Ballantine*: | After the first week. |
| *Eugenia*: | Yes. |
| *Serj Ballantine*: | He put his hand into your penny, and put your hand on his penny? |
| *Eugenia*: | Yes. |
| *Serj Ballantine*: | What did you mean by telling me that you did not know whether it was his finger or his penny? |
| *Eugenia*: | I was not certain, but I believe it was his finger. |

The judge, no doubt confused, sought some clarification:

| | |
|---|---|
| *Baron Bramwell*: | I must ask you a question, because it is left in some uncertainty. You said that the first week he used to come and |

| | put his finger to you, as you have told us? |
|---|---|
| *Eugenia*: | Yes. |
| *Baron Bramwell*: | And that he also put your hand to his? |
| *Eugenia*: | Yes. |
| *Baron Bramwell*: | How did he do that? Did he do both at one time, or first one and then the other? |
| *Eugenia*: | Yes, first one and then the other. |

Serjeant Ballantine and the Judge were both trying to establish the exact detail of what Eugenia was alleging. They were attempting to probe any weakness in the story and weigh the reliability of the evidence. Given the explicit details, it is perhaps not surprising that Serjeant Ballantine did not persist in establishing exactly what was done and in what order. Eugenia was, after all, only eleven years old, and her description of what was done made it all sound quite credible given the circumstances. Further questioning might well have been to the defence's disadvantage. Ballantine now questioned her on what happened in the Hatches' bed...

| *Serj Ballantine*: | Now just tell me about the occasion when you went into his bed: was it then that he put his finger into you? |
|---|---|
| *Eugenia*: | He did it on my bed as well. |
| *Serj Ballantine*: | When did he begin to do it in your bed? |
| *Eugenia*: | He did not do it the first week I was there. |

| | |
|---|---|
| *Serj Ballantine*: | But he did it also when you were in bed with him and Mrs. Hatch, did he not? |
| *Eugenia*: | Yes. |
| *Baron Bramwell*: | He did it when [you were] in bed with him and Mrs. Hatch? |
| *Eugenia*: | Yes. |
| *Serj Ballantine*: | You have been in bed with both I understand you to say? |
| *Eugenia*: | With Mr. and Mrs. Hatch both. |
| *Baron Bramwell*: | She has not said so today. |
| *Serj Ballantine*: | I understand her to say so. |
| *Baron Bramwell*: | I have got it that Mrs. Hatch was in the room washing Lucy, and that she went into the bed with him. |
| *Serj Ballantine*: | Just let us understand. Tell me, did you go into bed with him and Mrs. Hatch? |
| *Eugenia*: | When I went in first, but after I had been there a little while, Mrs. Hatch got out of bed to wash Lucy. |
| *Serj Ballantine*: | But when you were in bed with him and Mrs. Hatch, did he do this? |
| *Eugenia*: | Yes. |
| *Serj Ballantine*: | When you were in bed with both of them? |

*Eugenia*:              Yes.

*Serj Ballantine*:      Whilst she was lying beside him?

*Eugenia*:              Yes.

*Serj Ballantine*:      Very much?

*Eugenia*:              Yes.

*Serj Ballantine*:      Why did you not cry out?

*Eugenia*:              I don't know. I thought he would do it the more.

*Serj Ballantine*:      Was that when you were in bed; how was he lying at the time?

*Eugenia*:              When I was in their bed, he was lying on his back.

*Serj Ballantine*:      Then he was not lying across you then?

*Eugenia*:              No, not when I was in their bed.

*Serj Ballantine*:      But you were lying by his side?

*Eugenia*:              Yes.

*Serj Ballantine*:      And then he put his finger into your person and hurt you very much?

*Eugenia*:              Yes.

*Baron Bramwell*:       Where was Mrs. Hatch lying then?

*Eugenia*:              Lucy was the other side of me and Mrs. Hatch was the other side of Lucy. I was between Mr. Hatch and Lucy.

| | |
|---|---|
| *Serj Ballantine*: | How often did he do it when he was lying beside his wife: how often did he hurt you in that way when he was lying beside his wife? |
| *Eugenia*: | He was not by his wife; he was not by Mrs. Hatch. |
| *Serj Ballantine*: | But when his wife was in bed? |
| *Eugenia*: | Then he was not by Mrs. Hatch either. |
| *Serj Ballantine*: | Why? |
| *Eugenia*: | Because I was by him, he was at the outside of the bed, I was on the other side of him. |
| *Serj Ballantine*: | How often did he do it while you were in that situation? |
| *Eugenia*: | He done it every morning. |
| *Baron Bramwell*: | You got into his bed every morning then, did you? |
| *Eugenia*: | Except the first week. |
| *Serj Ballantine*: | And then, with Mrs. Hatch in the bed, he hurt you in the same way every morning? |
| *Eugenia*: | Yes. |
| *Serj Ballantine*: | Then he must have done it six or seven times there? |
| *Eugenia*: | Yes. |
| *Serj Ballantine*: | How often did he do it when you were in your bed? |

| | |
|---|---|
| *Eugenia*: | He done it every night. |
| *Serj Ballantine*: | In your bed? |
| *Eugenia*: | Excepting the first week. |
| *Serj Ballantine*: | Every night he did it in your bed, and every morning in bed with his wife? |
| *Eugenia*: | Yes. |
| *Serj Ballantine*: | About what time was it in the morning you used to go into his room; was it light? |
| *Eugenia*: | About seven. Yes, it was light. |
| *Serj Ballantine*: | And in the evening, when he came into your room, did he bring any light with him? |
| *Eugenia*: | Yes. |
| *Serj Ballantine*: | He brought a candle with him? |
| *Eugenia*: | Yes. |

And now to the events of 25ᵗʰ August (the day the Plummers brought Stephana)…

| | |
|---|---|
| *Serj Ballantine*: | Just tell me what you told your mother in the water-closet. I was asking you what it was you told your mother in the water-closet? |
| *Eugenia*: | I told her that he put his "penny" into my hand; that was all I told her in there. |
| *Serj Ballantine*: | But did you tell her that he had done so every day? |

| | |
|---|---|
| *Eugenia*: | Yes; I told her he had done so every night. |
| *Serj Ballantine*: | You told her that he had put his "penny" into your hand every night? |
| *Eugenia*: | Excepting the first. |
| *Serj Ballantine*: | Are you sure you did that? |
| *Eugenia*: | Yes. |

Eugenia had told Mr Metcalfe that she only cried and asked to be taken home when she saw her mother in the closet on the day Mrs Plummer brought Stephana. Serjeant Ballantine and Eugenia may have misunderstood each other on the date – the day in question, 25$^{th}$ August, or the following day when both girls were both taken away. Mr Metcalfe was to clarify which day it was during his re-examination, since Mrs Plummer's actions in leaving both daughters at the Hatches' after being told what Eugenia had just alleged would have been quite inexplicable.

Baron Bramwell though, was confused on other matters and sought some more clarification from Eugenia:

| | |
|---|---|
| *Baron Bramwell*: | You remember that you said that after you had been there a week he used to do two different things to you; first one and then the other; that he used to put his finger to your penny and to put his penny into your hand. Do you remember saying so? |
| *Eugenia*: | Yes. |
| *Baron Bramwell*: | Which did he do first; you say that he did the one after the other? |

| | |
|---|---|
| *Eugenia*: | He put his penny into my hand first. |
| *Baron Bramwell*: | And then put his finger to your penny? |
| *Eugenia*: | He did not do that until after I had been there a week. |
| *Baron Bramwell*: | But you say that when he used to come to your bed of a night he used to do both those things after the first week? |
| *Eugenia*: | Yes. |
| *Baron Bramwell*: | And when he did that, did he put his penny first into your hand? |
| *Eugenia*: | Yes. |
| *Baron Bramwell*: | And then afterwards he put his finger to your penny? |
| *Eugenia*: | Yes. |
| *Baron Bramwell*: | Then you say your hand used to be wet? |
| *Eugenia*: | Yes. |
| *Baron Bramwell*: | Well, was that when he took his penny from your hands, and before he put his finger? |
| *Eugenia*: | Before. |
| *Baron Bramwell*: | Then after your hands were wet, he used to put his finger to your penny? |
| *Eugenia*: | Yes. |

Mr Metcalfe now re-examined Eugenia. He must have been

117

gratified at the amount of detailed extra evidence that had emerged from Serjeant Ballantine's questioning. Nevertheless, he immediately sought to clarify which day in the closet Eugenia had told her mother that Henry had put his 'penny' into her hand…

| | |
|---|---|
| *Mr. Metcalfe*: | You have talked about going into the water-closet with your **mother, did you go into the water-closet once, or more than once?** |
| *Eugenia*: | **I went both days.** |
| *Mr. Metcalfe*: | On the first occasion when you went into the water-closet, did you tell her anything about this? |
| *Eugenia*: | Not the first time. |
| *Mr. Metcalfe*: | Merely cried and wished to go home? |
| *Eugenia*: | Yes. |

And on the 26th August, when the Plummers came to take both children away, Stephana having only been there one night…

| | |
|---|---|
| *Mr. Metcalfe*: | In the morning, after that night, had you any conversation with your sister? |
| *Eugenia*: | Yes. |
| *Mr. Metcalfe*: | You must not tell us what it was, but did you make any communication with your sister? |
| *Eugenia*: | Yes. |

| | |
|---|---|
| *Mr. Metcalfe*: | And in the middle of the day, did your mother come? |
| *Eugenia*: | Yes. |
| *Mr. Metcalfe*: | And take you away? |
| *Eugenia*: | Yes. |
| *Mr. Metcalfe*: | Did you then make a complaint to your mother? |
| *Eugenia*: | Yes. |
| *Mr. Metcalfe*: | Did you make a complaint to anybody before that day – before your mother came to take you away? |
| *Eugenia*: | Only to my sister. |
| *Mr. Metcalfe*: | But before your sister came, did you tell anybody, Mrs. Hatch or anybody? |
| *Eugenia*: | No. |
| *Mr. Metcalfe*: | Why did you not tell Mrs. Hatch? |
| *Eugenia*: | I thought she would tell him of it. |
| *Mr. Metcalfe*: | But supposing she had told him? |
| *Eugenia*: | I thought he would do it the more. |
| *Mr. Metcalfe*: | Was there a governess there? |
| *Eugenia*: | Yes. |
| *Mr. Metcalfe*: | Did you say anything to her at all? |

| | |
|---|---|
| *Eugenia*: | No – not to anybody. |
| *Mr. Metcalfe*: | Why did you not tell the governess? |
| *Eugenia*: | I thought they would all tell Mr. Hatch of it. |
| *Mr. Metcalfe*: | They were all strangers to you, were they not? |
| *Eugenia*: | Yes. |
| *Mr. Metcalfe*: | Had you ever seen any of them before that? |
| *Eugenia*: | No. |
| *Mr. Metcalfe*: | Not one of them? |
| *Eugenia*: | No. |
| *Mr. Metcalfe*: | On the second occasion, when your mother came to take you away, did you then, before you went away, go into the water-closet with her? |
| *Eugenia*: | Yes |
| *Mr. Metcalfe*: | And was it then, on the second day, that you told her what you have told Serjeant Ballantine? |
| *Eugenia*: | Yes. |
| *Mr. Metcalfe*: | On the second day you say it was that you told your mother these matters in the water-closet? |
| *Eugenia*: | Yes. |
| *Mr. Metcalfe*: | What made your mother come the second day? |

| | |
|---|---|
| *Eugenia*: | Because she thought there was something the matter, she thought it did not seem right, the day she came with my sister. |
| *Mr. Metcalfe*: | You say you spoke to her in the water-closet? |
| *Eugenia*: | Yes. |
| *Mr. Metcalfe*: | What did she say to you? |
| *Eugenia*: | She said she would take me away, when I told her of it the second day. |
| *Mr. Metcalfe*: | And what did she do? |
| *Eugenia*: | She took me away. |
| *Mr. Metcalfe*: | At once? |
| *Eugenia*: | Yes. |
| *Mr. Metcalfe*: | Without speaking to Mr. Hatch? |
| *Eugenia*: | She told them she was going to take me away. |
| *Mr. Metcalfe*: | She did? |
| *Eugenia*: | Yes. |
| *Mr. Metcalfe*: | You heard her? |
| *Eugenia*: | Yes. |
| *Mr. Metcalfe*: | Did she say why? |
| *Eugenia*: | No, she did not say why. |

This completed the examination of Mary Eugenia Plummer. Eugenia was four months short of her twelfth birthday, so her performance even with Mr Metcalfe was creditable.

Against the might of the judge and Serjeant Ballantine it was magnificent. One suspects, though, that she must have been mature for her age. She corrected the Serjeant when he repeated back what she had said if the detail was incorrect or might be misunderstood.

Although it is not clear from the record, it was probably her sister Stephana Augusta Plummer who was next examined – by Mr Cooper.

| | |
|---|---|
| *Mr. Cooper*: | How old are you? |
| *Stephana*: | Eight years old. |
| *Mr. Cooper*: | Do you remember going to Mr. Hatch's with your mamma? |
| *Stephana*: | Yes. |
| *Mr. Cooper*: | Your sister was there when you arrived? |
| *Stephana*: | Yes. |
| *Mr. Cooper*: | On going there, where did you sleep at night; you know where your sister slept, do you? |
| *Stephana*: | Yes; I do. |
| *Mr. Cooper*: | Where did you sleep? |
| *Stephana*: | I slept in the next room to Mr. Hatch. |
| *Mr. Cooper*: | And your sister slept where? |
| *Stephana*: | In the next room at the other side of mine. |
| *Mr. Cooper*: | Do you remember going to bed that night? |
| *Stephana*: | Yes. |

| | |
|---|---|
| *Mr. Cooper:* | How long had you been in bed before anybody came to you? |
| *Stephana:* | Rather long. |
| *Mr. Cooper:* | Then who came to you? |
| *Stephana:* | Mr. Hatch. |
| *Mr. Cooper:* | When he came to you was he dressed or undressed? |
| *Stephana:* | He had his night-shirt on. |
| *Mr. Cooper:* | Were you asleep when he first came? |
| *Stephana:* | No. |
| *Mr. Cooper:* | On his coming into the room you were lying in bed were you? |
| *Stephana:* | Yes. |
| *Mr. Cooper:* | What did he do? |
| *Stephana:* | He put his penny into my hand. |
| *Mr. Cooper;* | How long was it there? |
| *Stephana:* | Not long; rather long it was. |
| *Mr. Cooper:* | Did he say anything to you? |
| *Stephana:* | No. |
| *Mr. Cooper:* | Where was your hand when he first came into the room? |
| *Stephana:* | Out of the bed because I was warm. |
| *Mr. Cooper:* | Which hand did he take? |
| *Stephana:* | I do not know: it was this one, I think (the right.) |

| | |
|---|---|
| *Mr. Cooper:* | After he did this, what did he do then? |
| *Stephana:* | He laid across me. |
| *Mr. Cooper:* | During this time did he say anything to you? |
| *Stephana:* | No. |
| *Mr. Cooper:* | Did he do anything else besides this to you? |
| *Stephana:* | No; I do not think he did. |
| *Mr. Cooper:* | Then after he had done this, did he say anything before he left you? |
| *Stephana:* | No. |
| *Mr. Cooper:* | And then when he had done this, where did he go? |
| *Stephana:* | Into his bed-room. |
| *Mr. Cooper:* | Do you remember what room he came from when he first came into your room? |
| *Stephana:* | I think, out of his room, where he slept. |
| *Mr. Cooper:* | Do you remember the next morning? |
| *Stephana:* | Yes. |
| *Baron Bramwell:* | Did he go to bed when he went into his own room do you know, or go down stairs? |
| *Stephana:* | He went to bed. |

| | |
|---|---|
| *Mr. Cooper*: | Was Mrs. Hatch there? |
| *Stephana*: | Yes. |
| *Mr. Cooper*: | You saw her there did you? |
| *Stephana*: | I saw her. |
| *Mr. Cooper*: | How often did he come into your room? |
| *Stephana*: | Only once. |
| *Mr. Cooper*: | Had he been into your room before that, do you know? |
| *Stephana*: | Yes; I think he had. |
| *Baron Bramwell*: | I do not understand; you say he only came once, and you think he had been once before? |
| *Stephana*: | Yes; I think he came once before. |
| *Mr. Cooper*: | Did he do anything to you the first time? |
| *Stephana*: | No; he did not do anything the first time. |
| *Mr. Cooper*: | Did you hear him before he came into your room talking to anybody? |
| *Stephana*: | No. |
| *Mr. Cooper*: | After you got to bed did you talk to your sister? |
| *Stephana*: | No. |
| *Mr. Cooper*: | Did you hear anyone in her room talk? |

| | |
|---|---|
| *Stephana*: | Yes; I heard Mr. Hatch. |
| *Mr. Cooper*: | When was that? |
| *Stephana*: | Before he came to me. |
| *Mr. Cooper*: | Do you remember the next morning? |
| *Stephana*: | Yes. |
| *Mr. Cooper*: | Did you go next morning into the school-room? |
| *Stephana*: | Yes. |
| *Mr. Cooper*: | Do you remember being alone with your sister in the school-room? |
| *Stephana*: | Yes. |
| *Mr. Cooper*: | The governess had left had she? |
| *Stephana*: | Yes. |
| *Mr. Cooper*: | When alone with your sister, did your sister state to you anything? |
| *Stephana*: | Yes. |
| *Mr. Cooper*: | Something about Mr. Hatch? |
| *Stephana*: | Yes. |
| *Mr. Cooper*: | On her stating that to you, what did you say? You said something to your sister? |
| *Stephana*: | Yes. |
| *Baron Bramwell*: | It seems to me very questionable whether this ought not to be given. I very much doubt whether, |

in cases of this description, you
have not a right to ask it.

This intervention from Baron Bramwell may have been in
response to an unrecorded objection from Serjeant Ballantine
to the effect that what Stephana's sister told her was hearsay
and therefore not admissible. Baron Bramwell evidently
disagreed.

| | |
|---|---|
| *Mr. Cooper*: | On your sister making a communication to you, what did you say to her? |
| *Stephana*: | I said, he done it to me. |
| *Mr. Cooper*: | Was this said to you, and did you say this to your sister in the morning? – Did you tell that to your sister in the morning? |
| *Stephana*: | Yes. |
| *Mr. Cooper*: | What time in the day did your mamma come afterwards? |
| *Stephana*: | I can't hardly recollect. |
| *Mr. Cooper*: | Was it after dinner? |
| *Stephana*: | Yes. |
| *Mr. Cooper*: | And then, on her coming to you, did she take you and your sister away? |
| *Stephana*: | Yes. |
| *Mr. Cooper*: | And did you then tell your mamma and papa – make a communication to them? |
| *Stephana*: | Yes. |

| | |
|---|---|
| *Mr. Cooper*: | Was that as you went home? |
| *Stephana*: | Yes. |
| *Mr. Cooper*: | And after you reached home, did you tell them again? |
| *Stephana*: | Yes. |

Stephana was now cross-examined by Serjeant Ballantine…

| | |
|---|---|
| *Serj Ballantine*: | Tell me what you did tell your sister? |
| *Stephana*: | Do you mean in the school-room? |
| *Serj Ballantine*: | I mean what your sister told you? |
| *Stephana*: | She said, he put his penny into my hand. |
| *Serj Ballantine*: | Go on. |
| *Stephana*: | And then I said he done it to me. |
| *Serj Ballantine*: | Did she say anything about his lying across her? |
| *Stephana*: | No. |
| *Serj Ballantine*: | Are you sure about that? |
| *Stephana*: | Yes. |
| *Serj Ballantine*: | Did she say anything about any wet – about being wet? |
| *Stephana*: | No. |
| *Serj Ballantine*: | Did she say anything about his having hurt her at all? |

| | |
|---|---|
| *Stephana*: | No, she did not. |
| *Serj Ballantine*: | You did not very much want to remain at that school, did you? |
| *Stephana*: | No. |
| *Serj Ballantine*: | You did not like coming, did you? |
| *Stephana*: | No. |
| *Serj Ballantine*: | Your sister did not like going did she? |
| *Stephana*: | No. |
| *Serj Ballantine*: | You liked a good deal better staying at home, did not you? |
| *Stephana*: | Yes. |
| *Serj Ballantine*: | Did you feel anything when he put your hand to him? |
| *Stephana*: | Yes. |
| *Serj Ballantine*: | He did put your hand to him? |
| *Stephana*: | Yes. |
| *Serj* Ballantine: | Did you feel anything? |
| *Stephana*: | Yes. |
| *Serj Ballantine*: | Wet? |
| *Stephana*: | No, I did not feel it wet. |
| *Serj Ballantine*: | Did your sister? |
| *Stephana*: | Yes. |
| *Serj Ballantine*: | How do you know that? |
| *Stephana*: | She told me so. |

| | |
|---|---|
| *Serj Ballantine*: | Did she tell you so in the school-room? |
| *Stephana*: | No, I heard her tell mamma of it at home. |
| *Serj Ballantine*: | You heard her tell everything to your mamma, did you? |
| *Stephana*: | Yes. |

So according to Stephana, Henry had assaulted her too. Serjeant Ballantine, though, was careful to establish that Stephana had heard her mother and sister discussing the details of what Henry had allegedly done to Eugenia.

From the press reports, the children gave their evidence in a 'simple and artless manner...', and were 'subjected to a severe cross-examination by Serjeant Ballantine but very little appeared to be elicited from them that in any way tended to invalidate their testimony...'

The last witness for the prosecution was Mrs Caroline Plummer, the mother of the two girls:

| | |
|---|---|
| *Mrs. Plummer*: | [Responding to an unrecorded question from Mr Metcalfe] My eldest child told me, on the first night she was there, they were out in the garden waving their handkerchiefs to me and papa, which was very natural, to wish us good bye, and him as well, till we were out of sight, and then he took me round the garden. We saw them take a turn; he took her round, and he told her to put her hand in his pocket, which she did; but she found it was not like papa's pockets, they |

|  | were not sewn up, and she found something there that she thought was like a 'broken bone'. |
| --- | --- |
| *Mr. Metcalfe*: | That took place in the garden? |
| *Mrs. Plummer*: | During the time before they went into the house, after they had bid us good bye. |
| *Mr. Metcalfe*: | You say, when you went away you saw them in the garden and they were waving their handkerchiefs to you? |
| *Mrs. Plummer*: | To me and my husband, Mr. Plummer. We were going along in the fly [cab], and, as far as we could see them, Mr. Hatch and my child and his adopted child, as he told me, watched us out of sight. |
| *Mrs. Plummer*: | [Responding to an unrecorded question from Mr Metcalfe regarding the alleged nightly visits to Eugenia's bedroom.] [On the first night at the Hatches']... I had ordered my child to stay up to supper; I thought it would please her. She had been very much indulged at home, and after the first night they put her to bed, and every night after that, as near as I can recollect, he went to my child's bed. He first began by unbuttoning his trowsers, which the child tells |

me were fastened in front, and making her take what I have just mentioned into her hand and keeping his hand a-top of hers. He did that several nights, till the Sunday had passed, for some few nights before the Sunday following. He began by degrees it appears by the child; he then ventured to take the bed clothes off her and lay across her, and on two or three occasions he hurt her with something, she said his finger, to that degree that he made her sick, and at times he hurt her with his finger or something else, I do not know what, and she was sick, - very extraordinary that a child should feel sick.

Mrs Plummer here contradicted her daughter's evidence; Eugenia had insisted that Henry had not removed the bedclothes from her when he 'laid across her'. Hence the exchanges with Serjeant Ballantine when he pointed out that if Henry was lying across the bedclothes then it could have only been his finger that was used to hurt Eugenia...

Mrs Plummer commenting on the towel...

*Mrs. Plummer*: Every night she [Eugenia] was obliged to get out of bed and wipe her hands on the bed-room towel, and every morning it made her sick, because her dear face was wiped on the same towel that she wiped her hands on.

| | |
|---|---|
| *Mr. Metcalfe*: | When you left your child there, did you understand that she was to go into the bed of Mr. Hatch of a morning? |
| *Mrs. Plummer*: | They told me they always had Lucy in a morning, and they should make a pet of her. Eugie is rather a nervous child, and I thought that that would please her; but of course I did not dream of such a thing as this. I certainly did allow it, and I sanctioned it, you may call it, because there should be no jealousy, and I was thankful for my child to be made a pet of, because I like my children made pets of, but not in that way. I said, very well, make her think she is at home; it all seemed as natural as possible. There was one other thing; when Mrs. Hatch was out of bed washing this little girl Lucy, my child was left in bed with him, and he would raise up the bed clothes by keeping his knees up, and her eyes would be under the bed-clothes, you understand; and she there saw something very long, standing upright. |

Again this conflicts with Eugenia's evidence. She had claimed that her mother had said that when Eugenia came to the Hatches, it was *not* right, for her to go into the Hatches' bed.

*Mr. Metcalfe*: This is all what she told you?

*Mrs. Plummer*: That is what she told me.

*Mr. Metcalfe*: On the day when you went with the youngest girl, you had an opportunity of speaking to the elder girl?

*Mrs. Plummer*: I found I could not, which I thought very strange.

*Mr. Metcalfe*: How do you mean?

*Mrs. Plummer*: Because whenever I went into the bed-room either Mr. or Mrs. Hatch followed us; in fact both of them, everywhere; I thought it very unusual; it never happened anywhere before.

*Mr. Metcalfe*: Did you get an opportunity of speaking?

*Mrs. Plummer*: Yes; I embraced an opportunity as soon as possible.

*Mr. Metcalfe*: In what way?

*Mrs. Plummer*: Of course I took her to the only place where they could not follow me, and that was the closet. I felt very uneasy; she looked ill, and I took her there purposely.

*Mr. Metcalfe*: In the closet, did she say anything to you at all?

*Mrs. Plummer*: She had scarcely entered when she leaned against the wall

|   |   |
|---|---|
|   | and began crying, and said she was very sorry I had brought Stephana there, for she was very unhappy there, she disliked it. |
| *Mr. Metcalfe*: | Did she say any more at that time? |
| *Mrs. Plummer*: | No, but repeated the same words, entreated me to take her home; nothing more than that. |
| *Mr. Metcalfe*: | And was crying while she entreated you? |
| *Mrs. Plummer*: | All the time, and I cried too. |
| *Mr. Metcalfe*: | But ultimately you left her, and left the other little girl? |
| *Mrs. Plummer*: | I did; I told her, papa and I had brought her sister; I would come again in a week, and she must try and see how she got on; but I had not seen her bed-room yet, and I would see what I could do; I would perhaps try to get papa to take her back, because I found the child disliked it. |
| *Mr. Metcalfe*: | What induced you to go? [back the next day] |
| *Mrs. Plummer*: | I cannot tell – the child's crying: and besides, I saw that they had not fulfilled the promises they had given me in their arrangement. I felt very unhappy, and I was determined to go and take them away. |

| | |
|---|---|
| *Mr. Metcalfe*: | Then you did go the next day; and on going the next day, did you try to see the elder child alone, or the two children alone? |
| *Mrs. Plummer*: | I went instantly, and I asked to see Mr. and Mrs. Hatch, for I was come to take them away. I thought we had better part before it was too late, for the child was not happy, I was certain. I went with that determination. I told them so before I sat down. |
| *Mr. Metcalfe*: | Did Mr. Hatch say anything to that? |
| *Mrs. Plummer*: | He begged me to try to let them remain till Christmas, and they would endeavour to do according to my plan – to act up to it – and I said no – I have come with that determination, for I had only laid down two hours, I felt so unhappy: it was no good to shake me, I was determined to take them away – they both begged me. |
| *Mr. Metcalfe*: | Was anything further said? |
| *Mrs. Plummer*: | Am I to tell without your asking me – When they were busy collecting the books and various things together, I then took my child to the same place – told her to dry up her tears. |

| | |
|---|---|
| *Mr. Metcalfe*: | You mean to the closet? |
| *Mrs. Plummer*: | Yes: again while the servant was bringing down the portmanteau, I said to her, "Are you not glad my dear?" She said, "Oh! Yes, mamma, for Mr. Hatch is such a disgusting man!" I said, "A disgusting man, dear! Well he does not appear as pleasant as he was when I first came to look at the place – but what do you mean by disgusting, dear?" "He is mamma, for he has such a curious penny." |
| *Mr. Metcalfe*: | Was anything further said? |
| *Mrs. Plummer*: | I said, "Oh! dear, dear what do you mean my child", or something similar to that: she said, "He has mamma, for I have seen it", that was when the things were preparing for our departure – mind, after I had gone to take them away. |
| *Mr. Metcalfe*: | Did you say anything then? |
| *Mrs. Plummer*: | Certainly not, what could I say to the child. |
| *Mr. Metcalfe*: | Did she say anything further? |
| *Mrs. Plummer*: | Nothing more; but I went back to the dining-room and appeared very pleasant – and I was very pleasant. I felt vexed, but I thought perhaps that he |

had, by accident, been out in the
garden, and the child might have
been popping round and caught
sight of it by accident, and there
it ended – so that we paid and
came away.

This was the most glaring and important contradiction between
Eugenia's evidence and that of her mother. Eugenia had not
said that she had just seen Henry's 'penny', but that he had put
it into her hand. Mrs Plummer could hardly have confused the
difference between what might have been an accidental sight
of Henry peeing in the garden, with what Eugenia said she told
her mother. In addition to which, it was Eugenia's version of
events that was related in the Plummers' letter to the bishop
when they first accused Henry of assaulting their daughters.

Mrs Plummer was now cross-examined by Serjeant
Ballantine for the defence, and he immediately sought to
confirm the contradiction …

| *Serj Ballantine*: | From what your daughter said in the water-closet, you thought she might have seen what she mentioned by accident? |
| --- | --- |
| *Mrs. Plummer*: | Yes; that was the second day when I went to fetch them away. |
| *Serj Ballantine*: | She did not say anything about it at first? |
| *Mrs. Plummer*: | No, I thought it was an accident in the garden. I thought Mr. Hatch might have been in the garden, as gentlemen may go, and that the child might pop round and see it by accident, |

| | so that I did not feel much disturbed; still I should rather for her not to have seen it. |
|---|---|
| *Serj Ballantine*: | Why did you not ask her [about it]? |
| *Mrs. Plummer*: | Oh dear, because I could not think it possible that it was anything but that. Of course I could not think that a man who had to educate two children would attempt to go to his little pupil's bed. |
| *Serj Ballantine*: | So you imagined it was merely accidental, seeing it? |
| *Mrs. Plummer*: | Yes. |

Mr Metcalfe, aware of the contradictory evidence between mother and daughter, now re-examined Mrs Plummer, and attempted to divert the jury's attention away from it. He proceeded to emphasize the assault on Stephana...

| | |
|---|---|
| *Mr. Metcalfe*: | My friend has asked why you kept up the younger child: [This question, presumably from Serjeant Ballantine, was not recorded] did she also make a statement to you? |
| *Mrs. Plummer*: | Yes, she was there but one night. |
| *Mr. Metcalfe*: | Did she complain of his conduct during that one night? |
| *Mrs. Plummer*: | Oh dear, yes. It thundered and lightened that night very heavily, |

and the dear child could not go to sleep. She was then in Eugie's room, and he came into Stephie's; he was dressed then, not undressed then, and Stephie thought he would be angry with her that she had not gone to sleep, but she was frightened at the thunder and lightning. At that time, he had a light, and she thought he would be angry not to see her asleep, so she shut her eyes. She then heard him go out of her room into Eugie's, and he was there half an hour, and was then lying across my child and hurting her.

*Mr. Metcalfe:*  But I am asking about Stephie?

*Mrs. Plummer:*  Then he told Eugie that Stephie was asleep, but she was not; she shut her eyes because she was fearful he would be angry with her; and when he came up to bed and undressed himself he went into Stephie's room, and Mrs. Hatch was in her room undressing, and he unbuttoned his trowsers, the same as he had done in the first place with Eugie, and he took up her little hand and put his penny into her hand and laid across her, and hurt her very much.

*Mr. Metcalfe:*  I thought it was the eldest?

*Mrs. Plummer:* It was the youngest that one night, and Mrs. Hatch called, 'Henry, why don't you come?' He said, 'I am coming presently', and he at that time was lying across her with his legs on the floor, and he was reaching over to see, as she said, because she is a very sensible child. He fancied that Mrs. Hatch was looking at him, and as he leaned round to look through the door he pressed her chest the more, but he did not take the bed clothes off of her, for I asked her, but that was but one night.

This completed the evidence from the main three prosecution witnesses. There were a number of significant discrepancies between the evidence of Eugenia and that of her mother, mainly in respect of what she told her mother in the closet; there were also major differences between their evidence, and what was said in the Plummers' letter to the bishop (which formed part of the evidence). There was no claim that Lucy put her hand in her father's pocket in the garden, or 'touched' him when she and Eugenia were sitting one on each knee during the story. Also, Mrs Plummer claimed that Stephana had been 'hurt… very much' when Henry visited her in her room, although Stephana, in her evidence, made no such claim.

Constable Taylor, who arrested Henry, proved that a warrant for the arrest of Henry John Hatch was placed in his hands on 29th October, and on finding him not at his residence, he was finally apprehended at the hotel in Holborn. He repeated the questions Henry had asked regarding the nature of the charges and the likely sentence. Serjeant Ballantine asked him if he realized that

> so far from the defendant having purposely kept out
> of the way...he had been in communication with Mr.
> Pratt [the Plummers' solicitor] and went to the hotel
> by arrangement...to give himself up.

The constable said that he was unaware of that.

Serjeant Ballantine called Mr Pratt to confirm that in response to a communication from Mrs Hatch, he had arranged to meet the defendant at the hotel to give himself up.

Richard Onslow, the governor of Wandsworth prison, was then called. He confirmed that Henry John Hatch had been chaplain of the prison for eight years. In consequence of the communication sent by the Plummers to the Bishop of Winchester, the visiting justices of the prison were to investigate the affair on the 28th October when the parents of the children would also be present. Henry Hatch was informed of this fact. The investigation never took place because the defendant resigned his position. Responding to questions from Serjeant Ballantine, Mr Onslow said that he had not advised Henry Hatch to resign, but had stated that whatever the outcome of the investigation, it might be difficult for him to carry on in the position. He had also heard that the defendant had been involved in some troublesome and costly Chancery proceedings.

In response to a question from the judge, Mr Onslow said that he did not make the previous observations from any thought that the defendant might be guilty, merely from the fact that

> even if his innocence should be established in the
> clearest possible manner, still the fact of a charge
> having been made against him would prevent his
> ministration being useful to the prisoners.

Serjeant Ballantine then addressed the jury on behalf of the defendant. He called upon them to acquit him, on the ground that the evidence in support of the charge could not be relied on, and that it had been trumped up by the two little girls in order that they might be taken away from the school, to which they admitted they had a disinclination to be sent. [The accusation made against the defendant was] of the most atrocious character, and, apart from the improbability that a clergyman and a man in the position of the defendant should have been guilty of such conduct, it appeared to be incredible and utterly unworthy of belief...Was it likely that a man would have acted in the manner described, almost the very first moment that a young girl was placed under his charge...and also [was] it not repugnant to human nature that such proceedings could have been adopted within the hearing and almost, if not actually, in the presence of his own wife?

He may well have called their attention to the contradictions between what Eugenia said she told her mother in the water closet, and what Caroline Plummer had said she said, as well as the differences in their evidence compared with what had been claimed in the letter the Plummers wrote to the bishop. Naturally, the newspapers were unable to print such details.

Serjeant Ballantine then, extraordinarily, did not call any of the material defence witnesses that were in court. The law then did not allow the defendant or his wife to give evidence on his behalf. But everyone in the Hatch household at the time of the alleged offences was present – Essie's mother, the French sisters, Martha Howe, Mary and Ellen the servants, and even little Lucy. Most of them had given evidence in the magistrates' hearing. Clearly, it was not possible to bring any witnesses against what might have happened when Henry was alone with Eugenia Plummer, but the first alleged offence took place whilst walking in the garden in full view of Mrs Dillon,

Martha Howe, the French ladies, the servant Mary, and Lucy, who was closest of all. They were adamant in statements made later, that what was alleged to have taken place could not possibly have happened because they would have seen it. If part of Eugenia Plummer's evidence could be shown to be false, then that would have created great doubt about the truth of the rest of it.

Nothing daunted, Ballantine proceeded to call a substantial number of *character* witnesses for Henry Hatch. These included the Rev Thomas Bullock, chaplain of Guy's Hospital, Captain and Mrs Robert Bridge, Edward Wise of Ryde, Isle of Wight, (who had arranged for Lucy's adoption), Dr James Booth, Vicar of Stone, Charles Wilkinson, surgeon of Wandsworth, the Rev Henry Dupuis, Vicar of Richmond, Surrey, George Annesley, Solicitor, Lincoln's Inn Fields (who was in the process of suing Henry in Chancery), Captain Sylvester Penrhyn and Charles Francis, Magistrates for Surrey, John Briscoe, MP for West Surrey, also a magistrate for Surrey, the Rev George Cotterell, Incumbent of Kingston Vale, near Richmond, and the Rev Joseph Gegg, Assistant Chaplain at Wandsworth House of Correction. All the witnesses had known Henry John Hatch for many years and gave him a 'high character for morality'. They also '...expressed an opinion that he was utterly incapable of committing the offence imputed to him'. Judge Bramwell commented, 'it is impossible for any man to have a higher character than had been already deposed to the defendant', and this closed the case for the defence.

Now came the judge's summing up. He said that it was certainly a most extraordinary thing if the story that had been told by these two children had been invented by them; but if the jury believed that story, there was no doubt that the defendant ought to be convicted. However if they were of the opinion that they could not safely rely upon the evidence, then they ought to acquit the defendant.

He commented on the extraordinary fact that, 'such a course of proceeding' should have started almost before the mother of the children was out of sight. Also, that the defendant should have 'acted as represented', while his wife was in the room, effectively making her an accomplice. At four o'clock in the afternoon, the jury retired to consider their verdict. They returned fifty minutes later, and found the prisoner guilty.

Baron Bramwell addressed Henry John Hatch. He said that he had been found guilty of about as hateful an offence as could possibly be imagined. It was impossible to conceive a worse crime, than for a man to take advantage of his position, and act in such a manner towards two poor little children who had been placed under his protection. He therefore felt it his duty to pass upon him the extreme sentence of the law for such an offence.

Henry John Hatch was sentenced to two years hard labour for each offence; sentences to run consecutively. Henry then addressed the court 'with great excitement', the only time he was allowed to speak:[1]

> The children have been telling abominable lies. The sentence passed upon me must, in my position as a clergyman, crush and ruin me. I will never have a chance of retrieving my character. I must of course submit to the verdict of a jury of my countrymen, but if it is the last word I have to say, I declare my innocence of the crime, and the time will come when this will be made out...

Henry was then taken down to Newgate to begin his sentence. The weather was cold; it was just one degree above freezing in London.

---

1   Henry's words have been transposed into the first person.

# Newgate

**N**ewgate! '...massive, dark, and solemn, arrests the eye and holds it...a stranger in the capital would fix on it at a glance, for it is one of the half dozen buildings, in this wilderness of bricks and mortar, which have a character; of all the London prisons, except the Tower, it alone has an imposing aspect.' So wrote Hepworth Dixon in 1850. Newgate Prison had existed since the twelfth century, built from the proceeds of the will of a medieval Lord Mayor of London, one Richard Whittington. The old gaol was gutted during the Great Fire of 1666, only the stone walls surviving; it was repaired in 1672. A new building was erected about 100 years later only to be burned once more during the Gordon Riots of 1780. Again it was rebuilt, and Dickens described its dismal and forbidding interior and occupants in his 1836 essay. Most fortunate for Henry John Hatch, the interior of the prison for male convicts had been remodelled just months before he arrived. In 1859, individual cells had been provided for the prisoners to replace the previous dormitories. This was not out of concern for prisoner welfare, but a manifestation of the Separate System. The Reverend John Davis, Ordinary of Newgate, in his 1859 report on discipline in the prison, remarked upon the

> great improvements that had been effected on the male side of this establishment...The only mode of confine-
> ment that gives the offender a hope of reformation, and

at the same time most severely punishes him, is that by which both day and night, he is kept entirely by himself...the depravity of a mass of incorrigible convicts is beyond all conception...how little do many flimsy and flippant writers and talkers about the criminal population know of their real propensities.

No liberal reformer he. Evidently the Rev Davis relished his occupation, which then included ministering to condemned men still publicly hanged outside the gaol on Mondays.

Henry had to get used to his new environment, John Davis and all. Hard Labour at Newgate consisted of picking oakum; Henry was required to complete around three pounds weight per day. If he was lucky, he might have learned from the prisoners at Wandsworth the trick of wetting the picked oakum in order to make it weigh more. His food ration was basic. He received bread and a pint of porridge for breakfast, and the same for supper; at dinner (midday meal) on alternate days, either three ounces of meat, more bread and potatoes, or a pint of soup and bread. One hopes that he was fond of bread.

It must have been of no consolation either, to know that Henry was a special prisoner. Newgate was not a penitentiary; that is to say it was not a prison where sentences were served. Like the county gaols, it held prisoners committed for trial or on remand, as well as those sentenced to penal servitude and awaiting transportation. It also held some debtors as well as those condemned to death. Persons convicted at the Old Bailey of offences committed in Surrey, would normally have been removed to Wandsworth to serve their sentences. According to *The Observer* newspaper, the Home Secretary had decided that it would be a 'painful and unnecessary aggravation of [Henry's] sentence to be sent back [to Wandsworth] as a criminal', so it was decided to keep him at Newgate for the time being. *The Morning Post* was more forthright:

> The authorities have so strongly felt, from the beginning, the inadequacy of the evidence for the prosecutor, that Mr. Hatch has been allowed to remain at Newgate since his conviction.

Nevertheless, being locked up in Newgate in the depths of winter, living on prison rations, and picking oakum until his fingers were numb (oakum picking was most difficult in winter), must have been a living nightmare for Henry. He had lost his reputation, his livelihood and his liberty. His wife and adopted daughter were destitute, and he was incapable of offering them any protection. He had been found guilty of a detestable crime and was unable to do anything about it. There was no Court of Criminal Appeal in 1859.

At least if he was thinking clearly he would have realized that the jury, given the evidence presented to them, and notwithstanding the significant discrepancies in that evidence, would have had little alternative other than finding him guilty. How could girls of seven and eleven possibly have had knowledge of the sickening details of the encounters they described, unless they had actually experienced them? Henry's resignation as prison chaplain in order to forestall the magistrates' hearing made it look as though he was trying to hush the matter up. And when it seemed as though it would all come out and a warrant was issued for his arrest, he appeared to abscond from home! To cap it all, when he was finally apprehended, he asked the arresting constable to be lenient with him and wanted to know what the penalties were for the crimes for which he was charged. Against this damning evidence, all that could be offered in defence was a series of character witnesses.

In as much as the jury had weighed the evidence as presented, it was a fair trial. In fact, it had been a travesty. Firstly, most of the evidence for the prosecution had been in the form of the word of Eugenia, Stephana and Caroline Plummer, against that of Henry and Essie Hatch. And neither Henry nor Essie was allowed to testify. Their evidence was inadmissible, so the jury were unable to hear their denials, qualifications or counter-charges. Secondly, and this reflected woefully on Henry's defence team, no material witnesses had been called for the defence – as they had all been for the magistrates' trial. Some of the allegations made by Eugenia Plummer were of events that had taken place in the presence of others. They would have been able to confirm or otherwise the truth of her statements. If only one piece of Eugenia's sworn evidence could have been shown to be false, then very significant doubts would have arisen regarding all her other claims.

On 5th December, *The Daily News* reprinted an editorial from *The Morning Post* expressing severe misgivings on the outcome of the trial. If Henry was guilty, it said, almost no punishment was severe enough. On the other hand, if he was innocent, then '...was there ever a calamity more dreadful than has befallen this clergyman?' The paper went on,

> Is he, then, guilty, or is he not? If guilty, his crime is beyond the execration of human speech; if innocent, no human compassion can console the unspeakable hardship of his case.

It continued,

> The jury has decided that he is guilty. This verdict we do not wish to impugn, for we have not the materials for forming a correct conclusion ourselves. But we confess that we are puzzled; and after a most thoughtful sifting of the evidence so far as it has transpired, we cannot resist the temptation that it is not so conclusive as it ought to be...the details of this case are properly withheld from the public, and all argument about it... must be from the premises of probability...

The editorial commented on the not unnatural wish of the 'elder child' to be removed after two weeks from a school that she did not like, and her complaint of 'improper treatment' to justify that removal. It then listed the improbabilities: first, the defendant's previous character 'vouched by the highest testimony'; secondly, the 'absence of all motive' (a slightly dubious point, unless the paper was assuming that if the sexual appetite that motivated the 'improper treatment' existed, then it must have manifested itself previously, and would already have destroyed Henry's character.) Thirdly, the allegation that Henry's wife was present during some of the offences, and was thus an accomplice. The paper called for a review of the case, noting that the Secretary of State could do so, as he had done for Dr Smethurst (of whom more later), and commented on the lack of a Court of Criminal Appeal. The article then called for evidence of the character of the two Plummer girls, compared with that of Henry, and finished by saying,

> If Mr. Hatch's crime were a capital one, would the country consent that he should be hanged on this testimony? And if not, ought it to sanction any lesser punishment?

It was powerful advocacy for a review – not even mentioning the lack of defence witnesses – and may well have encouraged Henry's many friends, who were absolutely determined to help him. He had to be got out of prison quickly, and the only way to accomplish that was to petition the Queen for a free pardon. Henry completed his notes for the petition, and it was issued on 29th December 1859. Not only that, his friends pulled off a quite brilliant coup. They managed to contact the twelve jurymen who had convicted Henry, and show them the draft petition containing his defence. Following this, eleven of the jury signed a declaration that was appended to the petition. This stated that had they been aware of the evidence presented in the petition to the Queen, they would never have convicted Henry!

In the petition, Henry provided evidence that would have been given in court if he had been allowed to speak. The material was laid out in seventy-three articles, the key ones of which are reproduced here, together with the declaration from the jury:

### To the Queen's Most Excellent Majesty.

The humble petition of the jury who tried the indictment of the Queen on the Prosecution of Thomas Plummer against the Rev. Henry John Hatch, at the sessions holden [sic] at the Central Criminal Court in the month of November 1859 [it was actually December].

Showeth, - that having read and carefully considered the petition of the said Rev. Henry John Hatch to your Majesty, we do hereby declare that had the contents of such petition been proved at the trial of the said indictment, we should have acquitted the said Henry John Hatch, and that we now believe him wholly innocent of the charges made against him. That it is a subject of extreme regret to your petitioners that the statements set forth in the said petition were wholly withheld from their consideration.

That notwithstanding such omission, and in order that justice may be done, we humbly pray that the truth of such allegations contained in such petition may be enquired into, and, in the event of their proving correct, that your Majesty will be graciously pleased to accede to the prayer of the said Henry John Hatch.

And your petitioners will ever pray.

Samuel T. Keene, Foreman.
William Hyde.

William Hart.
Samuel M<sup>c</sup>Lellan.
William H. Parsons.
Marmaduke Dent.
Robert Helsdon
Alfred H. Hunt.
Walter Heath.
Theodore Bates.
Joseph B. Strong.

Surely it must have been unprecedented, to have persuaded eleven of a twelve-man jury within a month of having delivered a verdict, to sign a document saying that that verdict was wrong. The statement damns Henry's defence team completely. All of the information in the petition was known at the time of the trial. Some of it was sworn to at the magistrates' hearing. Why did Henry's defence team not use the information to good effect?

It is interesting to attempt to identify the one dissenter from Henry's jury, and therein lies small mystery. Ten of the jury are as written in the Old Bailey court book. However, there was no *Walter Heath* in the court book instead there was a *Wm Head* and a *Chas Saul*. One of the jurymen must have been switched at the last minute. The name *William Head* might have been mistaken for *Walter Heath*; they had the same initials, and the first three letters of their surnames were the same, so whether it was William Head or Charles Saul who refused to sign the petition cannot be known.

### To the Queen's Most Excellent Majesty.

The petition of the Reverend Henry John Hatch, late of Wandsworth, in the County of Surrey, but now a prisoner in Newgate under sentence,

Humbly Showeth…

The first eight articles relate to Henry and Essie's personal circumstances, the details of which have been covered elsewhere in this narrative…

9.   That a conversation ensued in your petitioner's drawing-room relative to the said Eugenia Plummer, [following the arrival of the Plummers and Eugenia on 11th August 1859] when her mother stated in the presence of all the before mentioned ladies, [Mrs. Hatch, Mrs. Hatch's mother, Miss Howe, and the two French ladies] your petitioner and Mr. Plummer, that her daughter Eugenia was untruthful and deceitful, and that since her return from her last school she saw a great change in her manner, and that she was reserved and unconfiding.

10.   That Mrs. Plummer afterwards said to Mrs. Hatch, she should like to go upstairs and see the room Eugenia was to occupy, and so strange was the manner and conduct of Mrs. Plummer, that Mrs. Hatch whispered to your petitioner, that she was afraid of Mrs. Plummer, and begged your petitioner to accompany her up stairs, and accordingly Mr. and Mrs. Plummer went up stairs with Mrs. Hatch and your petitioner.

11.   That whilst there Mrs. Plummer expressed a wish to have some brandy and water, which was accordingly furnished to her by the servant Mary, under the direction of Mrs. Hatch.

12.   That among other injunctions given by Mrs. Plummer as to Eugenia, was one, that the doors of her bed-room should always be kept wide open. She even wished them to be taken off the hinges.

13.   That Mr. and Mrs. Plummer and Eugenia dined

with your petitioner and his family on the said 11th August, and during dinner Mrs. Plummer, addressing your petitioner's wife, said, that Eugenia was accustomed to be petted, and to be taken into her bed of a morning, and that Eugenia had done so when at Mr. and Mrs. Brighton's [a previous school where Eugenia had been] and that she, Mrs. Plummer, wished Mrs. Hatch to do the same thing.

14. That neither your petitioner nor his wife ever stated to Mr. or Mrs. Plummer that Lucy was accustomed to go to your petitioner's bed, such not having been the fact.

15. That prior to the departure of Mr. and Mrs. Plummer on that day, Mrs. Hatch prepared and offered them tea, which they declined, from the necessity of their leaving at once to be in time for their train at Paddington.

16. That Mrs. Plummer was very much excited upon leaving her daughter. She cried and screamed in a loud and violent tone – threw her arms about, and behaved as a person out of her mind.

Article 14 conflicts directly with Caroline Plummer's evidence that it was the Hatches who suggested taking Eugenia into their bed in the morning. Mrs Plummer is heard in front of several witnesses saying that Eugenia was untruthful and deceitful, and Mrs Plummer's need for brandy and water in the bedroom, and her behaviour when she departed, casts doubt upon her stability of character. There is also the question of the need to keep Eugenia's doors open at all times. Did Mrs Plummer suspect her daughter of questionable behaviour? Had something happened before? And of course, Mr and Mrs Brighton could have been called to confirm whether or not they allowed Eugenia into their bed previously…

The next few sections contain Henry Hatch's version of events in the garden after the Plummers had left. He said that Eugenia seemed to be out of spirits, so he invited her and Lucy to run after him in the garden, maintaining that his wife, Mrs Dillon, and Martha Howe were watching from the drawing-room window, while the servant, Mary, was standing at the front door. Henry maintained that he and the children could be seen at all times either from the window, or the front door, until they were called into tea. Henry denied that his pockets had holes in them, and denied that any act – as described by Eugenia – ever took place.

And as to the doors of Eugenia's bedroom...

25. That in accordance with the wish of the said Mrs. Plummer, the two doors opening into Eugenia's bedroom were constantly kept wide open, except when she was being bathed by the servant Mary every morning.

26. That with a view to secure the privacy of your petitioner's bed-room, a large screen was placed by your petitioner's bed on the side nearest the door of Eugenia's room.

The veracity or otherwise of article 25 – in direct conflict with Eugenia's evidence – could have been proved by the servant Mary.

The alleged incident when Henry took Eugenia on one knee and Lucy on the other has quite a different form when described by him...

27. That your petitioner had some friends to see him on the evening of Thursday, the 18th day of August last; upon which day your petitioner went into his bed-room before his expected guests arrived, for the

purpose of washing his hands, and there found the servant Mary, who was finishing dressing the children Lucy and Eugenia.

28. That Mary left the room for a few minutes, and the children remained with your petitioner, who was requested by the said adopted child Lucy to tell them a story, which your petitioner consented to do.

29. That your petitioner took the said Eugenia on one of his knees, and Lucy on the other, and told them the desired story but before it was concluded, a master Francis Coghlan came up stairs to the said bed-room, the door of which had been left ajar by Mary, and remained so, and knocked at the said door, whereupon your petitioner bade him "Come in." He told your petitioner that he and the children were wanted below; whereupon the said child Lucy asked your petitioner not to go until the said story was finished, which your petitioner having assented to, told Master Coghlan they would be down shortly, and having concluded the story almost immediately, your petitioner went down stairs with the said children.

In article 30, Henry strenuously denied the story Eugenia told concerning that incident.

Next, the issue of the night time visits to Eugenia's bedroom was discussed. It turns out that Henry *did* visit Eugenia in her bedroom when she was in bed, but for a purpose quite different from the one that she described...

31. That your petitioner's invariable custom, when at home of an evening was to remain with the ladies in the drawing room, and to exert himself for their comfort

and amusement, either by conversation, reading, or music, and now and then, at their request, to join them in a round game at cards. On such occasions your petitioner, prior to commencing the game, went up stairs to his bed-room to wash his hands. This used to be so soon after the children had gone to bed, that your petitioner always found Lucy awake, and the servant Mary about the rooms completing her work.

32. That it was Lucy's custom on such occasions to claim from your petitioner a kiss before he left the room, and that Eugenia hearing it would say, "and me too, Mr. Hatch"; and that your petitioner would immediately after return to the drawing-room in time to commence the said game at cards, having only been absent therefrom a few minutes.

The ladies would have been able to confirm whether Henry's statement about being absent for a few minutes was correct or not. In addition, the servant Mary must have been witness, on some occasions, to him washing his hands and kissing the children.

Article 33 contains a denial regarding Eugenia's charges of what Henry did to her in her bedroom. And now the question of the morning visits into the Hatches' bed was dealt with...

34. That in compliance with the express request of Mrs. Plummer but in opposition to the wish of your petitioner, he permitted Eugenia to come to his bed for a few minutes in [the] morning, whilst Mrs. Hatch was there. That Lucy, who was always jealous of any attention in which she did not share, was admitted to the same privilege. That it was almost an invariable rule that Lucy came to the side of your petitioner, and Eugenia to Mrs. Hatch. That neither of the children

were ever on any occasion permitted to come into your petitioner's bed, but were invariably placed outside the blankets, and then covered with the counterpane. That both children regarded the indulgence as a great privilege, and whilst there seemed very happy; they generally amused themselves by naming the first and last letters of anything in the room and then spelling the word. As an ordinary rule, Mary used to fetch Eugenia first, but if by any chance Mrs. Hatch got up before Mary came, and began to dress Lucy, Eugenia would remain on Mrs. Hatch's side of the bed, and be taken from there by Mary.

35. That on several occasions your petitioner, as well as Mrs. Hatch and Mary, have remarked the avowed unwillingness of Eugenia to leave the bed and go to Mary, when requested to do so, for the purposes of being dressed.

So according to the Hatches, the children were only under the counterpane with Eugenia nearly always on Mrs Hatch's side. And Eugenia, it transpired, did not like getting out of bed in the morning. Was this the kernel of her dislike of the regime at the Hatches', and her determination to make an issue out of what happened in the bed? The servant Mary could have testified as to the arrangements in the bed. Yet again, Henry denied Eugenia's charges.

Now, the circumstances of the Plummers' visit on the 25th August were described:

38. That the said Mr. and Mrs. Plummer arrived at the house of your petitioner, at Wandsworth, with their youngest daughter Stephanie, on Thursday, the 25th of August, and dined with your petitioner and his family.

39. That Mrs. Plummer, before dinner, went up

stairs as before, and had some brandy and water, and behaved in much the same wild and unaccountable manner as on previous occasions, complaining to your petitioner and his wife, that her daughter, an heiress to £15,000, should only have calico sheets to her bed.

40. That during dinner your petitioner explained to Mrs. Plummer, that in compliance with her wish, Eugenia had been allowed to come to the bed of your petitioner and his wife, with Lucy of a morning, at which Mrs. Plummer expressed her satisfaction, and observed that Eugenia had been accustomed to do the same when at Mr. and Mrs. Brighton's.

41. That Mrs. Plummer also said at dinner, that Eugenia was heiress to £15,000, and was betrothed to her medical man, whereupon Eugenia observed, "Yes, and when I am 17, I mean to marry him."

42. That Mr. and Mrs. Plummer left your petitioner's house about seven o'clock in the evening to return home, Mrs. Plummer's conduct being more outrageous than before.

43. That after their departure, there was a severe thunderstorm. The children were placed in the care of the nursemaid, who superintended their going to bed.

44. That during the whole evening your petitioner remained in the drawing-room, but fearing the children might be alarmed by the lightning, Miss Howe and Mrs. Hatch went up several times to look at each of them; and Mary, the housemaid, remained the whole evening on the first floor, where the said children slept.

45. That prior to undressing on that night, your petitioner and Mrs. Hatch went together to the bedside of each child, to see them safe, and having done so, your petitioner went direct to his bed-room with Mrs. Hatch and did not leave it again until the following morning.

Once more, Henry's movements could have been corroborated by Miss Howe and the servant Mary, who was on the first floor the whole evening. And once more, Henry denied the statements from both Eugenia and Stephana regarding what they allege he did to them in their bedrooms.

Now as to the Plummers' unexpected return the following day. The Hatches' version of events is very similar to that of the Plummers…

47. That on the following day your petitioner was surprised at finding Mr. and Mrs. Plummer again at your petitioner's house, the more so, when they explained that their object was to take away both their said daughters.

48. That upon your petitioner demanding the reason of so sudden a determination, Mrs. Plummer said, "She could not sleep during the preceding night, and fancied that the storm was a judgement of God against her for having separated herself from her daughters, and that she had promised her mother to take them back with her;" and Mr. Plummer added he was very sorry, but he could not help it.

49. That Mrs. Plummer afterwards went up stairs with her children and Mrs. Hatch, whilst your petitioner remained below with Mr. Plummer.

50. That when Mrs. Plummer came again to the drawing-room, she appeared in a better humour and

better spirits than your petitioner had before seen her; and before leaving, she presented Lucy with a Noah's ark, in addition to the doll she had given the child on the preceding day.

51. That Mrs. Plummer on going away said to your petitioner, that he was to write to her and let her know whether he would receive the children again, if she changed her mind.

52. That on leaving, both Mr. and Mrs. Plummer shook hands in a very cordial manner with your petitioner, who was also kissed by Eugenia and Stephanie, the former of whom promised she would write to your petitioner; and, so far as your petitioner believed, the said Mr. and Mrs. Plummer and their children, parted with your petitioner and his wife, with every outward appearance of good feeling and satisfaction.

So no revelations here at least, except to note Mrs Plummer's apparent good humour and spirits when she knew she was taking the children back.

In the next two articles, Henry related that the first he knew of any complaint against him from the Plummers, was a letter from the Bishop of Winchester (at the beginning of October) which he acknowledged expressing surprise. On 8th October, he was given a copy of the Plummers' letter. On 11th October the letter was brought to the attention of the visiting magistrates at Wandsworth, who appointed 28th October as the day when an investigation would be carried out. From 11th October, Henry was given leave of absence.

In the next few articles, Henry stated how the charges against him, so unexpected as they were, seemed to overwhelm him and paralyse his powers of action and thought. Nevertheless, he was determined to attend the magistrates hearing on 28th

October. He then described the interview with Mr Onslow the prison governor, the outcome of which was that he resigned his chaplaincy. Then:

62. That at this date [28th October] your petitioner was threatened with an attachment from the Court of Chancery in reference to a claim made against him by the General Indemnity Insurance Company, then in course of being wound up by the said court, in respect of a call of £1 per share upon 200 shares, held by your petitioner in the said company, and which said call your petitioner was unable to satisfy.

Henry had purchased 100 shares at £2 each (rather than 200 at £1 each); there were also shares issued at £5 each and he may subsequently have purchased some of these also, the call being only for part of the value. Most likely, he just made a mistake.

63. That, such claim hanging over his head, your petitioner believed it would be enforced against him the instant it transpired that your petitioner had resigned his said appointment, and thereby place him in a position of still greater difficulty. In order therefore, to obtain time for the arrangement of these claims, and avoid the threatened attachment against his person, your petitioner, with the concurrence of his wife, before he had any knowledge that any criminal proceedings on the part of Mr. Plummer had been instituted against him, left his home on Friday 28th October last, and took lodgings in Poplar, and forthwith commenced arranging his said accounts with a view to the settlement thereof, so as to enable him to return to Wandsworth without fear of molestation.

So, it was fear of the debtors' prison, not the bailiffs, that had prompted Henry to leave home. If evidence of the date of the Chancery claim could have been presented, this would have negated the charge of absconding to avoid arrest. Henry then explained what happened next...

> 64. That your petitioner ascertained from his said wife on Monday, the 31st October last, that a warrant had been taken out against him upon the charge of Mr. Plummer, whereupon your petitioner at once determined to surrender and meet the said charges the moment he had completed his said accounts, which he concluded early on the morning of Saturday the 12th November, and on the same day, your petitioner went to the hotel in Holborn where Mr. Pratt the solicitor of the prosecutor was staying, and surrendered to the said warrant.

> 65. That your petitioner never had any intention to avoid the said charge, or to attempt to leave the country, which he had ample opportunity of doing.

Article 64 is the weakest item in the petition. Henry knew that there was a warrant issued for his arrest, and yet he spent a further twelve days doing his accounts! One has to apply some understanding to his position though. He had practically no money, he was facing three writs from Chancery – one from Cochrane in respect of his brother-in-law's bankruptcy, one from his solicitor against his sister's debts, and one for the insurance shares for which he faced imprisonment. He had resigned his job, his one remaining source of income, and he was facing the most appalling charges for sexual assault against children. He was also worried about his family, who without him had no means of support. It is little wonder that he was not thinking clearly.

Article 65 though is significant. Henry could easily have fled the country with his family before it became known that he was a wanted man. The fact that he did not do so, suggests that he knew he was innocent and thought that he could still prove it, while at the same time salvaging some element of his wrecked financial affairs. Of course it could also be claimed that he did not leave the country because he could not afford to.

In article 66, Henry confirmed the conversation with Constable Taylor after his arrest, and claimed he surrendered only because he (Henry) was 'assured of his entire innocence'.

In the next article, Henry denied that he had made a confession since the trial…

> 67. That your petitioner has learned with sincere regret, that it is supposed your petitioner has, since his conviction, made some kind of confession or admission of his sentence, or rather of the guilt of your petitioner: but this your petitioner wholly and solemnly denies, and will refer with confidence to the Reverend gentleman to whom, such admission is supposed to have been made, for a complete refutation of such a supposition.

If Henry *had* confessed his guilt at any time, then it would have been as good as pleading guilty in court. It would have exonerated the strategy of his defence team in presenting only character witnesses in order to mitigate the sentence. Who the 'Reverend gentleman' was to whom he is supposed to have confessed, is not known. It might have been Joseph Gegg, Henry's deputy, or it may have been one of the other clerics called to provide him with a witness of character. Who it was, was never revealed, although there *was* a later claim that he had confessed to the Plummers' solicitor, Walters Freake Pratt.

In the next three articles, Henry detailed his good works as a priest, as prison chaplain at Wandsworth, and in respect of many 'societies for the benefit of his fellow creatures'. He also stated that his pecuniary distress was mainly due to losses suffered on being obliged to give up ownership of his journal, *The Philanthropist*.

In article 71, Henry referred to the evidence given at his trial as to his excellent character – as confirmed by Judge Bramwell. In article 72, he declared the entire falseness of all the charges brought against him. He claimed that the charges arose from the 'wicked [and] diseased imaginations' of the two girls.

And the final article...

> 73. That your petitioner is prepared to prove, by satisfactory evidence the precise truth of every allegation in this his petition, and shall for ever in this world regret, that the learned counsel who conducted his defence thought so lightly of the case for the prosecution as to determine not to produce to the jury, the witnesses on behalf of your petitioner, then in attendance and ready to be examined.

And then...

> That under the circumstances aforesaid, your petitioner humbly prays that the allegations contained herein may be duly enquired into; and that upon the truth thereof being made apparent, your Majesty's most gracious pardon may be forthwith extended to your petitioner, and he be released from his present dreadful and unmerited degradation.
>
> And your petitioner will ever pray, &c.
>
> Henry J Hatch,
> 29th December 1859.

All of the evidence that Henry would have given in court, had he been allowed to, was detailed here. Attached to the petition were sworn statements from the various witnesses.

The additional declaration from eleven of the jury, must surely have tipped the sternest of judges into admitting that a gross miscarriage of justice had taken place.

Henry's new solicitor, Mr Holt, circulated the petition and the sworn statements to the press in an attempt to get a newspaper to take them up and publicize them. The declaration of the jury was published on 31st December in *The Morning Chronicle*. The petition was published in full on 9th January 1860 in *The Morning Post*. On the same day, *The Morning Star* published the statement from the jury; the next day *The Guardian* reported *The Morning Post* story, also reproducing the jury statement.

On 11th January, *The Daily Telegraph* having taken a couple of days to consider its response, published a long and thoughtful editorial summarising the material contained within the petition, together with other evidence relating to the case. It compared the Hatch case with that of Dr Smethurst but declined to declare an opinion on Henry's guilt. The newspaper lamented the lack of a Court of Criminal Appeal, questioning,

> is it better to have an organised tribunal than the independent, secret and irresponsible caprice of a Home Secretary who may allow his political, religious or social prejudices to bias him?

*The Daily Telegraph* was of the opinion that further investigation was warranted; it continued,

> Half the circumstances, it is clear, were not brought forward [at the trial] at the advice, it seems, of Mr. Ballantyne [sic]; but what could have been his reason for keeping them out of sight we cannot conjecture.

It was a sober and balanced offering, considering the extraordinary nature of the 'revelations'.

However it was a journal called *The Detective*, not so sober, and perhaps not so balanced, that not only reproduced the petition in full on 14th January, but in subsequent issues over the next few weeks, published in detail virtually all of the collateral defence material. It also printed some interesting background information on the Plummers, having placed an advertisement in *The Times* on 11th January, requesting anyone with information on the case to contact its editor.

In passing, it is sad to note that although *The Philanthropist* understandably said nothing regarding Henry Hatch's conviction, neither did it publish a single item of information related to the action to get him released, following the publication of the petition to the Queen.

*The Detective* had commenced publication in December 1859. It was a fortnightly journal, similar to *The Philanthropist* in size and layout, and devoted to articles on criminal detection, adulteration (of food etc), swindling, quacks, reformatories, parish defaulters, prisoners' aid, immoral literature, street ruffianism, strikes, health insurance, prostitution etc. The back page of the first edition laid out its mission:

> The object of The Detective is primarily to be the antagonist and castigator of fraud, whatever form it may assume; to detect and expose it in its incipient stages, and to frustrate its nefarious designs by nipping them in the bud.

It was printed and published by Thomas Danks. *The Detective* was discontinued in March 1860 after only fourteen editions, but if it did nothing else in its short life, it did at least document much of the otherwise unpublished material on the Hatch case. It thus played a crucial role in drumming up public support for action to reverse such a clear miscarriage of justice.

It is appropriate at this point, and thanks to *The Detective* which printed it, to outline the evidence confirming where relevant the truth of Henry Hatch's submission to the Queen. This consisted of sworn statements by members of his household, sworn to specifically in support of the petition.

There was no material submission from Essie. Although the petition to the Queen was from Henry, Essie must have participated in its preparation. In any event, it is clear from later court appearances that she supported Henry in every word of his evidence. Probably *The Detective* omitted Essie's submission since it mirrored what was said in the petition.

Essie's mother, Esther Dillon, established her own probity as a witness by stating that she was a solicitor's wife, her husband being in practice in New South Wales. She confirmed that Mrs Plummer criticized Eugenia's character and behaviour in front of herself, the Hatches and Martha Howe. She also confirmed Mrs Plummer's strange behaviour when she left Wandsworth after the first visit, and stated that Henry Hatch and the two girls (Eugenia and Lucy) had been in her full view, and could also be seen by Essie, Martha Howe and the two French ladies, the entire time they were in the garden. She said that Henry was running around with the children after him. If either child had put her hand into Henry's pocket, she must have seen it, and she declared unequivocally that they did not. The whole incident had, in any case, lasted barely one or two minutes because she was waiting for her tea – as was Martha Howe – and she called for Henry to come in so that they could eat. She stated that her bedroom was opposite the Hatches' room, and she could also see the door of Eugenia's bedroom. She confirmed that Eugenia's door leading into the passage was, in compliance with Mrs Plummer's wishes, wide open every night when she (Mrs Dillon) went to bed, and wide open in the morning when she left her room. She also mentioned that on account of her ill health, Mary the housemaid slept with her in her room, and spent much time on that floor of the house, constantly passing and re-passing Eugenia's door. She confirmed that while Eugenia was in Wandsworth, and in the evenings after she and Lucy had gone to bed, the five ladies – Essie, Mrs Dillon, Martha Howe and the two French ladies – assembled in the drawing room. Henry then 'exerted himself' to entertain them with diverse activities – conversation, reading aloud, music (Henry played a small accordion as well as the piano), and occasional card games. Before the card games, played on only two or three occasions, Henry would go upstairs to wash his hands. Mrs Dillon confirmed that had Henry been gone even so much as a quarter of an hour, especially on consecutive evenings, then she would have noticed it, his efforts at amusing the ladies being so constant. In addition to that, Henry's health was indifferent, and he suffered from fits of severe cramp. She stated that, 'his absence therefore would have excited our alarm, and immediate enquiry would have been made after him'. She confirmed the story at dinner of Eugenia being an heiress to £15,000, and being betrothed to her doctor whom she was going to marry when she was seventeen. She claimed that on the one night that Stephana stayed at Wandsworth, the night of the storm, Stephana slept in Eugenia's usual room – next to the Hatches' room – with the door wide open, as was the door to the room in which Eugenia slept that night. She further claimed, that on that particular night Henry never left the drawing room from the time the children went to bed, until she (Mrs Dillon) retired. However, Miss Howe and Essie went up several times to check that the children were not frightened. She stated that when the Plummers departed, after having left Stephana at Wandsworth, Mrs Plummer behaved in an even more extravagant way than before, and confirmed the events of the following day when they returned to take both girls away.

Finally, she said that Mr Hatch had been a most kind husband to her daughter; they lived on terms of happiness and mutual affection. She esteemed and respected him very highly, and believed him to be a good and honest man 'wholly innocent in thought as well as deed of the abominable acts charged against him'. She was also confident that her daughter 'would not, and never has for an instant during her life countenanced any act of impropriety or indecency'.

Given the circumstances, it was perhaps not surprising that Mrs Dillon painted such a rosy picture of her daughter and son-in-law. Nevertheless, her evidence directly contradicted what Eugenia had said about what happened in the garden, as well as confirming that Henry would not have had time to make the alleged visits to Eugenia in her room. She also refuted the claim that the bedroom door to the passage was shut, and insisted that Henry had never left the drawing room on the night of the storm.

Martha Howe, the governess, was a truly independent witness. She was in the employ of the Hatches for two and a half months from 11th August 1859, until Henry's departure on 28th October. She confirmed what Caroline Plummer had said about Eugenia's behaviour, as well as Mrs Plummer's excited state when she 'cried and screamed very loud' on leaving the house. She confirmed that she was watching Henry and the children running about in the garden, and that Mrs Dillon had called out to Henry to come in because she wanted her tea. She also stated that she observed Henry and the children the entire time they were running around in the garden, which was not more than a few minutes, and that neither child put their hand into Henry's pocket. 'Had they done so, I must have seen it.' Martha Howe slept on the second floor, and confirmed that she passed Eugenia's room every night, and that every night the door was wide open just as Mrs Plummer had requested. She claimed that Mr Hatch only left the ladies in the drawing room on two occasions while Eugenia was in the house, and then only for a few minutes to wash his hands. Her picture of the Hatches' married life was similar to that of Mrs Dillon. She stated that, 'Mr. Hatch lived on terms of the greatest affection with his wife, and they presented to my mind a true picture of a happy marriage.' She commented that Eugenia never wrote home until she encouraged her to do so; she finally wrote one letter to her father. She never heard Eugenia complain about Mr Hatch, quite the contrary: 'I thought she was attached to him as she used to race with Lucy who should first greet him on his return home.' She also confirmed a very important point. The day the Plummers came with Stephana, they had all dined together. Henry explained how they had complied with the Plummers' wishes in letting Eugenia come into their bed together with Lucy in the morning. Mrs Plummer had replied that she was pleased, as Eugenia had been accustomed to do the same when at Mr and Mrs Brighton's. On the same day, Mrs Plummer, who had been in tears at the thought of leaving her daughters, was once more in an excited state and made everyone around her feel uncomfortable. Miss Howe claimed that she was unaware that Eugenia had expressed any wish to leave the Hatches, and did not believe that she had been crying that day. She confirmed that Henry had not left the drawing room on the night of the storm, although she herself went up several times and saw each of the children, confirming that the servant Mary was also up there. When the Plummers returned unexpectedly to Wandsworth the next day, the Hatches were out. Martha Howe was in the school-room with Eugenia and Stephana and Lucy came in with Mrs Plummer who addressed Miss Howe 'in a loud and angry voice, and excited and offensive manner', questioning why her children were in the school-room and Lucy was in the hall. (Lucy had probably just gone to see who was at the door.) Miss Howe confirmed the details of the Plummers' departure, observing only that Eugenia had said that she did not want to go. Miss Howe then stated that she had heard the charges against Mr Hatch by Eugenia and Stephana, and she

> believe[d] them to be utterly without foundation and to be wholly destitute of truth. [Mr Hatch's character was] irreproachable and distinguished by unaffected piety, Christian piety, modest demeanour, and extreme

kindness to all around him. [Mrs Hatch was possessed of] the highest sense of virtue, truth and honour; [was] most affectionate to her husband, [and was] a kind friend and good mistress…altogether incapable of countenancing much less encouraging any impropriety or act which could in any manner be unbecoming a lady and a good Christian.

Truly, in the eyes of Mrs Dillon and Miss Howe, the Hatches were a model couple of the very highest character.

The final and critical evidence was provided by young Lucy. She started, 'I, Lucy Harriet Hatch, do hereby solemnly and sincerely swear that I shall be eight years old on the 20th day of February 1860.' (She was only seven and a half when the alleged offences were committed.) She had lived with the Hatches since 26th July 1856, having been placed with them by Mr 'Wyse' (Mr Wise of the Isle of Wight). She called Mrs Hatch 'Mamma' and Mr Hatch 'Papa'. On the day of Eugenia's arrival, she remembered them both running a short while after the cab taking the Plummers to the station, following which they went back to the garden, Eugenia crying a little. Henry laughed, and played with them; they ran after each other for a few minutes after which he took each of them by the hand, and they went in to tea. She never lost sight of Henry or Eugenia and

nothing happened but our play…Papa did not ask me to put my hand in his pocket, nor did I do so. I did not hear him ask Eugenia to put her hand in his pocket, and I am sure she did not do so. Eugenia never told me she had done so. Had she done so, I must have seen it.

Eugenia, it transpired, was not interested in Lucy's dolls and playthings, and did not like 'childish games nor children', preferring to be a companion to 'grown-up people such as Mamma'. (More evidence of her maturity…) Lucy confirmed the sleeping arrangements: Eugenia slept in the bedroom next to the Hatches' that used to be hers, and Lucy had a bed in the room with the Hatches. The door between Eugenia's room and the Hatches', as well as the door to the passage was open. On the night of the party, Lucy and Eugenia saw Henry washing his hands in his bedroom, and Lucy demanded a story. Lucy sat on one of Henry's knees and Eugenia on the other; they both had their hands on their laps while Henry related a story about a lion and a little boy. Master Coghlan came to the door – which was ajar – to tell Henry that he was awaited, at which point Lucy insisted that he finish the story, which he did with a loud roar. She continued,

> Nothing whatever took place except his telling us the story whilst we were in the room, and Papa neither wished us to do anything, or shewed us anything.

Lucy went to bed first, followed by Eugenia, after which the servant Mary was in and around the rooms doing her work. Since the door between the two rooms was open, Lucy could hear all that happened there. She related how when Henry came to wash his hands she demanded a kiss, to which Eugenia would respond, 'And me too, Mr. Hatch.' She said that Eugenia had told her that she did not like Mr Hatch as much as Mrs Hatch, but nevertheless, she would always race Lucy to get the first kiss when Henry came home. Lucy was sure that, apart from the goodnight kisses, Henry was never in Eugenia's room. She clarified the morning visits to the Hatches' bed which she never made until Eugenia came. When they went to the bed it was always between the blankets and counterpane and only for a few minutes, and Lucy always went to Henry's side. Further, she confirmed that on the night of the storm, Henry never came up to either room, although Mary Ann was in the rooms for a long time.

The evidence of Mrs Dillon, Martha Howe and even Lucy

was quite clear. Each one of Eugenia's charges was shown either not to be true or to have been impossible to have taken place.

All of this material was published by *The Detective*. The journal could not contain its indignation. Starting in somewhat melodramatic style, it observed,

> We have risen from the perusal of these documents with overwhelming sensations of astonishment, shame and indignation. We feel as though half-waking from some terrible dream, the prominent incidents of which cling to us, and seem to be real, though reason forbids the belief in their reality. [No doubt Henry Hatch thought that too...] Can it be, that when the march of human intellect is elsewhere going forwards with giant strides, that in the administration of criminal law, the credulity and the iniquity of the dark ages are to live again?

After more extravagant invective, *The Detective* then proceeded to examine the character of Eugenia and her parents, having received some communications addressed to its editor. First Mr Plummer:

> It was generally understood that Thomas Plummer, the father of the two children, was a Wiltshire gentleman of wealth and good position in the county...It turns out, however...that Thomas Plummer is a man whose education is greatly below the standard of a butler or gentleman's coachman.

Apparently, Mr Plummer had written a three page letter to the editor of *The Detective*

> without the introduction of a single stop in the whole course of it, and his knowledge of orthography may be judged of when we state that an 'h' is prefixed to those

words which begin with the letter 'a'.

Still, it is no crime to be ill-educated even if one is wealthy – as remains the case today.

Mrs Plummer however, was beyond the pale. She was, it was claimed, illegitimate – hardly her fault – although this charge was retracted in a later edition. Worse than that though, she had form. Before she was married, Caroline Plummer, née Taylor, had

> locked up one Martha Kennett (living in her service) for a whole day and night, in a bed-room without food, and then dragged her out by the hair of her head down stairs, using most foul and disgusting language, which she was in the habit of doing.

For these excesses she was tried at the petty sessions at Cricklade, convicted, and fined £5 and costs. James Lovatt, an attorney of Cricklade who provided this information on oath, further claimed that no servant had lived with the Plummers for the previous three or four years on account of the 'violent, disgusting, and unnatural conduct of the said Caroline Plummer'. Mrs Plummer's mother, apparently, provided the services of servant.

Phoebe Easell, of Bathford, Somerset, stated on oath that she worked for the Plummers as a servant for over eighteen months. The Plummers frequently threw buckets of water over her, and 'obliged her to stay in wet clothes all day and all night'. She claimed that on one occasion, Caroline Plummer had taken her husband's razor and threatened to cut the children's throats with it. Mrs Plummer had once cut off nearly all of Phoebe's hair, and locked her in the cellar for the night. As a consequence of this Phoebe was under medical treatment for several months, paid for by the Plummers, who also gave Phoebe's mother a sum of money to 'stay legal proceeding'. Mr & Mrs Plummer were, she claimed, 'frequently the worse for liquor'.

Notwithstanding the error regarding Caroline Plummer's birth status, these testimonies had been sworn to, and Mrs Plummer's conviction for the assault on Martha Kennett was a matter of record. The Plummers sounded like the dysfunctional family from hell…

Having disposed of the reputations of Mr and Mrs Plummer, *The Detective* now turned its fire on the principal prosecution witness. Mary Eugenia Plummer had been a pupil at a ladies' 'seminary' kept by Susan Spiller of Bath. She claimed that Eugenia showed 'constant bad conduct…and [a] general want of truth'. Susan Spiller had visited the Plummers at Holcroft House, and commented on the 'want of delicacy and intoxication' that she saw there. She said she would not believe Eugenia on oath, and the child was removed from her school after two and a quarter years at her (Susan Spiller's) request.

Another school-keeper in Bath, Eliza Gordon Gray, had the pleasure of Eugenia as a pupil between October and Christmas 1858. She too claimed that from Eugenia's conduct and behaviour, she would not believe her under oath. (In *The Daily Telegraph* article, it had also been stated that Mrs Gray, Mrs Spiller, and Mrs Spiller's servant, Mary Gore, all testified to the 'intractable, cunning, and false disposition of the little girl Eugenia…')

The two main prosecution witnesses in Henry's trial were thus shown to be of very questionable character. Mrs Plummer was a heavy drinker given to using foul language, threatening the children, and committing violence against the servants. She also had a conviction for assault. Eugenia's word, on the evidence of two ex-schoolteachers, was not to be trusted. *The Detective* had not only publicized counter evidence to destroy the prosecution case in Henry's trial, but it had also demolished the character of its two main witnesses.

The issue remained, however, why were no defence witnesses called in the trial? It was not only *The Daily Telegraph* that was exercised on this point. An article in *The Law Times*

– partially reprinted *The Detective* – also expressed incredulity with the outcome of the case and provided a professional assessment and explanation of what had happened. *The Law Times* had access to the trial notes of the prosecution evidence, together with copies of the signed statements of Henry Hatch's putative defence witnesses; it commented thus:

> Having read them attentively our astonishment is increased that, upon such testimony, any jury could have convicted any man, however vile his previous character...Let us add that it inspires alarm also; for what security has innocence if it be possible for a man to be found guilty of such a charge upon such evidence?

Leaving aside the lack of credence given to the possibility of the assaults taking place in the Hatches' bed with Essie present, *The Law Times* made the further entirely obvious point:

> The defence was overwhelming. Every person in the house was there [at the trial] ready to prove that they had seen nothing approaching to impropriety, and that some of the statements of the girl, where she could be contradicted, were certainly false.

The journal then referred to Eugenia's original deposition at the magistrates' hearing, this deposition being appended to the court reporter's record of the prosecution case:

> Extract from a deposition made by Mary Eugenia Plummer at the Wandsworth Police Court, on 14th November 1859. 'I didn't like the Hatches. I told mother this tale for the purpose of taking me away. When mamma brought my little sister, she intended me to remain. I wished to go away, and I told mamma this tale.'

And getting to the nub of the issue:

> Now comes the question, why the witnesses for the defence were not called…It is the reply given to the prosecution, by calling witnesses for the defence, that in this, as in so many other cases, prevented the whole of the evidence on both sides – that is to say, all the materials from which the judgement is to be formed – from being submitted to the jury. Practitioners in criminal courts rightly hold no maxim in greater reverence than this – 'Never give a [defence] reply if you can help it'. Experience shows that there is nothing so dangerous as a reply. One reason is, that the ingenuity of [prosecution] counsel can always dress up a case and present it in such a form as to lead the minds of the jury to look upon it as conclusive of guilt. Another reason is, that by calling witnesses for the defence, you raise a new issue, and the jury try – not whether the prosecution has proved guilt, but whether the prisoner has proved innocence. The [prosecution] reply usually addresses itself to this, and if it can cut the defence to pieces, it cares not how weak the case is for the prosecution. Hence prudent counsel will not call witnesses for the prisoner, save in the last extremity…

And that was the explanation of why Serjeant Ballantine had not called witnesses for the defence. The burden of proof (of Henry's guilt) was with the prosecution. Handing them some nice juicy defence witnesses to dissect – all genteel ladies whose behaviour when presented with the truly shocking and explicit details of the case might be unpredictable – was too much of a risk. The article continued,

> In the case of Mr. Hatch, the prisoner's counsel were

properly of the opinion that the case for the prosecution had broken down [the substantial inconsistencies between the evidence of Eugenia, her mother, and the letter to the bishop], and therefore they resolved not to call witnesses for the defence, and give to a powerful advocate the immense advantage of the last word. The consequences we see. The jury convicted; but they now say, that had they been aware of the defence, they should have acquitted. [The incident was] not uncommon, happening every day in the criminal courts...There is not an assize or quarter session at which counsel and attorneys acting for prisoners are not compelled to choose between the suppression of a defence and the danger of a reply; and as a general rule, they seldom resolve in favour of entering upon a defence without having cause to rue the resolution... The Scotch law is more just to prisoners. Not only does it not give the last word to the prosecution, but in all cases the prisoner has the last word.

The article went on to argue the case for a change to the law, so that the last word is always given to the defence.

*The Manchester Examiner and Times* then waded in with its view of the Hatch case. This article was also reprinted in *The Detective*. Equally indignant in its condemnation of the verdict in the Hatch trial, it did, however, make an important point. The facts of the case and the detailed evidence against Henry, could not by their nature be reported. Thus an informed public debate about what might or might not have happened could not take place. The newspaper also commented that such a crime, '...utterly abhorrent to human nature...', and as '...unmitigatedly gross...', as Henry Hatch was accused of, had a habit of 'sticking' regardless of the evidence, precisely because it was so hideous. This further weighed against Henry in public opinion.

It is noteworthy that the main national newspaper, *The Times*, while having reported as much as decency permitted of the Old Bailey case, was entirely silent following the publication elsewhere of Henry's petition to the Queen, together with the sworn witness statements. No comment was made on the petition; no debate took place in its columns; no clamour for a review or the institution of a Court of Criminal Appeal, a clamour that could hardly have been ignored in Parliament. Indeed, on 2nd February 1860, *The Times* published an editorial fiercely *in opposition* to a Court of Criminal Appeal. It is appropriate to comment on this later.

Henry's friends, meanwhile, having assisted in the production of the petition, were looking to see what could be done to get it accepted as quickly as possible. Edward Wise was the chairman of this group and Joseph Gegg, Henry's assistant chaplain at Wandsworth, was the secretary. There were also William T Blair, a magistrate of the city of Bath and Somerset, Dr Gridwood of Paddington and Charles Wilkinson, the surgeon at the prison.

On 17th January 1860, Joseph Gegg and two of the others had a meeting with the Home Secretary, Sir George Cornewall Lewis. Henry's petition to the Queen had to be considered first by the Home Secretary; it was his decision whether or not to recommend that a free pardon be granted. Sir George told them that he had heard from someone 'in high authority', that Mr Hatch had made a confession of his guilt to Walters Freake Pratt. Mr Pratt, it may be remembered, was the Plummers' solicitor who visited Essie and tried to get her to admit to Henry's guilt, and tell him where Henry was hiding. He also told her that if Henry admitted his guilt and apologized, then the action would be dropped; he asked Henry the same thing the following day, when Henry surrendered to him. Sir George had had an interview with Mr Pratt on the subject of the alleged confession, and Mr Pratt had '...declined to give any explanation except on oath...' (And this to the Home

Secretary, no less.) The implication was that Henry *had* made a confession to Mr Pratt, and this was the impression left on Sir George. Not only that, the story gradually emerged that Mr Pratt had told the prosecuting counsel at Henry's trial, Mr Cooper, that Henry had confessed to him. And even worse, Mr Cooper then whispered the fact into the ear of Serjeant Ballantine during the trial. Ballantine later confirmed that the story was circulating in court, and he thought that some of the jury might even have heard it.

This was highly damaging; Serjeant Ballantine had already decided not to call witnesses in the trial, so the report of a confession was unlikely to cause him to change his strategy – except to determine more than ever not to call witnesses. But if the jury heard of it, no matter how poor was the prosecution case, they could hardly find Henry not guilty...

Henry's friends had to decide what to do. If there was any doubt in Sir George Cornewall Lewis' mind that Henry might have confessed to the crime, then the petition would not be granted. It is possible that he invited Mr Gegg and the others to the meeting in order to tell them that he *had* decided to reject the petition, unless it could be shown that no confession had been made. Time was of the essence. Henry's friends needed a pretext to get Walters Freake Pratt into court in order to swear, under oath, that Henry had not confessed.

A new legal team was briefed and told what was needed. They concluded that the approach to adopt was to charge that Mr Pratt had acted outside of the law when he suggested first to Essie, and then Henry – in front of witnesses – that the case could be dropped if Henry confessed. If, as part of the proceeding, Mr Pratt could be induced to swear that Henry did *not* confess, then surely that would satisfy the Home Secretary. And if, at the same time, he could be censured in some way or even found guilty of misconduct, then that too would be to Henry's advantage. The question remains though, why did the team reject the primary charge of misleading the

Home Secretary? Possibly, they thought that such a charge
would be very difficult to prove. After all, Mr Pratt had not,
strictly speaking, broken the law, and was not responsible
for Sir George Cornewall Lewis' conclusions following the
interview…

The case of Walters Freake Pratt was called before Lord
Chief Justice Cockburn, and Justices Crompton and Hill,
sitting in banco (in full court at Westminster), at the Court of
Queen's Bench on 23rd January 1860.

Sir Alexander James Edmund Cockburn, 58, twelfth
baronet, had been appointed Lord Chief Justice in 1859. A
few years later, he was turned down for a peerage on account
of the Palace's view of his 'notoriously bad moral character…'
(ODNB) (He had fathered two illegitimate children.) Cockburn
was not a judge with the 'highest reputation', rather he was a
'man of the world who knew how to master detail by hard
work' (ODNB). Sir Charles Crompton, on the other hand, was
said to have a '…profound knowledge of the law…' He had
been a Queen's Bench judge since 1852. A few years older
than Cockburn, he was '…quick-witted, sarcastic, kind and
humane…' (ODNB). The third on the bench was Sir Hugh
Hill. He was the same age as the Lord Chief Justice and had
been appointed judge to the Queen's Bench in 1858. He was
a QC and a Serjeant-at-Law. Poor health forced him to retire
shortly afterwards in 1861.

Pleading to this formidable triumvirate, Henry's friends
had assembled Mr Edwin James, QC, together with Mr Garth
and our old friend Serjeant Ballantine. Richard Garth, later
Sir Richard Garth, chief justice of Bengal, was called to the
bar in 1847, and had been a contemporary of Henry Hatch's
at Eton. Edwin James was a curious choice to lead the team.
A sometime actor with the appearance of a prize-fighter, he
had been called to the bar in 1836, but his '…knowledge of
the law was very limited…'; his main talent seemed to be in
dealing with 'common juries' where he '…freely appealed

with conspicuous success to their ignorance and prejudices…' (ODNB). Despite (or perhaps because of) earning £7,000 a year, he was bankrupt the following year (1861) with debts of an astonishing £100,000. Shortly afterwards, he was found guilty of obtaining money by misrepresentation, disbarred, struck off and had his Queen's Counsel appointment cancelled. Since the Queen's Bench hearing was without a jury, and justices Cockburn, Crompton, and Hill had between them a considerable knowledge of the law, and nearly 90 years experience, variously as barrister and judge, Edwin James would seem not to have been a brilliant choice to plead Henry's case.

Nevertheless, he moved for a rule (a ruling) calling upon Mr Pratt to '…show cause why he should not answer the matters of the affidavits on which the learned counsel moved'. Mr Garth outlined the details of the Hatch case, saying that he could make no comment on Mr Hatch's guilt or otherwise, since the case was under the consideration of Sir George Cornewall Lewis, Secretary of State for the Home Department. However, he called the attention of the court to the conduct of Mr Pratt during his visit to Essie. This was '…of the grossest and most culpable manner…' He then read to the court from an affidavit that Essie had provided. Her husband had left home on 28th October 1859 after having resigned from Wandsworth in a 'very desponding state of mind…' She was afraid that he would be tempted to destroy himself, and despite her entreaties he refused to tell her what he was charged with. On or about 31st October, she found out that a warrant had been issued for his arrest on a charge of indecently assaulting Eugenia and Stephana Plummer. A gentleman named Pratt called upon her on 11th November; she declined to see him alone on hearing that he was the solicitor for the prosecution. A friend who was with her, Amelia Grove, was asked to hear what Mr Pratt had to say, but he wished to speak to Essie confidentially, so Amelia Grove left the room. He then proposed to Essie that she might have her husband back within a few days and 'nothing more be said about the prosecution', if she would tell him Henry's address, and declare in writing that she considered her husband to be guilty and that he should make an apology. She responded that she could not give him her husband's address without his authority, and would not admit that he was guilty since it would not be true (notwithstanding the fact that she knew nothing about the details of the charge). Essie became alarmed at Mr Pratt's '...extraordinary conduct...', and sent for Mr Onslow, the prison governor, who then spoke with Mr Pratt alone. The two were apparently already acquainted – probably as a result of the case. Mr Onslow then repeated to Essie, on her own, what Mr Pratt had proposed, and added that if she declined to reveal Henry's whereabouts, his name would be advertised in *Hue and Cry* with a £100 reward for information. She then saw Mr Pratt again. He repeated his offer, and threat, and said he would return the next day. This he did, and saw Essie in the presence of one of Henry's friends, Walter Coward. Once more Mr Pratt proposed that 'an apology be made and the matter hushed up...' Essie was very distressed at the tone and manner of Mr Pratt, and 'declared that she could never admit her husband's guilt'. Mr Pratt then replied that she had mistaken him. He wished Mr Hatch to make the admission and to surrender himself. Essie replied that her husband would not admit his guilt, for he was not guilty, and that he was ready to meet the charge, and he would give himself up. It was then agreed that Henry would surrender that same evening at 7:30 at Ridler's Hotel in Holborn where Mr Pratt was staying. Mr Pratt added helpfully, that he would have police officers present, and it would be better than coming to Wandsworth to be publicly arrested. Essie then, and in much distress, cried, 'What do you want? Is it money? If so, we have none...' And upon adding, '...Oh what shall I do?', Mr Pratt offered her assistance saying, '...I pity you, and if you want any private professional advice I will give it to you.' An affidavit from Mr

Onslow confirmed all that Essie had said regarding the events when he had been present.

The Lord Chief Justice then enquired whether it was suggested that Mr Pratt had acted from corrupt motives, to which Mr James said that it would appear by and by.

Mr Coward's affidavit also confirmed Essie's account regarding the offer to 'hush up the proceedings' if Mr Hatch would surrender and acknowledge his guilt.

Most importantly, an affidavit from Henry Hatch was now read. This was Henry's first opportunity to make any statement in his defence in court. It said that on his arrest, Mr Pratt had asked him to confess his guilt, 'promising that if that were done the proceedings should be made to cease...' Henry 'distinctly' refused.

And now an affidavit from Mr Gegg was referred to. It described the meeting with Sir George Cornewall Lewis and Mr Pratt's refusal to confirm or deny that Henry Hatch had confessed to him except under oath. The Lord Chief Justice then observed, '...and that, no doubt, is the reason why this application is made', to which he added that otherwise, it should have been made much earlier. (But, of course, that was not the reason for the application.)

Mr James, who may have been wondering whether that *should* have been the reason for the application, continued, while avoiding the rhetorical question. The issue was, he said, whether Mr Pratt had been guilty of the grossest misconduct. He wondered what Mr Pratt's motive in making the visit might have been. Was it to compromise a felony, or get an apology in order to 'arm himself against a subsequent action', if so, it was misconduct and an abuse of his powers. He pointed out that a policeman taking the same action 'would have been reprehended by the bench...' Mr Pratt was, under the circumstances, representing the Crown.

When asked what he wanted the court to do, Mr James said he wanted Mr Pratt to confirm that he had, as an officer of the court, visited Mrs Hatch and stated that the prosecution would be stayed if Mr Hatch confessed, referring again to the affidavit from Mr Hatch wherein he stated 'most unequivocally that he refused to [confess].'

Mr Justice Hill then questioned whether Mr James 'said anything as to Mr Pratt's motives…', to which Mr James said that he did not. The Lord Chief Justice said,

> …it may be that he [Pratt] was anxious to protect Mr. Hatch…Perhaps the promoters of the prosecution would have rested content with an apology on the truth of the case being sifted [examined]…

To which Mr Justice Crompton added,

> Were it not for the peculiar nature of the charge, one might come immediately to such a conclusion. Still, [we] every day heard of common assaults, and such cases being settled on an apology being given. It might turn out that Mr. Pratt's great fault was his tenderness towards the defendant.

The Lord Chief Justice then commented,

> …at the same time this was not a prosecution which ought to have been stopped, and, in the mildest view of the case, the attorney had committed a gross error of judgement. If the court granted a rule, it was a matter which ought to be disposed of without delay…especially as its decision might have a material bearing upon the determination of the Home Secretary.

Although Mr James wanted answers from Mr Pratt by the next day, The Lord Chief Justice declared that '…Mr. Pratt must be allowed abundant time to prepare his answer.' That answer to be supplied to the court by Friday (this being Monday), for consideration on Saturday, and a rule nisi (a conditional rule or decision) was granted.

The hearing was re-convened on Monday, 30th January 1860, having slipped from Saturday. Mr Justice Wightman joined their Lordships Cockburn, Crompton and Hill on the bench. Sir William Wightman had 'a sound knowledge of the law, combined with patience, courtesy, and clear reasoning' (ODNB). Mr Macaulay QC, and Mr W Cooper appeared for Mr Pratt. Mr Macaulay reminded the court that after the warrant had been issued for Henry Hatch's arrest he had absconded, and Mrs Hatch had written to Mrs Plummer appealing to her for mercy. He read the letter out in court. Chief Justice Cockburn, evidently moved, said that he wished that the letter had been read out in court when the rule was applied for.

Mr Macaulay then described Mr Pratt's visit to Essie, emphasising Mr Pratt's 'delicate' feelings in going himself rather than sending a policeman. Being 'deeply impressed with the misery in which he saw Mrs Hatch', he said that Pratt admitted that he had said that the charge would be dropped in exchange for a confession. The following day when Mr Hatch surrendered, Mr Pratt asked him whether he would 'make an apology to the prosecutor, Mr Plummer... he said he would not...' Then he said, '...Deal with me as leniently as you can...', adding the words, '... I was mad...', or, '...I am mad', Mr Pratt could not be sure which. The implication – left unsaid – was that this was Henry's confession. Mr Macaulay proceeded to paint Mr Pratt's visit to Essie Hatch as youthful and inexperienced generosity – he was only twenty-nine years old – in going himself rather than sending the police to arrest Henry. He was inexperienced in criminal matters; he had no improper motive in visiting Mrs Hatch, and it was only his sympathy for Essie that prompted him to offer to withdraw the prosecution in exchange for a confession. (The point about not sending the police was completely spurious. Constable Taylor had already been to Wandsworth to try to arrest Henry. Henry was not there, and Pratt knew he was not there.)

Mr Edwin James said that Mr Pratt's conduct *had* been most improper throughout. Mrs Hatch's letter had been included in his (James') affidavit, but he had not read it out because he did not think it was material. In any case, when she wrote it, she did not know the nature of the charges against Henry. Mr Pratt had not denied the offer to withdraw the prosecution in exchange for a confession. Henry's comment on being arrested, 'Deal with me as leniently as you can', could have applied to the immediate treatment he was to receive from the police officer rather than to the charge itself. However, Mr Pratt had not answered the point that he had declined to state to the Home Secretary, except on oath, whether or not Mr Hatch had made a confession. That left the Home Secretary with the impression that Mr Hatch had made a confession.

Chief Justice Cockburn observed that it would have been 'more correct and generous to have stated what he knew; but that was not the charge on which this rule was granted'. Mr James reiterated that Mr Pratt had left Sir George Cornewall Lewis with the impression that a confession had been made, and now it was clear that this was not so. Chief Justice Cockburn, collecting his thoughts, observed that Mr Hatch's statement on being arrested was ambiguous, but he questioned whether Mr Pratt's refusal to make a statement was misconduct. (So Henry's friends were correct when they concluded that Mr Pratt's conduct with the Home Secretary was an unsuitable subject for the action.) Mr James said that it *was* misconduct in an attorney to go to Mr Hatch's wife and say that he would withdraw the charge if a confession were made.

Chief Justice Cockburn's next contribution makes it clear where his sympathies lay. He said that Mr Pratt's motive in visiting Mrs Hatch was her letter to the Plummers. He repeated that the letter ought to have been brought to the attention of the court. Mr James stated that he had no desire to keep it back – it had been part of his original affidavit – but it was written before Mrs Hatch knew the true facts of the case. (If Mr James had been awake, he could have pointed out that Pratt's first visit to Essie was made fifteen days after the letter was written – hardly an urgent response to a heart-rending appeal, particularly considering Essie's request to respond by return.) Then, the Chief Justice

> …expressed himself with great warmth in condemnation
> of the course adopted in making Mr Pratt's visit to Mrs.
> Hatch a ground of charge, after she had written that
> touching appeal to the compassion of Mrs. Plummer.
> His Lordship thought it a most ungrateful return…

Justice Crompton added that he thought that Mr Pratt had 'acted with great leniency in not making any statement when he was called to do so'. The Lord Chief Justice had made up his mind.

Mr Garth, trying to maintain some semblance of the prosecution case, declared,

> The impression on the mind of the Home Secretary,
> that Mr. Hatch had made a confession, must have been
> produced by something that Mr. Pratt had circulated;
> and to leave the Home Secretary under the impression
> that a confession had been made when none had, in
> fact, been made, was misconduct.

An indisputable point, but not, as Chief Justice Cockburn had already pointed out, the charge upon which the rule was granted. Besides which, Chief Justice Cockburn said, 'Mr. Pratt might have honestly believed that Mr. Hatch had made a confession…' (Notwithstanding the ambiguity of the 'deal with me as leniently as you can' comment, Henry had 'particularly declined' to make a confession when arrested, but this was the Lord Chief Justice's view.) It was, he said, unnecessary for the court to rule whether Henry's words on being arrested amounted to a confession, although he would offer an opinion if it was requested. Apparently, it was not.

Then came the summing up. Lord Chief Justice Cockburn, in a mind-numbing triple negative, said,

> I would not go to the length of saying that Mr. Pratt might not have acted in a manner not well advised and judicious [Mr Pratt 'might' have acted in a manner 'not well advised and judicious'] but an attorney undertaking a prosecution [has] to…steel himself against every consideration of humanity, ignoring letters written imploring mercy etc.

Chief Justice Cockburn thought that the application (for the rule to be made absolute) was unfounded. Mr Pratt had no improper motive. If he erred '…it was on the side of tenderness and mercy…' The rule should never have been granted had the facts been known (the content of Essie's letter). Mr Justice Wightman then spoke for the first time and said that there was not the slightest imputation on Mr Pratt, other than he was too humane. The rule was discharged, and that was that.

The case cost Henry's friends around £400 to bring and they were lucky. When Mr Macaulay (for Pratt's defence) asked for costs, having won, Justice Crompton responded that it was '…hardly worth while to ask for them, but it must not be supposed that they were not granted because there was any blame remaining…' Perhaps that was their Lordships' way of firing just the lightest of shots across the bows of Mr Pratt's team to remind them of the pitfalls of being too humane…

To a twenty-first century mind, the ruling seems astonishing. Walters Freake Pratt *was* guilty of gross misconduct. He misled the Home Secretary in a matter that was absolutely central to a petition to the Queen! And he avoided censure on a point of law, that being that it was not his misleading of the Home Secretary that was the reason the case was brought. And even if it *had* been the central charge, the Lord Chief Justice had questioned whether Mr Pratt's ambiguous response was really misconduct.

Not only that, Pratt was effectively representing the Crown when he visited Essie. Thomas Plummer had already brought a charge of indecent assault against Henry – an indictable offence – and a warrant had been issued for Henry's arrest. Such a charge could not be dropped just because the person so charged had made an apology, and yet their lordships decided that this action was merely youthful indiscretion. Walters Freake Pratt was guilty of misconduct, bordering on the criminal, and he got away with it.

Despite the fact that the action was lost, Henry's legal team did get a result. They established from two sworn statements – by Henry John Hatch and Walters Freake Pratt – that Henry did *not* confess to the assaults. Establishing that fact was the primary objective in bringing the case. It should have satisfied Sir George Cornewall Lewis in his decision on Henry's petition to The Queen.

Naturally, *The Law Times* commented on the case. And once more, it is helpful to get its view of the proceedings. On 4th February 1860 the paper commented,

> Mr. Pratt has been relieved by the Queen's Bench from the charge of having dealt unprofessionally with the prisoner; but his conduct is not wholly free from blame in this respect, that he did give his own counsel to understand that the prisoner had made a confession to him, whereas in truth the fact was the very reverse

of this…and yet by what he said to the counsel for the prosecution, and afterwards by refusing to answer a question in that significant manner which is usually taken as a tacit admission, he produced on the Home Secretary also the impression that the story that a confession had been made to him was true…

The fact that Walters Freake Pratt had told the prosecution counsel that Henry had made a confession, was amplified in a letter written to *The Star* newspaper, reproduced, once more, by *The Detective*. John Passmore Edwards was a newspaper proprietor, philanthropist, and social reformer. Evidently he was acquainted with Henry's band of friends, and it may be that they encouraged him to further their cause by writing to the newspapers; it was clear, though, that he did not fully agree with their strategy. In any event, he related what had happened. Following the meeting with the Home Secretary, Mr Gegg had asked Serjeant Ballantine, Henry's defence counsel, why he had not called the defence witnesses that were ready in court during Henry's trial. Ballantine told him the story of Henry's alleged confession that he heard from Mr Cooper. Exactly as predicted by *The Law Times* earlier, Serjeant Ballantine had taken the view that in not calling the defence witnesses and allowing them to be shredded by the prosecution, he was increasing Henry's chances of a 'not guilty' verdict, relying instead on the jury disbelieving the two girls and their mother. His decision was reinforced by the suspicion that Henry might have made a confession.

Passmore Edwards then summarized the benefits of the Pratt hearing, lost as it was: that Mr Pratt told the prosecution counsel that he had a confession – or something construed as a confession – from the prisoner; that on Mr Pratt's sworn statement Henry declined to confess and avoid prison, and this was the best evidence in Henry's favour; and that from Essie's letter to the Plummers, she was unaware of the details of the charge and therefore could not have been an accomplice to her husband. If she had been, she would surely have made some reference to it in the letter. He finished his letter somewhat critical of Edwin James' strategy in the Pratt hearing, but profoundly convinced of Henry's innocence, and delighted with the 'moral victory'.

Nevertheless, the full story was now out at last. Henry had been denied what would undoubtedly have been a winning defence case because his counsel, Serjeant Ballantine, had misjudged the dangers of bringing defence witnesses into court; a decision reconfirmed, if he was in any doubt, by the report that Henry had made a confession. Added to which, one or more members of the jury may have heard of the alleged confession.

Unfortunately, the Walters Freake Pratt effect was not finished. On 18th February 1860, Sir George Cornewall Lewis, Second Baronet, Eton and Christ Church, Oxford, Secretary of State for the Home Department, '...declined to interfere...' That is to say,

> He was not prepared after giving the whole matter his most anxious consideration, to say that the two children...have wilfully and maliciously sworn that which is false.

Henry's petition to the Queen had been rejected. Sir George noted only, that it was open to Henry to bring an action for perjury against Eugenia Plummer; the implication being, that a successful outcome would lead to a reassessment of his petition.

How had Sir George Cornewall Lewis come to this decision? Every charge against Henry had been refuted by sworn witness statements. The horseplay in the garden had been seen by several independent witnesses, each one stating that no indecency had, or could have, taken place. The nightly incidents in Eugenia's room could not have happened. Henry was only away from the drawing room on two or three occasions while Eugenia was staying at Wandsworth, and then for only short periods; in addition to which, the servant, Mary, was in and out of the rooms doing her chores, and both doors to the bedroom were wide open. Lucy swore that the alleged assault, when Eugenia and Lucy were perched on Henry's knees listening to the story, did not take place, and in any case, Master Coghlan knocked on the door in the middle of the story and was told immediately to 'Come in!' Of the incidents in the Hatches' bed in the mornings, Lucy swore that it was *she* who was always on Henry's side of the bed. In addition to all of that, Henry swore, and this was acknowledged by Walters Freake Pratt, that he was innocent and had never made a confession. There were also the sworn affidavits regarding the characters of Eugenia and Mrs Plummer published in *The Detective*, and there was the declaration from eleven of the original jury, that had they seen the contents of the petition, they would never have found Henry guilty.

With this overwhelming weight of evidence, Sir George Cornewall Lewis yet declined to allow Henry's petition. Were Henry's words, 'I was mad…deal with me as leniently as you can…', at the back of his mind? Was there a suspicion that, after all, Henry might have implied that he was guilty?

Another factor may have told on the Home Secretary's decision. Sir George Cornewall Lewis had received first class honours in classics, and second class honours in mathematics at Oxford. He was interested in political economy and had entered Middle Temple. He was also an expert in ancient and modern languages. Perhaps as a scholar and a lawyer, he insisted on exactness and due process before the major step of reversing the verdict in a trial could be taken – notwithstanding that eleven of the trial jury had already declared themselves to have been wrong. Possibly this was true, and may in any case have weighed with Sir George in his consideration. But there was something else also, and references in *The Morning Chronicle*, *The Observer*, *The Daily Telegraph*, and *The Detective* to another criminal case that was still very fresh in his mind, may possibly throw some light on the decision.

In an article published on 1st January 1860 in *The Observer*, parallels between the Hatch and Smethurst cases had been drawn. The Smethurst case had come to a final close just one day before Henry himself was tried at the Old Bailey.

Thomas Smethurst was a doctor who had been found guilty of the murder of his recent and bigamous wife, Isabella Bankes, by poisoning her with arsenic or antimony. He was sentenced to death. The prosecution counsel was, as it happens, Serjeant Ballantine. The case had come to the Old Bailey on 7th July 1859. The following day it was halted, much of the prosecution case having already been presented, and reported in the press, on account of the illness of one of the jurymen. The jury were discharged, and a new trial commenced six weeks later. The details of the case were truly extraordinary. At the time of Isabella's death, Smethurst was still seeing his 'real' wife regularly and sending her money. She was twenty-five or thirty years older than he was, and she even wrote to *The Times* when he was under sentence of death declaring him to be innocent. The burden of proof that he poisoned Isabella Bankes rested on 'chymical' analysis, some of which was found subsequently to be wrong, and there were no poisons found in Smethurst's possession even though he was a doctor. Letters flooded *The Times* from medical and scientific men, pointing out that the analysis was faulty, and there was no scientific proof that Isabella had been poisoned – the symptoms leading to her death being explained as natural causes. There was some quite incriminating circumstantial evidence – Isabella's will, hastily drawn up by Smethurst in his favour, and signed while she was actually dying. And of course, there was the bigamous relationship, and the fact of his on-going and apparently cordial relationship with his first wife. Nevertheless, there was no *proof* that Isabella Bankes had been poisoned.

A public outcry ensued, and a few days before he was due to be executed, Thomas Smethurst was reprieved. Several months later, on the very day that Henry Hatch was appearing before the Surrey magistrates, Sir George Cornewall Lewis confirmed that Thomas Smethurst was to be granted a full Royal Pardon. The scientific evidence against Smethurst had been considered, and although there were suspicious circumstances, there were also sufficient doubts as to the prisoner's guilt. After considering the evidence for four days, Sir George granted Smethurst a free pardon. He did say, however, that Smethurst would be indicted for bigamy, which he duly was. Smethurst was found guilty, and received a sentence of one year's hard labour the day before Henry Hatch's appearance at the Old Bailey.

The six week delay in Smethurst's original trial saved his life. It allowed a public opinion head of steam to build up regarding the inadequacy of the scientific evidence, and this led directly to the reprieve and pardon. He was convicted on the 20th August, and was due to be hanged on the 6th of September. Without that delay, he would undoubtedly have suffered Marie and Frederick Manning's fate on the roof of the entrance gate of Horsemonger Lane Gaol. The gallows had already been serviced ready for the event.

Although not relevant to the murder case, there were some fascinating revelations at the subsequent bigamy trial. It had been established that Smethurst's marriage to his first wife, Mary Durham, had taken place in 1828 when he was seventeen and she was forty-five. Since Mary was still alive in 1858 when he married Isabella Bankes, the second marriage must have been bigamous – *if the first marriage was proper*. But the defence showed that at the time she married Thomas Smethurst, Mary had been for some time the apparent wife of another man, Johnson, and the son of that union was brought into court as a defence witness! The defence then attempted to show that the bigamy had been committed on Smethurst by his first 'wife', not by him on Isabella Bankes. The defence failed, because it was proved that Johnson, whose real name was Laporte, was already living with a lawful wife and family, spending only part of his time with Mary Durham. And piling confusion onto perplexity, one of Laporte's lawful sons with his wife was also called as a witness, and Mary Durham's son by Johnson/Laporte proved her signature to the marriage to Thomas Smethurst!

The Smethurst case had been a shambles. The jury had convicted a man to be hanged on the basis of faulty scientific evidence reinforced by circumstantial evidence. One of the jury had even written to the newspapers to allay fears that the judge's summing up had influenced them. He said that eleven of the jury had already made up their minds that Smethurst was guilty before the judge started his summing up! There was a barrage of letters to the newspapers claiming that the scientific evidence was worthless. And when Smethurst was finally granted the Royal Pardon – even though the evidence against him was 'suspicious' – there were further revelations of his private life illustrative of his general contempt for the law.

There was a danger that the Smethurst case could have undermined public trust in the bedrock of British justice – trial by jury. In addition, the one safety net existing for criminal cases – the Royal Pardon – had been clearly tainted. A man subsequently convicted of a serious criminal act – bigamy – had been pardoned, albeit for another crime. *The Times*, in an editorial following the bigamy trial, felt it necessary to spell out that the two crimes – bigamy and murder – were quite independent of each other. The fact that Dr Smethurst was clearly guilty of one did not devalue the pardon for the other. When the Hatch case came along a few weeks later, again with a questionable decision by the jury – and one which eleven of the jury now maintained was wrong – and again requesting a Royal Pardon, it is little wonder that Sir George Cornewall Lewis was wary of interfering. Imagine! Supposing the Royal

Pardon was granted to Henry John Hatch, and subsequently it was shown that he *was* a child-molester! Supposing it could be shown that he *had* confessed, even if he had subsequently retracted his confession, then serious questions would have to be asked about the British Criminal Justice System, and those charged with its proper conduct.

There was, unfortunately, yet another and far more prosaic reason why consideration of Henry's petition might not have received the full force of Sir George Cornewall Lewis' undeniable intellect. He was ill. The decision to deny the free pardon was announced on 18th February 1860, but Lewis's diaries and correspondence indicate that he was quite unwell during most of the month. Initially, it was 'neuralgia of the brain', identified at the time as possibly malaria on account of the poor state of the drains at the Home Office. After this he developed influenza which he suffered with for a further ten days. His diaries indicate that during this period he was overcome with a 'great depression' and could do little work. Sir John Trelawney noted in his diary on 26th February, that Lewis seemed to be half asleep when speaking in the House of Commons. It was another cruel twist of fate for Henry Hatch; at this critical time, the Home Secretary's judgement may have been significantly compromised by ill health.

Now it is appropriate to consider the entire lack of comment on Henry's trial in *The Times* newspaper, following publication elsewhere of his petition to the Queen. The Smethurst murder trial received blanket coverage in the press in general, and *The Times* in particular, before and during, but particularly after the conviction. Of course it was a juicy murder trial of a medical man, with gruesome details of tests on body parts for arsenic and antimony, and a will signed by a dying woman, all spiced up with illicit relationships. But as more and more information emerged regarding the questionable scientific evidence, so the clamour grew for action. Not so with the Hatch trial. The publication in *The Detective* of Henry's petition to the Queen was advertised in *The Times*, but following the 'astounding revelations' mentioned in the advertisement, there was no editorial and not a single letter of comment published in *The Times*.

The editor of *The Times*, John Thadeus Delane, had been in the job for twenty years. He ran the newspaper like a '...great department of state'; he had a 'close relationship' with Viscount Palmerston (the Prime Minister), and was adept at 'journalistic curvature' whereby opinions were steered in directions '...his political antennae told him that governments would follow...' (ODNB). Delane even advised Palmerston on the composition of his government, advice that was accepted in the appointment of Sir Robert Peel (the third baronet, son of the famous Robert Peel) as Chief Secretary for Ireland. Delane regularly corresponded and dined with members of the government, including Palmerston and Cornewall Lewis, and like Cornewall Lewis, he was a sometime lawyer. It may be that quiet words were spoken about the inadvisability of encouraging another debate about a faulty jury decision and Royal Pardon, so soon after public trust in the system had been shaken up over the Smethurst case. If there was collusion no one was going to admit it, but it does seem to be a likely explanation for the deafening silence in the pages of *The Times* on the Hatch case.

The failure of Sir George Cornewall Lewis to recommend the Royal Pardon for Henry John Hatch was a major setback, and it condemned Henry to at least another three months in gaol; but Henry's friends were not to be put off by the Home Secretary. A short while later an order was obtained from Mr Baron Bramwell, coincidentally the original trial judge, to 'prefer a Bill of Indictment for Perjury against the child Eugenia Plummer'. Meanwhile, Henry had to languish in Newgate, awaiting events outside as they took their slow but inexorable course. He hoped that the wait would be worth it.

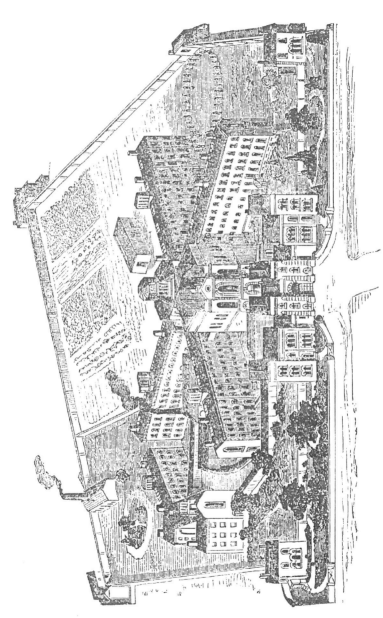

1. The New Surrey House of Correction at Wandsworth around 1852. The prison chaplain's house is immediately to the right of the main gate,

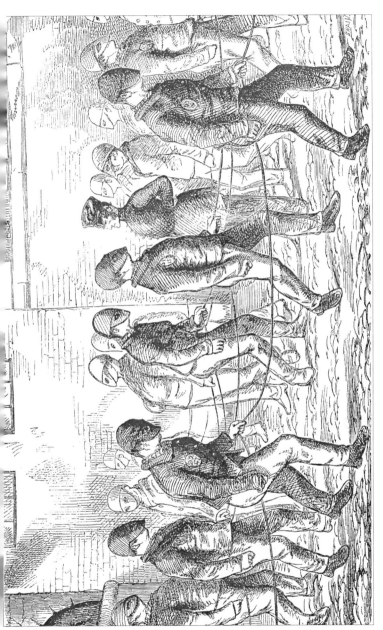

2. The Separate System in operation at Pentonville. Masked prisoners are being exercised holding on to ropes to ensure a proper distance was maintained between them.

3. A cell at the Surrey House of Correction. The prisoner is working on his Labour Machine – the handle needed to be turned 10,000 – 12,000 times per day. Note the wash-basin and water closet, the gas light over the table for reading, and the prison rules on the wall. Sleeping was done on a hammock – not shown – slung between the walls.

4. The chapel at the Surrey House of Correction. The chapel, only part of
   which is shown, could hold up to 400 prisoners. The person on the raised
   platform – which looks quite precarious – could see each prisoner, and be
   seen, but the prisoners could not see each other.

5. The memorial to Richard Boyle, 2nd Viscount Shannon, in St Mary's
   Church, Walton on Thames. It was sculpted by the notable Louis
   François Roubiliac, and erected in 1759.

6. The prison chaplain's house and garden at the Surrey House of Correction around 1852. The chaplain's house is on the left, with the surgeon's house at the extreme right. Between them is the garden with its shrubs before the carriage drive was built. The drawing is somewhat idealized; the distance from the chaplain's drawing-room widow (at the right side of the house, and not visible) to the end of the garden was actually 258 feet – about 79 metres.

7. An illustration from John Mildred – 'Papa tells his story'. Papa's unusual appearance – high forehead, large pointed nose, clean shaven with sideboards, suggests that this might be an image of Henry John Hatch....

8. The Church of St Mary's, Little Stambridge. The dilapidated state of the porch roof suggests that the picture was taken shortly before the church was demolished in 1891.

9. A few gravestones are all that remain now.

# Some Justice

Henry's first month in Newgate – when he had time from his oakum picking – was spent preparing the submission to the Queen for his free pardon. After that was finished, and when the case against Walters Freake Pratt failed, followed shortly afterwards by Sir George Cornewall Lewis' decision not to recommend him for a free pardon, it became clear that Henry's stay in prison would be longer than he had hoped. His main concern, apart from getting his freedom, was how to provide for his family. He decided to write a book and sell subscriptions forward, hoping to cash in on public sympathy. The book was called *John Mildred or Love One Another*, and it was published in April 1860. The author's name was given simply as 'H.J.H.', and it was written for a 'much-loved child of eight years old' called Lucy; the last sentence of the preface says it all:

> Should this offering have this effect [to lead the young mind to the true fountain of wisdom…Jesus Christ, who is the Way, the Truth, and the Life…], the writer will have additional cause to thank God for the awful and heavy calamity under which he was suffering at the time when it was written.
>
> H.J.H.
> April, 1860

John Mildred is a simple tale, in verse, of a boy who has to support his mother and himself through difficult times after his woodcutter father is press-ganged into the navy. Whilst continuing to do good to all around him, he helps an old woman, a stranger, who falls over in the snow when other boys throw snowballs at her. Having befriended her, and after a number of stereotypical fairy-tale coincidences, he discovers that not only is she his grandmother, but that she had secretly eloped with the local squire's eldest son forty years previously. John's father, who turns up on the doorstep just at this point, after years at sea, is thus welcomed by the current squire as his brother's long-lost son, and everyone lives happily ever after. No doubt Henry Hatch wished that real life was just like that. Every good and proper act detailed in the book has a biblical reference, three or four to a page; it is a very noble and proper educational tool and a good story as well – for children at the time that Henry wrote it.

Of more interest than the literary content of the book is the list of subscribers, together with the number of copies that each purchased. Lady Birch, wife of Sir Richard Birch, Henry's aunt, bought five copies. Henry's sister Mrs Mary Cragie and her mother-in-law bought four copies, his sister Eleanora Durnford bought two copies, his sister Matilda Wooley bought 6 copies and sister Augusta Oliver bought 18 copies. Henry's Uncle Charles, just to show that there were no hard feelings over the Chancery case, bought five copies. Dr Thomas Dillon of Ireland, married to Henry's sister Adelaide, and probably related to Essie, bought 20 copies. The Bishop of Lichfield, who had ordained Henry, bought 10 copies and the Earl of Shaftsbury bought 50 copies. Notably absent from the list were Henry's other sister, Annamaria, as well as Uncle Henry at Sutton.

Altogether, 817 copies were pre-subscribed at two shillings and sixpence each, grossing over £100, with probably more sold post publication. This amount, less production costs, which would not have been much – the book was barely twenty pages long – would have at least provided Essie with sufficient funds to live on for a while.

There exists no likeness of Henry John Hatch that this author has managed to find. Henry was described on his admission to Newgate, as being five foot eight inches tall, slender, with brown hair and hazel eyes. However, *John Mildred* has illustrations. The first one shows a family group with *Papa* telling his story to *Lucy* while two other ladies, one young, and one somewhat older, also listen. *Lucy* looks older than Lucy Hatch's eight years, but the two ladies could be Essie and her mother. All of the females have the anonymous faces familiar from Victorian literature. But not Papa. His face has a large pointed nose, high forehead and swept-back hair with long sideburns. It is tempting to suspect that this might be a portrait of Henry John Hatch…

Meanwhile, outside Newgate Henry's friends were massing for a counter-attack. Having failed with Walters Freake Pratt, the action against Eugenia Plummer had already been started but they needed money. More than £400 had been spent on the petition and the Pratt case. Now they needed at least as much again, probably more, only this time they had to widen the scope of appeal. On 25th February 1860, one week after the petition to the Queen had been rejected, *The Detective* published their appeal for funds:

## Public Appeal

A very strong opinion being entertained that Mr. Hatch was not guilty of the infamous charges upon which he was convicted in December 1859, a committee (many of them strangers to Mr. Hatch and to each other) was formed for the purpose of instituting a thorough investigation into every detail connected with the allegations made against him. The result of that enquiry (conducted at serious expense) in every respect confirmed the belief of the committee in Mr.

Hatch's perfect innocence, which view was likewise entertained by the eleven convicting jurymen, to whom the evidence collected by the committee was submitted. On the 28th December 1859, that evidence was laid by the committee before the Right Honourable the Secretary of State for the Home Department in support of the petitions then presented to Her Majesty by Mr. Hatch and the aforesaid jurymen. And on the 18th inst. Sir George Lewis communicated his reply to the chairman of the committee, whereby he intimated that he could not properly advise the Crown to interfere in the present position of the case, as Mr. Hatch had a legal remedy of which it was competent for him to avail himself. The committee having no other object than to ensure 'strict justice', have determined that Mr. Hatch shall be placed in a position to avail himself of the remedy alluded to by Sir George and by presenting himself, and all other witnesses whose statements have been laid before the Home Secretary to the test of public examination, set at rest the painful doubts so extensively felt whether or not an innocent man is now suffering a severe and degrading punishment.

The expense attendant on these proceedings will necessarily be very considerable and the penniless condition of Mr. Hatch precludes the possibility of his bearing any portion of it.

Under such circumstances and for the purpose of securing a further judicial enquiry into the details of this most extraordinary case, the committee confidently appeal to the public in the name of justice and of truth for sympathy and support.

Edward Wise, Chairman

Joseph Gegg, Secretary

*The Detective* had done sterling service to the Hatch case, publishing as it did the petition as well as the key witness statements and material on the Plummers, but it had a limited readership. Henry's friends had to address a mass audience, inform the public at large of the facts of the case, start a debate, but more importantly get some money coming in. The way to do that was to advertise in *The Times*. The appeal printed in *The Detective* was able to finance a substantial advertisement carried by *The Times* on the 12th April 1860. Occupying nearly half a column on page 5, that newspaper carried the following announcement:

The Case of the Rev. HENRY JOHN HATCH.

– An appeal to BRITISH JUSTICE

Extract from Mr. Hatch's observations to the court after sentence passed:- "I maintain as I stand here, if it was the last word I was to speak, that these children have been telling abominable lies: and I hope and know that the time will come when God will prove this has been the case."

The list of subscribers to the fund for the thorough investigation of the Case of the Rev. H. J. Hatch contains the names of Englishmen eminent in every order of our society. Peers, prelates, merchant princes, professional men, authors – all sanction by their subscriptions the cause we plead.

A British citizen, a minister of religion, a fellow-creature, whose character – traced minutely from his youth to the moment of deposition, on oath, or under the hand of bishops, members of the Legislature, magistrates, and gentlemen of position, from intimate knowledge – has been vouched to be such as the Judge from the bench declared "most men might envy" is now undergoing a sentence of four years' imprisonment with hard labour.

The jury who (in the face of a charge for acquittal) convicted him now declare (by petition to the Queen) their belief that he is wholly innocent. The judge who sentenced him, has granted his warrant for leave to prefer a bill of indictment for perjury against the inculpatory witness. The Secretary of State declares the adoption of that course to be a condition precedent to the intervention of the prerogative of the Crown. The grand jury have found that there is a prima facie case against Mr. Hatch's accuser, by returning a true bill on the charge for perjury against her. The victim of her testimony is penniless – shall he therefore be without redress? He is "sick, and in prison" – shall Christians refuse to "visit even the least of their brethren?" He asks – not mercy, but bare justice – shall he not have it? The light has been shut out – he challenges inquiry – in the name of truth and charity we beg alms for the right.

The sole witness on whose deposition, totally uncorroborated at his trial, he was condemned, was a girl of 11, now in her turn to undergo the issue of her indictment. We cannot honestly blame Mr. Hatch's counsel for believing that his client's character and position afforded a conclusive answer to a filthy accusation so wholly unsupported. When the world has turned its back, when he is poorer than the poorest that are free, humble servants of the prison where he officiated for eight years are of the most zealous of his advocates; officials with whom he differed yet have the manliness to labour to do him justice; and those who knew him best are the most anxious for inquiry. What vouchers for the life and conduct of a citizen can be less fallible than these?

The 'officials with whom he differed' were, no doubt, Colonel Challoner and Captain Best, the Surrey magistrates whom Henry managed to offend by his editorial in *The Philanthropist*. The appeal continued:

But far more on public than on individual grounds we solicit your pecuniary help. If the word of one child of 11, about whose disposition, education, and parentage, no enquiry was made, and no testimony even offered – if the bare oath of an infant in the eye of the law, incapable of consent, of contracting liability, of managing her affairs – unvouched by one jot of fact, or tittle of testimony, is, in a British tribunal, to outswear the character of the whole life of an educated English Protestant divine, entrusted by our magistrates with a solemn charge demanding the highest moral qualities, living in the midst of them for eight years, who – the purest, the highest of us – is safe? If our property be insecure, we can lock it up; if wife or daughter be in danger, we can take warning, and keep them at home; but against the treacherous ingenuity of an unscrupulous accuser there is literally no possibility of protection; because it takes care to exclude the chance of contradiction, by the device of alleging the privacy of the offence. Common justice suggests that, where previous character is untarnished, the accused, even where both are on equal terms, is as well entitled to credence as the accuser, and that something more than mere individual naked assertion ought to be required to turn the scale. Common sense demands that if a citizen charges a neighbour, of good repute, with an improbable enormity, he should be made to prove it by something more than his own assertion. Our common faith, seeing the fallibility of human testimony uncorroborated by circumstances which neither err nor lie, has, both in the Old and the New Testament, required the oaths of two at least, and asks for those of three, witnesses to sanction the conviction of a citizen. It is true our jurisprudence has ignored that counsel – with how little reason too palpably demonstrated. The safe maxim of our law is, that every man is innocent until he is proved to be guilty; the practice too often is that no man shall be regarded as innocent whom anybody accuses.

The procedure against which this appeal is a protest strikes at the root of the securities of domestic life. If the appalling verdict under which Mr. Hatch suffers be carried into full execution, no citizen will be safe in venturing out of sight of a witness of his hourly life – no master of a household will be certain of his liberty while a female is under his roof – no teacher will be secure against the prurient fancy of a pupil – no loftiness of virtue or eminence of position will be above the higher reach of the safe calumny of a privileged prosecutor. Is the boasted impregnability of an Englishman's hearth and home to be penetrable at any moment by the inventiveness of morbid mendacity? It were better to entrench ourselves in the fastness of absolute isolation, than to live in daily peril of such a state of society.

If our fellow-citizens be like-minded we entreat them promptly to follow our example. Mrs. Hatch, an educated gentlewoman, is absolutely destitute. Her unfortunate husband has not a farthing in the world. We have not spared our own means to get bare justice for a fellow-creature. We solicit the liberality of our countrymen to redress an intolerable wrong, and to delete a stain upon our law which would be a libel on justice, and is an outrage upon the security of the social compact.

It is with reluctance that the necessity of the case has compelled us to anticipate by this appeal the judgment upon which a jury is yet to be called upon to give a verdict. Our procedure is entirely defensive. The object of the indictment is vindicatory, not vindictive. Mr. Hatch freely forgives, and we sincerely pity, a child who ought never to have been obtruded into the position which has left her victim no other course than that which the Judge and the Home Secretary have agreed to indicate, and which is justified by the return of the Grand Jury to the bill. When the claims of truth have been satisfied by rendering justice to the oppressed and the assertion of the right, considerate compassion for the infantile errors of a mis-educated child will be the duty and the sentiment of all concerned in these painful but indispensable proceedings.

By order of the committee,

EDWARD WISE, Chairman.

JOSEPH GEGG, Secretary.

Committee Room, Change-Alley-Chambers,
24 Cornhill; 30th March 1860.

The authors had summarized the essentials of the case, and appealed to Justice, Fair Play, Englishness and Christianity. Most importantly, they had informed the readership of *The*

*Times*, the Great British Establishment, that an enormous injustice had been perpetrated, and that (then, as now) money was required to purchase Justice for the wronged. The statement was dated 30th March, although the grand jury had not confirmed the 'true bill against the accused' until 3rd April, in addition to which, it appeared that in the jury's initial considerations, both Eugenia and Stephana were to be charged with perjury. The press report is not clear, but it seems that the decision was made to charge Eugenia only, perhaps because of Stephana's age. No doubt last minute changes were made to the announcement before it was published on 12th April.

One consequence of the advertisement, and indicative of nervousness in the Plummer camp, was a letter of response from them placed as an advertisement in *The Times* a few days later. Clearly, they were rattled. The material already published in *The Detective* made it clear that the enormity of the perceived injustice was not going to go away. All they could do was to attempt to mitigate the damage. The letter was from William Hitchcock, the agent of Walters Freake Pratt; apparently, he (Pratt) was still the Plummers' attorney, now acting in defence of Eugenia. Hitchcock started,

> With respect to [Henry's statement of his innocence from the dock]...it is very similar to what is heard every day at the Central Criminal Court from persons convicted...

(Perhaps so, but not from an Established Church clergyman of previously unblemished record...) He then claims that the jury said (in the petition) not that Mr Hatch was 'wholly innocent', but that they would not have found him guilty – and it was not the whole jury. He pointed out that none of the defence witnesses were called, but makes an interesting point about the trial judge, Baron Bramwell. It was Baron Bramwell, who granted the warrant for the indictment against Eugenia

209

Plummer, but,

> The judge himself…refused to hear the application until
> he was told it was made to him because he happened
> to be the judge in chambers…[he also] refused part of
> the application, and repeated more than once, it was
> to be understood that he had not expressed an opinion
> one way or another…

The letter was responded to a week later, in a letter – also placed
as an advertisement – from Joseph Gegg. He quoted from the
declaration of the jury in the petition to the Queen that 'we
now believe him to be totally innocent of the charges made
against him'. He reproduced the words of Baron Bramwell
allowing the indictment for perjury:

> Upon hearing Mr. Giffard…counsel for the said H. J.
> Hatch, and upon reading the several affidavits of the
> said H. J. Hatch, Essie Hatch, Esther Dillon, Martha
> Howe, Lucy Harriet Hatch, Mary Ann Reed and H. F.
> Holt [Henry's solicitor], I do hereby consent that the
> said H. J. Hatch may prefer a bill of indictment for
> perjury against Mary Eugenia Plummer.

So there.

Some skirmishing was to be expected. Mr Hitchcock's effort
was laudable enough given the few points upon which he could
challenge the tidal-wave of evidence in Henry Hatch's favour.
Also, one cannot blame Henry's friends for making the most
of the coincidence that it was the original trial judge, Baron
Bramwell, who happened to be the judge in chambers that
granted leave for the indictment against Eugenia Plummer.

Joseph Gegg's letter was published on 19th April, when
Henry Hatch had been in prison for more than five months. His
friends were working hard for him on the outside, but every day

he had to endure the grinding awfulness of the regime of hard labour and prison diet in Newgate. *The Detective* had pointed out earlier in the campaign that two felons of gentle birth, sentenced to the same duration in prison as Henry Hatch, had died there. Henry was not in good health, and his friends must have worried that the same fate might befall him. But it didn't, and finally on Wednesday, 9th May 1860, Henry got his day in court. As it happened, it was to be five days in court.

The trial of Mary Eugenia Plummer for Wilful and Corrupt Perjury commenced at 10 o'clock in the Old Court at the Old Bailey. Baron Channell presided, assisted by Mr Justice Keating. Sir William Fry Channell, 56, was described as 'conscientious, careful and learned...', but did suffer from severe asthma, and this made it difficult, sometimes, to hear what he said (ODNB). Sir Henry Singer Keating was said (in 1875) to be:

> ...a true disciple of the law...not on the alert for the just, the moral, the fair, the equitable, the conscientious and the expedient, those dangerous will-o'-the-wisps which lead judges astray from the beaten track of the law... [ODNB].

A modern layman's view might be that a judge's interpretation of The Law as an instrument for the achievement of Justice should have just those qualities. Nevertheless, whatever else happened in Eugenia Plummer's trial, it would be conducted strictly to the letter of the law.

The court was crowded; in fact it was full, and not only in the public areas. The Lord Mayor and Aldermen of the City of London had the right to sit on the bench and observe, although they took no part in the legal proceedings. It would be nice to think that it was the prospect of righting a terrible wrong that attracted the Lord Mayor and no less than six of his aldermen to the Plummer trial. It was certainly the trial of the year, and one hopes that it was not just prurient interest in the explicit nature of the evidence to be presented that attracted the presence of the Right Honourable John Carter, Lord Mayor of London, and aldermen Mr Copeland, MP, Sir Francis Graham Moon, Sir Robert Walter Carden, and Messrs Hale, Conder and Abbiss.

In the account of the trial that follows, the children's ages are sometimes given incorrectly by the barristers and others. At the time of the alleged offences in 1859, Stephana and Lucy were seven years old, although Lucy was four months younger than Stephana, and Eugenia was eleven. By the time of Eugenia's trial, Stephana and Lucy were eight and Eugenia was twelve.

Eugenia was brought into court by her father, and in deference to her age, was seated at the attorney's table rather than in the dock. The prosecution was conducted by Edwin James, who had led the unsuccessful prosecution of Walters Freake Pratt, with Mr Gordon Allen and Mr Giffard. Here, at least, Mr James would be able to use his theatrical training and ability to influence 'common juries' to the best effect. For the defence were Serjeant Shee, Mr Cooper and Mr Metcalfe. William Shee had been called to the bar in 1828 and made Serjeant of Law in 1841. In 1863, he was to be appointed to the Queen's Bench and was knighted the following year, '…the first Roman Catholic to be promoted to the English bench since the revolution of 1688… [His] breadth of legal knowledge and common-sense approach…' led to him acting as counsel in many notable trials of the time (ODNB). Messrs Cooper and Metcalfe had appeared for the prosecution in Henry's trial. Serjeant Shee requested that the witnesses present should retire from the court in order for them to be examined separately when called.

Addressing the jury, Mr James said that they would have to pay patient and careful attention to what was one of the most extraordinary cases to be investigated in court. He outlined Mr Hatch's background and circumstances, and the details of the case for which he was convicted and currently serving a prison sentence in Newgate gaol. He pointed out that the law forbade Mr Hatch's wife from giving evidence on his behalf, and there was no Court of Criminal Appeal. Mrs Hatch was, in any case, implicated in the alleged offence, so Mr Hatch's only recourse was to prefer the present charge of perjury against Eugenia Plummer. He then summarized Eugenia's original evidence. He stated that apart from the extreme improbability of the story, he would produce evidence which would show her entire story to be untrue, '…the result of a prurient and depraved imagination…' He ended his address by reminding the jury of the 'fearful issues' involved, and that the 'very existence of the prosecutor [Henry] depended on the result of the trial'. He was satisfied that when they had heard the evidence presented, the jury would come to a 'righteous conclusion'.

Mr Kemp, the Deputy Clerk of Arraigns, produced the original indictment against Henry along with the certificate of his conviction, and Mr Harker, one of the court ushers, proved that he had administered the oath to Eugenia Plummer.

At this point, Serjeant Shee observed that only character witnesses had been called for Henry Hatch, to which Mr James retorted that he was not aware that witnesses were 'in attendance to speak to facts'. (Mr James was being economical with the truth; he must have known that witnesses *were* in attendance for Henry's trial, but that Serjeant Ballantine had elected not to call them.) Next, Mr Barnard the court shorthand writer proved the depositions made by Eugenia from the original trial record.

At last, Henry John Hatch was brought into court to give his evidence.[2] In response to various questions:

I am the prosecutor in this case. I was convicted of an indecent assault upon the defendant Mary Eugenia Plummer. I am 42 years old and my father was vicar

2   Henry's evidence has been transposed into the first person.

of Walton-on-Thames. I was educated at Eton and Cambridge, and presented to a curacy and then an incumbency in Staffordshire by the Bishop of Lichfield. I was married in 1845 but have no family. In 1851 I was appointed Chaplain to Wandsworth Gaol and held the office until this charge was made against me...

A plan of his residence and garden were shown to him, and following some questions from Serjeant Shee, it emerged that the length of the garden from the drawing-room window was 258 feet, and there were some thick shrubs in the garden. Henry's residence was, he said, close to the gaol.

At this point, it is worth commenting that it seemed to have occurred to no one, not the defence nor the prosecution at either of the trials, to have performed a simple forensic analysis of the garden layout with its obscuring shrubs; who was watching and where, what were they able to see, and where Henry and the children were when the alleged offence occurred. There is a bird's-eye view of the front of Wandsworth prison, together with an annotated ground-plan, in Matthew and Binney's book. The houses of the governor and chaplain are positioned either side of the main prison entrance, backing onto the prison wall. The chaplain's house, on the right, has its garden running along the prison wall as far as the first corner, where the surgeon's house is situated. The picture shows only four prison wings having been built, so it must date from the opening of the prison in 1851 (a fifth wing was built around 1852-3); there are some large shrubs in the chaplain's garden, but no carriage drive. By 1859, a drive had been constructed, but it is clear that anyone observing the garden from the drawing-room window, which faced the garden, the front door, from which by looking to the left the garden could be seen, but more importantly, *anyone observing from the surgeon's house*, could have triangulated the whole garden, shrubs and all, there being virtually no part of it not visible.

Perhaps there was no-one in the surgeon's house looking. Nevertheless, the point could have been made that *had* Henry been doing what was alleged, he could not have known that he was unobserved from the surgeon's house. This must have reduced the likelihood of him committing the alleged abuse in the garden, even assuming that he was disposed to do so. Nobody thought to make this simple analysis; an analysis that could have proved the falsity of, or at least rendered highly improbable, at least one of Eugenia's accusations, and thereby have condemned all of her evidence as untrustworthy.

Continuing with his evidence, Henry mentioned the adoption of Lucy in 1856, and briefly outlined how the Plummers came to Wandsworth with Eugenia, and what had happened:

> ...Mrs. Plummer wished the doors of the bedrooms of the children to be left open, in order that they might have as much air as possible...[she] said that she liked her child to be petted, and that [Eugenia] had been in the habit of going into the bed of a former schoolmaster, and wished that we should allow her to do so, and we consented to it.

When the Plummers left to go back to Wiltshire, Eugenia was in low spirits; Henry said, '...I ran round the carriage drive and I told the children to catch me, and they ran after me...' He then took Lucy and Eugenia by the hand and led them into the drawing room. All the ladies of the family were looking out of the window at the time and the servants were also there. Regarding the charges of indecency, he denied in the 'most solemn manner', that he had ever committed them either on the defendant or her sister, continuing,

> ...the only occasions upon which I ever went into the child's bedroom were when she asked me to come and kiss her before I went to bed...I was never in the room

for more than a minute or a minute-and-a-half, and nothing improper ever took place...

Regarding the morning visits to the Hatches' bed, Eugenia was never allowed *in* the bed, only under the counterpane and Mrs Hatch was always present. When the Plummers brought Stephana, Henry said that they had every opportunity of talking to Eugenia if they had wished to. He then repeated Mrs Plummer's story about Eugenia and her £15,000 fortune, and the fact that she was to marry Mr Gay, her doctor, when she was seventeen. He recounted the Plummers' return the next day on account of Mrs Plummer thinking the thunderstorm had been a judgement on her. They had dined together, and the only complaint Mrs Plummer made was that Eugenia – as an heiress to a fortune – should sleep on calico sheets. There was some talk about the children coming again at Christmas, and the Plummers took an affectionate leave, giving Lucy a present of a toy, and the children kissing Henry, before they left. Henry continued, 'I heard nothing more until the letter from the Bishop of Winchester...' Following this, he had a consultation with Mr Onslow, resigned from his post, and was subsequently arrested, tried, and convicted.

Serjeant Shee now cross-examined Henry for the defence. Henry confirmed further details of his history and circumstances. He had no personal fortune, and was entirely dependent on his appointment (so by that time, his entire inheritance had gone). He said that during the fortnight Eugenie Plummer was at his house he was very kind to her, and she appeared to be fond of him. Generally, he said, '...she ran to me and kissed me when she came out of school...' He never scolded her, or ever made her cry:

> ...she was scolded once for behaving improperly to a gentleman in the house. I did not wish to insinuate that she behaved in any manner indecently...

(She was probably just rude to someone.) Henry continued, 'I saw nothing in her conduct different to what I should expect from a child of respectable Christian parents.' The Plummers were to pay Henry £50 a year for each of their children, and there was no dispute about the amount owing when they were taken away. Serjeant Shee pressed Henry on the question of Mrs Plummer not being left alone with Eugenia on the day she brought Stephana and other matters:

> I could not swear that the child Eugenia was left alone with her mother any part of the day...except when they were in the watercloset...I did not kiss the child in her bed more than four times...I had a distinct recollection that my mother [-in-law] was at the drawing room window when the children were running after me, and I had no doubt that my wife and the French ladies were also there...On the 18th August I did take the two children on my knee, but it was merely to tell them a story to amuse them. [Here, Henry swore that no indecency whatever took place.] When the child [Eugenia] came to our bedroom in the morning, she had nothing on but her nightdress...I was also undressed, but of course covered with the bedclothes...

Henry then admitted that sometimes Eugenia was in the bed when Mrs Hatch was up and washing Lucy:

| | |
|---|---|
| *Henry Hatch*: | I would not have allowed the child to come to my bed if it had not been the express desire of her mother. I did not think it was right. |
| *Serjeant Shee*: | Thinking it wrong, why did not you, a clergyman and a man of |

|  | your age, competent to form an independent judgement, refuse to allow it to be done? |
|---|---|
| *Henry Hatch*: | I thought the child was accustomed to it, and she did not think any harm of it |
| *Serjeant Shee*: | But if you yourself thought it was wrong, why did you allow it? |
| *Henry Hatch*: | I did not think there was any absolute harm in it. |

Henry now responded to further questions from Serjeant Shee. He most likely kissed the child when she first got into the bed (Eugenia, when she got into the Hatches' bed in the morning). He positively swore that he never went into Stephana's bedroom dressed only in his nightshirt. Regarding Essie:

> I have always been on affectionate terms with my wife, I consider I can safely depend on her judgement in any matter of delicacy connected with her own sex...we were married at Sydney in 1845...I never told her the details of the charge until the day I surrendered myself, the 12th November...

He had shown Essie the first letter from the Bishop of Winchester received on 3rd October; the second letter, detailing the precise charges being made by the Plummers he did not show his wife. The main reason was that Lucy was mentioned in it, (implicated actually), and he was afraid that Essie might discuss it with her.

Serjeant Shee now asked Henry whether he had discussed the matter with anyone. He did not mention it to his brother chaplain at the gaol, although he subsequently wished that he had. He wanted advice, and he was on intimate terms with many clergymen in the neighbourhood, but he did not discuss it with any of them. He subsequently resigned his appointment at the gaol, his only source of income, rather than have the matter investigated by the visiting magistrates. This followed the interview with Mr Onslow, the prison governor, who told him that whatever the outcome of the enquiry, his position at the gaol would be impossible. He now realized that he should have faced the charges, and refuted them by the witnesses he could produce. He did not even mention it to his solicitor, thinking the matter could be hushed up – he realized now that it was all too late, and that he had made the wrong decision.

| | |
|---|---|
| *Serjeant Shee*: | Will you explain how you came to the conclusion that the matter would be hushed up, and no one know anything about it, when you must have been aware that you would have to leave Wandsworth and break up your establishment, and would be bound to give some explanation of the reasons for this proceeding? |
| *Henry Hatch*: | I did think so, and I can give no other explanation. |

When he left Wandsworth, Henry went to Poplar and initially his wife did not know his address. He knew she had written to the Plummers, and the letter was read out in court. Subsequently, Henry was made aware that a warrant had been issued for his arrest, but still he took no steps to get advice – his mind was very distressed and he did a great many foolish things. When he was arrested, he asked the officer what the punishment was for such an offence. He repeated that Mr Pratt offered at that point to abandon the charge in exchange for a confession, which he refused to do. He denied saying 'I am mad', or, 'I was mad'. He had resolved to meet the charges, and told Mr Pratt so distinctly. The only person with whom he discussed the charges was Mr Onslow, the Prison Governor, with whom he was on very intimate terms.

This was Henry's evidence; of itself, not terribly impressive. After all, it was mostly his word against Eugenia's. He admitted to consistently poor judgement: in allowing Eugenia in the family bed in the first place, in deference to Mrs Plummer and against his own wishes; in thinking that by resigning his post and not attending the visiting magistrates' hearing, he could somehow hush it all up; and in remaining in Poplar for eleven days, knowing that there was a warrant out for his arrest – Serjeant Shee could have made more of that fact but elected not to. He also did not pursue the remarkable coincidence that Henry had absconded, ostensibly to avoid arrest for debt, just one day before the warrant was issued for his arrest on the indecency charge. It was a pity that neither he, nor particularly Henry's defence counsel, Edwin James, thought to check and establish those dates on oath, thereby proving once and for all whether Henry did or did not know of the impending arrest warrant when he 'absconded'.

It was Henry's defence witnesses, now appearing for the prosecution, that were to make all the difference in the case. The first of these was called, Henry's loyal wife Essie:

I am the wife of the Rev. Mr. Hatch, the prosecutor of this indictment...I am 35 years of age. I was married to him at Sydney in 1845, and we staid [sic] there about a year afterwards, and then went to Walton on Thames of which parish my husband's father was vicar.

Essie then described the day the Plummers first came to Wandsworth with Eugenia:

> When the cab had started [taking the Plummers back to the railway station] I went into the drawing-room and stood at the window. My mother, the governess and the two French ladies were also there. I never lost sight of my husband or the two children, Eugenie and Lucy, until they came into the house. They were not in the garden more than two or three minutes – a very short time. My mother called out to Mr. Hatch that the tea was waiting, and he and the two children came in immediately. If any proceeding such as that spoken to by the child Eugenie had taken place, I must have seen it; it could not have happened without my doing so.

Regarding the incident of the story in the Hatches' bedroom on 18th August with a child perched on each knee, Essie recalled that, 'A gentleman named Coghlan went up to fetch them and they came down immediately…' (The press report states here that her evidence then contradicted that given by her husband 'in some other particulars', which were not detailed.) She continued on the question of the visits to Eugenia's bedroom:

> It was impossible for my husband to have gone to Eugenie's bedroom every evening during the fortnight she was at our house without my noticing his absence.

And on the morning visits into their bed:

> It was at the request of Mrs. Plummer that Eugenie was permitted to come into our bed to be "petted", but it was greatly against the wish of my husband. She was never allowed to come actually inside the bed, but only under the counterpane. Lucy used to come into

the bed too, and Mr. Hatch used to make them say the first and last letter of any article in the room that he mentioned. [Eugenia] never exhibited the slightest symptom of fear or distress upon any occasion when she was taken into the bed…

So unsurprisingly, Essie utterly refutes Eugenia's claims regarding the incident in the garden, the visits to her room, and the morning visits to the Hatches' bed.

On the day of the Plummers' visit on Thursday, 25th August, when they brought Stephana, Essie insisted that Mrs Plummer and Eugenia had had plenty of opportunities of being alone. Further, Essie commented, '…it is impossible for Mr. Hatch to have committed any act of indecency in our bedroom with the child without my seeing it.' (The press report may be confused here. From the context, 'the child' was Stephana, but she claimed that Henry visited her in her bedroom, Eugenia's old room, which was next to the Hatches' room. She did not claim that anything took place in the Hatches' bedroom.) Mrs Plummer left that evening on the most friendly terms with the Hatches. She returned the next day to remove the children after the 'judgement' of the thunderstorm, but when she departed she '…kissed me, and appeared to be very friendly…' Regarding Henry's general behaviour, Essie was quite clear:

During the whole time Eugenie Plummer was in our house, I never saw the slightest act of impropriety on the part of my husband towards her.

Henry handed her the first letter from the bishop but she did not read it, only becoming aware of the specific charges when he surrendered himself to the police. She had written the letter to Mrs Plummer after Henry had left; she then recounted the visit of Mr Pratt and the arrangement for Henry to surrender at Ridler's Hotel in Holborn.

Essie was now cross-examined. Lucy had been a member of the family for two or three years at the time of the Plummers' visit. They were very fond of Lucy and very kind to her – as they were to Eugenia:

> ...nothing was denied to her [Eugenia] that was reasonable for a child. I did certainly "stop her beer" (a laugh)...Her mother wished her to have beer, but I considered it was not proper for her.

(So Caroline Plummer had wished her daughter to have a daily ration of beer...) And once more regarding the morning visits into the bed:

> I generally used to get up first and dress Lucy, and during this time my husband remained in bed, and the child Eugenie with him, but I do not think she was ever there longer than three or four minutes. I never saw my husband kiss Eugenie while she was in bed with him.

And the alleged nightly visits to Eugenia in her bedroom:

> My attention was not called to the circumstances until nearly three months afterwards, and yet I can remember that during the fortnight Eugenie Plummer was in our house my husband did not leave the room any evening for so long a period as 10 minutes. I am sure he was never absent more than two or three minutes. I will swear that he was never absent for so long a period as 10 minutes.

Regarding her relationship with her husband:

> I believe that I enjoyed my husband's entire confidence, and he never kept anything secret from me, and always

consulted me in everything affecting his interest, except in reference to this transaction. When my husband received the Bishop's [first] letter he appeared very much distressed, and was about to put it in his pocket, but I insisted upon seeing it, and he gave it to me. I only glanced it over, but I saw that it referred to some charge of indecent assault upon the Plummers by my husband.

The court reporter said that Mrs Hatch,

…gave her evidence with great calmness and self-possession, although she was evidently deeply affected at the unhappy position of herself and her husband…

The case was adjourned, '…the father of the defendant renewing the recognizance he had entered into in the sum of £500 for her appearance on the following morning.' Henry was led away back to his cell in Newgate.

Henry and Essie had finally given their evidence in court. It is interesting to note that among Mrs Plummer's other wishes for Eugenia during her stay at the Hatches, Essie positively declined to allow her to have beer. Perhaps if Henry had shown the same strength of character as his wife, things might have turned out very differently. One even starts to wonder how well suited he was to the strictness, sound judgement and adherence to authority required of a prison chaplain…

The charge of perjury was only a misdemeanour (rather than a felony), so the jury were allowed home at the end of day one. Day two of the trial started with the evidence of Lucy Harriet Hatch, '…a remarkably interesting, pretty child [giving] her evidence in a very clear and straightforward manner'.

Lucy began,

I am eight years old. I remember going to live with Mr.

and Mrs. Hatch, and I used to call them mama and papa. I remember Eugenie Plummer coming to Mr. Hatch's with her father and mother. I first saw them in the drawing room. Mr. and Mrs. Plummer left about 7 o'clock in the evening...[when] the fly came to fetch them to the train.

She repeated what had happened in the garden and 'positively negated' any act of impropriety on the part of Mr Hatch having taken place. The governess, Miss Howe, had arrived on the same day, and the children's studies had started on the following Monday. Mr Hatch's study was turned into a schoolroom, the hours of study being from 9 to 12 o'clock and 2 till 4 o'clock. Lucy said that Eugenia Plummer had had plenty of opportunity to speak to Miss Howe if she had wished to. She then described what had happened when Henry took her and Eugenia, one on each knee, to tell them a story to amuse them – a story about a lion. Lucy said that she remembered the younger child, Stephana, being brought to Mr Hatch's on 25th August, and stated positively that 'Mr. Hatch never behaved improperly to her, and that she did not on any occasion make complaint that such a thing had occurred.'

Lucy was now cross-examined:

My papa went away about two months after Eugenie Plummer came, and no one ever spoke to me upon the subject during that period. I have told my papa, my mama, and Mr. Holt, the solicitor, what evidence I could give. I think the first person I spoke to about it was my papa, but I do not think mama was present. It was when he was at Poplar. My mama was away at the time. My papa asked me if I would undertake to say that Eugenie Plummer did not put her hand in his pocket; and I said I would, and he told me to be sure not to forget it, and he kissed me and was very kind to me. My mama afterwards spoke to me on the subject. I have told the same story to grandmama and Miss Howe. I remember my papa being tried in this court. When I was examined before the magistrate I said that on the first evening that Eugenie Plummer came I ran away from her and Mr. Hatch and left them together, and sometimes their backs were towards me.

Lucy was then further questioned on the detail of her evidence:[3]

I was at Poplar with my papa three days. My mother took me to Poplar and I told her the truth and the same story I have today upon my oath. I told the same story to mama and my grandmama and the governess and Mr. Holt the solicitor...

In response to a question, Lucy clarified the events in the garden and other matters:

When I said that I sometimes ran way, leaving Mr. Hatch and Eugenia behind, what I meant was I ran around the carriage drive, but I could see all that was going on. My papa was not more kind to me in Poplar than he was before. He was always kind...

How many moist eyes must there have been in court that day, listening to this eight year old child forthrightly defending her papa with a clarity and purpose some of the subsequent witnesses might have envied! Nevertheless, she was not questioned about what side of the bed she went into in the mornings, whether she went into the bed or under the

---

3   Lucy's evidence has been transposed into the first person.

counterpane, or even whether she had been allowed into the Hatches' bed before Eugenia came.

Mr Holt, the Hatches' solicitor, then deposed that he had taken a statement from Lucy the previous December, about three weeks after Mr Hatch's conviction, and '...reduced it to...a statutory declaration'. No-one else was present, she made the statement voluntarily and he took it down, 'from her own lips', for the purpose of obtaining a pardon. A number of other witnesses made similar statutory declarations, and all were transmitted to the Secretary of State, who suggested, nevertheless, that there should be an indictment for perjury. Mr Holt agreed that this was the only course to be taken, and the necessary steps were taken to prefer the said indictment. Copies of the statutory declarations had not been supplied to the defendant.

Mr Lewis of the firm Lewis and Lewis, solicitors of Ely Place, deposed that he had conducted Mr Hatch's defence in the original trial, that witnesses were in attendance on his behalf, but that counsel had decided not to call them.

Now Mrs Esther Dillon, Essie's mother, was called. She stated that on Thursday, 11th August 1859, she was standing at the drawing room window after Mr and Mrs Plummer had left, she could see all that was going on in the carriage drive, and she did not observe any act of impropriety. She saw the children running round the garden after Mr Hatch. When she told him that the tea was ready, he laid hold of the hand of each of the little girls and led them into the house. She added that if any act such as that suggested had taken place in the garden, she would have seen it. She also confirmed that Mrs Plummer had ample opportunity of communicating with her child, and that she made no complaint whatsoever.

Under questioning from Serjeant Shee, she stated that she was on the most friendly and confidential terms with Mr and Mrs Hatch, and was generally consulted by them in reference to their affairs. She knew nothing about the charge until Mr

Hatch was arrested; she knew 'something' was wrong. She first heard that there was something on Mr Hatch's mind, in reference to the children, about six weeks after they had left. She knew Mr Hatch had gone to Poplar, and that Mr Onslow had advised him to resign. She had not heard that the resignation would forestall any enquiry. She would 'undertake to say positively' that Mr Hatch and the children 'were not five minutes in the carriage drive after the cab had driven off with Mr and Mrs Plummer'. She was looking at them all the time, and was quite sure that the little girl Eugenie did not run away with Mr Hatch after her (meaning that it was the girls who were running after Henry, not vice versa). Her attention was, she said, not called to the subject until six weeks afterwards, yet she recalled all that had happened on that evening. On the question of Mr Hatch's visits to Eugenia's room, she stated that if Mr Hatch had left them in the evening for a longer period than nine or ten minutes she would have been alarmed, as he occasionally suffered from cramp. She was sure that Eugenie and her mother were alone together on 25th August, and that 'nothing was done to prevent them being so.' Mrs Dillon was not, apparently, questioned about Eugenia's door being open or closed, which was curious, since this should have been key evidence.

After a short recess Martha Howe was called. She went to the Hatches' on 11th August as governess to the children, and was introduced to Mrs Plummer. She said that Mrs Plummer was 'very anxious that the door of her children's bedroom should be kept constantly open'. Miss Howe stated that she was constantly with Eugenia and Lucy, and Eugenia had plenty of opportunities to speak to her if she so wished. Eugenia never made any complaint or suggestion that she had been improperly or indecently treated or hurt, either by Mr Hatch or anyone else. Miss Howe remembered the Plummers' departure on 11th August. Tea was ready and waiting, and Mr Hatch and the two children came into the drawing room in less than two or three minutes after the carriage left. She was watching them all the time from the drawing room window, and she was quite sure that no act of impropriety had taken place. She continued,

> The child, Eugenie, passed the rest of the evening in [my] company, and she did not make the slightest complaint of any kind, and did not exhibit the least appearance of having been disconcerted in any manner…

The other child, Stephana, arrived on 25th August, and at dinner, Mr Hatch told Mrs Plummer that Eugenia came into his bed in the morning as she had done at a previous school. The following day Mrs Plummer had returned in a very excited manner and rushed into the schoolroom exclaiming, 'What, my children in the study and Lucy in the hall?' She then took the two girls and walked in the garden. Mr and Mrs Hatch were out at the time, but returned later in the afternoon. Martha Howe remained in the Hatches' employ until November and she had many opportunities of observing Mr Hatch's conduct. She never saw anything in his behaviour to the children 'but that of a kind and good man'.

In response to questioning from Serjeant Shee, she stated that Eugenia appeared to be attached to both Mr and Mrs Hatch and to herself. There was nothing in Mr Hatch's appearance that induced her to watch him, and she did not suspect that anything was wrong. Regarding the alleged incident in the garden, she saw Mr Hatch running away from the girls, and them running after him and that was all she saw. She knew nothing of the particulars of the charge against Mr Hatch until she was examined at the Wandsworth magistrates' court. She added that the whole of the front garden was visible from the drawing room window.

Mary Ann Reed, the Hatches' maid, was called next. She was employed by Mr and Mrs Hatch having been previously employed by another clergyman. She showed Mrs Plummer the bedroom arrangements when she arrived with her daughter on the 11th August. After the Plummers' departure, she was standing on the doorstep; she saw the children running around the carriage drive after Mr Hatch, and then catch him. She watched them all the time that they were in the garden and 'that was all that occurred, and if anything else had happened, [I] must have seen it'. They were not in the garden more than two or three minutes. She said that Eugenie Plummer never made any complaint whatsoever to her. During her time in Mr Hatch's service, she 'never saw anything in his conduct unbecoming a clergyman and a gentleman'.

Cross-examined by Serjeant Shee, she did make one observation regarding the morning events in the bedroom. Upon some occasions, she said, she saw Eugenie and Mr Hatch in the bed after Mrs Hatch and Lucy had left. Another servant, Ellen Farr, then gave 'evidence of a similar character'.

Mr F R Coghlan then gave evidence regarding the night of 18th August, when the Hatches had a party of friends. In the course of the evening, Mrs Hatch asked him to go upstairs and fetch Mr Hatch. He went to the bedroom whose door was ajar, knocked, and Mr Hatch told him to come in. '[I] did not go into the room, but merely asked [Mr Hatch] to come down', to which he replied that they would be down directly. Mr Hatch and the children came down two or three minutes later.

Baron Channell asked for some clarification; he (Mr Coghlan) had been at the Hatches about half an hour before Mrs Hatch asked him to go upstairs. He had seen Mr Hatch in the drawing room, but could not tell when he had left. Mr Hatch had called, 'Come in!', the instant he had knocked at the door.

Next to be called were the two French ladies who were staying with the Hatches at the time in question. First, Leonie Raffiel. She too had been in the drawing room when Mr and

Mrs Plummer had left on 11th August. She saw what had happened in the garden and gave an account similar to the other witnesses. She stated positively that '...no act of impropriety was committed by Mr Hatch towards either of the children...' She added that while at the Hatches', she had no particular reason for watching Mr Hatch, but she never saw anything in his conduct unbecoming the character of a gentleman and guardian of children. Mr Hatch always appeared to treat the children with the greatest possible kindness. Her sister, Valerie Raffiel, gave similar evidence, adding that it appeared to her that Mr Hatch

> did everything in his power to make his home happy and comfortable to everyone in it...Mr Hatch was exceedingly kind to both the children. He acted more like a father than a tutor...

The Court was then adjourned. It had been full during the day, with many people refused admission. The evidence as presented was not as overwhelmingly unequivocal as might have been expected from the material published in *The Detective*. Nevertheless, at least three of the alleged assaults were shown by multiple witnesses not to have been possible. The first of these, the events in the garden – all along the most unlikely given the practical difficulties involved – had been witnessed by Essie, Martha Howe, Mary Ann Reed, Leonie and Valerie Raffiel and Mrs Dillon (and, of course, Lucy). All were quite clear: they were watching all the time and Henry and the children had only been there for a few minutes. No doubt the spectacle of a clergyman running around the garden being chased by children was not that usual, but nothing untoward had taken place. The original case should have been decided on that incident alone. So many people had seen it; all were agreed that nothing had happened, and in any case, the whole incident took no more than two or three minutes. That

Eugenia insisted, nevertheless, that what she described *had* happened, should have damned her as an untruthful witness.

The incident of the story on Henry's knee was likewise contradicted by the evidence of Lucy herself but principally by Mr Coghlan. If any impropriety had been taking place, Henry would hardly have said, 'Come in!', so promptly. Nevertheless, Lucy was an eight year old child, and Mr Coghlan, described in *The Detective* as *master* Coghlan, may also have been quite young.

The nightly visits to Eugenia's room were discounted by the evidence of Essie and her mother, although since both were closely related to Henry, some independent evidence would have been useful. Since both Martha Howe and the French ladies were present in the drawing room, their comments on Henry's absence might also have been of assistance; these, apparently, were not forthcoming. Perhaps they genuinely could not remember. After all, it was a relatively trivial fact and had taken place nine months previously.

The morning visits to the Hatches' bed were the most problematic. Henry had stated that they were done against his better judgement, and both he and Eugenia were only dressed in their nightwear. He admitted that he and Eugenia sometimes stayed in the bed after Essie and Lucy had got up, and Mary Ann Reed said that she had seen them in bed together, '...after Mrs Hatch and Lucy had left'. It would have been helpful to have had evidence from Martha Howe and Mary Ann Reed regarding the night of the thunderstorm; what they did, and where they were.

Day three of the trial opened with the examination of the last prosecution witness, the Hatches' gardener James Downe. His contribution was to the effect that he had seen strangers (the Plummers) walking in the garden, with one of the children, on the day that the two girls were taken away.

This closed the case for the prosecution. Serjeant Shee, opening the defence case, now addressed the jury on behalf of the defendant Mary Eugenia Plummer. He summarized the facts of the original case against Mr Hatch, who was defended by 'a gentleman of the highest talent at the bar – Serjeant Ballantine'. Knowing the facts of the case and the defence witnesses that were available in court to testify, yet the defence called only character witnesses. Mr Hatch was duly convicted and sentenced and, no doubt, 'disgraced and degraded'. In order to secure his freedom, he 'got up' what were called statutory declarations in order to obtain a pardon. This was refused by the Secretary of State, without an indictment of perjury against the child who now stood before them. Serjeant Shee went on,

> It [is], no doubt, a question of great importance to the prosecutor; but it [is] equally clear that, whether innocent or guilty, it [is] a matter of dreadful calamity to Miss Plummer that at her tender years she should be connected with such a transaction, and that she should be subjected to the charge of having conspired with other persons to get up a charge of this dreadful description.

This was the first time that any mention of a conspiracy had been made. Probably Edwin James had made this charge while summarizing Eugenia's evidence. From the prosecution's perspective, a conspiracy, with the involvement of an adult or adults unknown, was the only credible explanation for Eugenia's apparent knowledge of sexual matters.

Serjeant Shee continued.[4] The fact that Mr Hatch was a forty-two year old clergyman with an unblemished character spoke to his favour. But the jury should not forget that the defendant was

---

4    Some of Serjeant Shee's remarks have been transposed into the first person.

the daughter of respectable and wealthy parents, careful of her education and morality, who placed her with a clergyman for the express purpose of carrying out that object; and if the question was asked on which side guilt was likely to exist, it might be difficult to come to a conclusion, but I believe I will be able to satisfy you that Mr. Hatch's story was without any corroboration, while the tale of the children was confirmed in many most material particulars.

Serjeant Shee ignored the existence of *Henry's* material and corroborative witnesses, and given the evidence that was to come regarding the Plummers' respectability and their '[care]... of [Eugenia's] education and morality', Serjeant Shee might profitably have declined to comment on that point...

He went on to concentrate on what was the most difficult aspect of the proceedings if Henry was really innocent: how could children of eleven and eight [sic] years of age be acquainted with such abominations as had appeared in this case? This was a difficulty with which the jury must struggle before they

> came to the conclusion that would destroy the prospects of this unhappy child for the remainder of her existence...what could possibly be the motive that operated upon the minds of two such young children to induce them to make such a charge to ruin a respectable and innocent man?

Since it had been universally deposed that Mr Hatch treated the children with the greatest possible kindness, and behaved more like a father than anything else what motive could they have for making the charge? And what motive could Mr and Mrs Plummer have either? Mr Hatch was a stranger to them, they knew he was a most respectable man and there was not the slightest disagreement between them. They were induced to make the accusation by a sense of duty to the public and to protect the children of other parents 'from undergoing similar pollution'. Even then, they wrote 'a most temperate and proper letter' to the Bishop of Winchester.

Serjeant Shee continued; he would attempt to treat the evidence fairly and dispassionately, but it seemed to him that no answer had been given to the evidence of Eugenia Plummer. Mr Hatch was aware of the evidence against him, and yet now, for the first time, an attempt was made to show that the first act of indecency was committed on the carriage drive. She was not asked the question at the former trial, but if she had been, she would have said that the offence had been committed behind the shrubbery and not in a position where anyone in the drawing room could have seen (but *could* have been seen from the surgeon's house. In addition to which, Eugenia deposed in her evidence in Henry's trial, that they were 'walking round the garden' not 'behind the shrubbery'...) If there was any foundation for the charge – that Mr Hatch and the children were in full view of the drawing room window in the carriage drive – he asked the jury how was it that the witnesses were not called at the original trial. He then commented that the evidence to that effect, now given, was of very little use, since if Mr Hatch were really guilty, he would hardly have 'selected a spot for the accomplishment of his purpose where the eyes of several people were upon him...' The witnesses had completely failed to establish that Mr Hatch had not left the carriage driveway and that he was absent for not longer than three or four minutes. (One wonders what further evidence would have satisfied Serjeant Shee on this point other than the word of Lucy Hatch, Essie Hatch, Mrs Dillon, Miss Howe, Leonie and Valerie Raffiel and Mary Ann Reed...) He went on,

What possible inducement could all these grown-up women have to witness the departure of Mrs. Plummer?

She was an entire stranger to them, and in all probability they were glad she was gone; and as to speaking positively for a minute or two it was absurd, and it appears to me that the evidence was clearly the result of an agreement between the parties with the object of saving a clergyman from disgrace and punishment.

(Of course it was the children chasing after Henry that everyone was looking at, and to suggest that they had all conspired was, itself, somewhat absurd. But Serjeant Shee pulled no punches, as was clear from his comment about the witnesses' gladness that his client's wife had departed.)

Serjeant Shee continued; Mr Hatch had admitted frequently going into the bedroom of this little girl and kissing her whilst in bed which was a '…somewhat extraordinary and unusual proceeding in the case of a man in the position of Mr. Hatch with a girl of twelve years old'. The child 'represented that he did more than kiss her, and I cannot see a tittle of evidence to contradict her testimony'. Regarding the evidence that Mr Hatch was not absent upon any evening for more than eight or nine minutes, he said that it was ridiculous to suppose that: 'such a circumstance could be remembered after a lapse of three months'. He went on,

I am most sorry to say one single word that could possibly give pain to Mrs. Hatch, who, I believe, is a lady of the utmost purity and virtue, and, as I have anticipated, if any acts of indecency were committed in the bedroom, it is quite clear that Mrs. Hatch was in such a position at the time that she could not by any possibility have witnessed them.

Serjeant Shee now examined the question of whether Eugenia was in the bed or just under the counterpane. This was, he said, the first time that such a suggestion had been made, although,

...from the first the child had distinctly stated that she was in the bed, and not outside it, as was now attempted to be shown, to answer the purposes of the present accusation.

(That was not true. Henry made the claim in his petition to the Queen less than a month after his conviction. Since only he and Essie could have positively confirmed the fact, and since neither was allowed to give evidence, the petition was the first time that it could be stated.) Serjeant Shee went on,

If Eugenia Plummer had really told a falsehood when she stated that she was taken into the bed with Mr. Hatch, do you believe, when he was aware that there were witnesses who could have contradicted her, that he would not have insisted upon their being examined, or that his counsel could have had any discretion in the matter? [Henry had, of course, tried to 'insist', but had been overruled by Serjeant Ballantine assisted by Mr Lewis] The prosecution have said that the story was improbable, but their own evidence clearly made out that it was perfectly possible that everything that was represented to have occurred might have taken place.

Henry's conduct was now commented upon at length: the fact that he concealed the nature of the charge against him from his wife and intimate friends, and whether this was 'consistent with his being an innocent man'. Serjeant Shee then detailed Henry's conduct in giving up his appointment and leaving his family destitute. This was, he said,

...evidently dictated by a desire to hush the matter up and prevent it from coming to the knowledge of the public, and it was utterly inconsistent with his innocence...

237

Serjeant Shee's 'most eloquent and powerful address to the jury' took more than three hours. When he finished, there was a burst of applause which was 'quickly suppressed by the officers of the court'. Without delay, the first of the defence witnesses was called, Stephana Augusta Plummer, Eugenia's eight year old sister. Described in the press reports as an 'interesting child', she gave her evidence, summarized as follows:

> I remember my sister going to Mr. Hatch's, and I remember going there too a few days afterwards. We arrived at Wandsworth in the afternoon, and I and my papa and mamma went into the drawing room and saw Mrs. Hatch there. Mr. Hatch was not at home. My papa and mamma went away in the evening, and soon afterwards I and Lucy Hatch were put to bed together. My sister slept in an adjoining room, and I could hear her come to bed. I could not sleep, and began to cry because my mamma had gone away. After some time Mr. Hatch came into my room. He was alone. He asked me how it was I was not asleep, and I made no answer. He then came up to my bed. [As before, the specific details of what she said happened could not be reported]…Mr. Hatch had nothing but his night shirt on, and I think he came from his own room…after this he wished me good night and left the room. I had heard him go into my sister's room a few minutes before he came into mine. On the following morning my sister told me that Mr. Hatch had done something to her, and I said he had done the same to me. Mr. Hatch called me into his bedroom on the same morning, and Mr. Hatch fetched my sister from her room and she got into his bed. Mrs. Hatch was in the bed at the same time. We all five were in the bed together – myself, Mr. and Mrs. Hatch, my sister, and Lucy Hatch. Mrs. Hatch got out of bed first and she then

dressed Lucy, and I and my sister were dressed by the servant. My papa and mamma came to Mr. Hatch's on the same day, and I saw my sister go with my mamma to the water-closet. After this, my papa, mamma, and my sister and I went into the garden, and Mrs. Hatch accompanied us. At this time I had told my mamma what Mr. Hatch had done. She asked me if I liked the place, and I told her I did not, and shortly after this we all went away in a cab to the railway station, and as we were going home, I heard my sister say how Mr. Hatch had treated her, and I also told what had happened to me. On the following morning, Mr. Gay, our surgeon, was sent for, and I and my sister told what had taken place in his presence. I have remained at home with my papa and mamma ever since.

Stephana was now cross-examined by Edwin James. In response to his various questions, she provided the following further information:

I had never been at school until Mr. Hatch's. I was on a visit to my sister once at a school in Southampton, and my mother came down and fetched us both away. [So, it had happened before…] I cannot read or write. My mother has never taught me either to read or write… My mother used to take me to church regularly every Sunday, but I have never been taught to read my Bible or Prayer-book.

Then she said, 'My sister first told me something Mr. Hatch had done. I knew what she meant.' Mr James asked her how she knew what her sister meant:

I don't know where I learned to know what she meant, but I did know. She did not say anything more at that time, and I told her he had done the same thing to me. I did not much like going to school, and I was anxious to get away. I did not tell my governess anything about what had happened. I don't think I said anything about it to my mamma while we were walking in the garden. I had told her before, and as we were walking about I heard my mamma tell my papa what Mr. Hatch had done.

So according to Stephana, not only did her sister tell her that Mr Hatch had 'done something', but she knew what it meant; Stephana told her mother while they were at the Hatches' on the day they were both fetched away, and in her father's presence, '…what Mr Hatch had done…', and she heard Mrs Plummer telling Mr Plummer in the garden 'what Mr. Hatch had done'. And after all this, 'We all had tea together, mamma gave Lucy 5s and a toy…' Then, in response to various further questions:

Eugenia did not say anything to me about Mr. Hatch until after school was over, at 12 o'clock. On this same day, I think, I was in my bedroom alone with my mamma, and I told her then what Mr. Hatch had done. My papa was present at the time and heard what I said. I asked my mamma to go upstairs as I had something to tell her. My sister heard what I said, but she did not say anything. Mr. Hatch had a candle in his hand when he came into my bedroom and he placed it on the washstand. My sister told all that had happened as we were going along in the cab, and also in the railway carriage, and before Mr. Gay, and before Mr. Pratt, the solicitor. I understood all that she meant, and that it was something very bad and wicked. My mother has talked to me about it several times, and she spoke to me about it just before I was called into court. I don't know what she said, I forget it. I was in waiting yesterday with my mother, and some times she talked to me about this matter. My sister Polly has told me what Lucy Hatch said yesterday. I call my sister Mary "Polly." A paper was read to us last night by papa. He did not read the whole of it. I don't know what newspaper it was that papa read to us. I am sure my mamma did not tell me what I was to say in court – not that I recollect. I saw Mr. Gay, the surgeon, yesterday, and he has been walking about with me and my mother.

She was then re-examined by the defence:

I don't think I have been told by anybody what I was to say when I came here. I have been waiting about the court to be examined, and when I was called, I came in.

It was becoming clear that who said what, and to whom, and when, was becoming critical. In alleging that Henry assaulted her also, was Stephana just doing a 'me too' after Eugenia had already told her what Henry had done? And had they really told their parents what Henry had done, before everyone sat down together and had a nice tea? Stephana was, of course, only eight, but many children of that age have a remarkable ability accurately to memorize facts and associate them with events.

Now, however, Stephana over-egged the pudding. In response to a question from Baron Channell:

| | |
|---|---|
| *Stephana:* | When Mr. Hatch was in my room I saw Mrs. Hatch in her own room. |
| *Baron Channell:* | Then she could see all that took place? |

| | |
|---|---|
| *Stephana*: | Yes. (This answer caused a great sensation in the court) |
| *Baron Channell*: | How far was Mrs. Hatch from you at the time? |
| *Stephana*: | Not very far. |
| *Baron Channell*: | As far as you are from me? (About 10 feet) |
| *Stephana*: | Not so far. |
| *Baron Channell*: | What part of the bed did you lie on? |
| *Stephana*: | I think it was on the blanket and under the counterpane. |
| *Baron Channell*: | Where was Eugenia? |
| *Stephana*: | I think she was on the blanket and under the counterpane too. |

It was clear that Stephana was just telling a story. She had confused Henry's alleged visit to her in her own room (Eugenia's old bedroom, next to the Hatches' room), with being in the Hatches' bed together with Eugenia. She also contradicted Eugenia's evidence in the first trial by saying that they were *on the blanket and under the counterpane*, not *in* the bed. This undermined Serjeant Shee's earlier argument, when he claimed that it was the prosecution who were now claiming for the first time that the children were only under the counterpane. What was also clear was that there was a suspicion that she was being coached, and if anyone had coached her in what to say, it was likely to have been her mother. The defence case had started to unravel.

Appropriately enough, and with Stephana's questionable evidence fresh in everyone's mind, it was her mother, Caroline Plummer, who next took the witness stand. In response to various questions from the defence:

> I remember taking my daughter, Eugenia, to Mr.
> Hatch's on 11th August. I had dinner, or rather I should
> say luncheon with them. I did not ask Mr. Hatch or
> anyone else in the house to allow my daughter to go to
> his bed in the morning, but I did say that she had been
> used to be petted, and I wished them to be kind to
> her. Mr. Hatch then said she should be treated as well
> as his own child, and she was in the habit of coming
> into his bed in the morning and Eugenia should do
> the same. I never made the suggestion that she should
> go to his bed. A fortnight after this I took my other
> daughter, Stephanie, to Mr. Hatch's, and during the
> whole day I had no opportunity of speaking to my
> daughter Eugenia alone; either Mr. or Mrs. Hatch was
> with us the whole time. When it was getting near the
> time for our departure I took the child to the closet,
> which was the only place I could get to be with her
> alone. She burst out crying immediately and asked me
> to take her home, and she appeared very unhappy. I
> returned the next day to Mr. Hatch's but I cannot tell
> what made me do so. (The witness, who appeared to
> be of a very excitable temperament then said) I am
> nervous, you know...

It is not really surprising that Mrs Plummer was nervous
given the publicity the case had already aroused, particularly
regarding her own background and behaviour. In response to
the question why she went back to Wandsworth the next day:

> I fancied something was wrong and I went back. I did
> not rush into the schoolroom, but went in quickly, and
> I said, "Holloa! Lucy running about the passage and
> my children in the school room, and I thought there

were no favourites here." I saw Mr. and Mrs. Hatch shortly afterwards, and told them I was come to take my children away. While the things were being packed up I went with my daughter to the closet, and she told me Mr. Hatch was "such a disgusting man." I asked her what she meant, and she made a communication to me. She did not state to the full extent what had occurred, and I said "Nonsense", and nothing more occurred. I spoke to my husband, and he entertained the same opinion that I did. There was no time for anything more to be said, as we had to leave by the 8 o'clock train. I am sure that Stephanie did not say anything to me in the house. I gave the child Lucy a Noah's ark and 5s before we left. We had hardly got out of sight of the house, in the cab, when Eugenia told us what Mr. Hatch had done to her. We did not arrive at our residence in Wiltshire until the middle of the night, and on the following morning we sent for our medical man; and Mr. Pratt, our solicitor, came on the same day, and after this we communicated with the Bishop. Our object in this was to spare our children the pain of a public exposure. We subsequently received notice to attend at Wandsworth before the magistrates, but on the day before we were informed Mr. Hatch had resigned, and that our attendance was not necessary, and we then obtained a warrant for Mr. Hatch's apprehension, but it could not be executed, because he went away. I afterwards received from Mrs. Hatch the letter that has been referred to.

Mr James, for the prosecution, now cross-examined Mrs Plummer. In response to his first question:

*Mrs. Plummer*:    Both on the 25th and the 26th I had no opportunity of being alone with Eugenia, except in the water-closet (The witness spoke this in a loud voice, and she at the same time said "I like to answer firm." (A laugh in court)) I swear I was not in a bedroom with Eugenia and my husband alone on either of those days. The "other party" was always present.

| | |
|---|---|
| *Mr. James*: | Who do you mean by the 'other party'? |
| *Mrs. Plummer*: | Mr. and Mrs. Hatch. |

Then, in response to various questions from Mr James:

Stephanie never told me in the bedroom that Mr. Hatch had behaved indecently to her. If anyone has said this, it is a deliberate falsehood. I am sure she did not tell me so herself. I swear that I did not walk round the kitchen garden with my husband and my two daughters on either of those two days, and that I told my husband what Stephanie had told me. She had not told me at that time. I may have stated at the former trial that Stephanie told me that Mr. Hatch was dressed, and that he unbuttoned his trousers, but if I did say so it is a mistake of mine. She never did say so. I remember the child told me that she noticed Mr. Hatch had a very shabby nightshirt on, or that it was pieced or mended. I don't know whether I have mentioned this before, but I was surprised that the child should make such an observation...

But, of course, Stephana *had* just deposed in her evidence that she had told her mother that Mr Hatch had 'done' something to her, and the gardener had sworn that he had seen 'strangers' walking around the garden... And now Mrs Plummer started to unravel. In response to an unrecorded question regarding the cab drive back to Paddington and other matters...

> I don't know whether my husband stopped the cab and bought me some beer. If he did it was not a criminal thing. I have not had any brandy and water today. I did have some yesterday, if I required it. To-day I have had sherry wine. I cannot remember whether I had any brandy and water yesterday, but I had the day before. I should like to have some brandy and water or sherry now (a laugh). I did not drink beer with the policemen after the conviction of Mr. Hatch. A bottle of stout was sent for, and I drank part of it, and the remainder was left for the policemen...

Having established Mrs Plummer's alcoholic preferences, Mr James now enquired about the Plummers' strategy regarding schooling for Eugenia:

| | |
|---|---|
| *Mr. James*: | How many schools has your daughter been at? |
| *Mrs. Plummer*: | As many as I thought proper to send her to – eight or 10, perhaps. She was only a fortnight at one. It was quite long enough. It is very probable that I threatened to publish a statement that the proprietress of that school had not kept her agreement with me. |
| *Mr. James*: | Did she go to school at Southampton? |

| | |
|---|---|
| *Mrs. Plummer*: | I dare say you know all about it. (A laugh.) |
| *Mr. James*: | Why did you take her away from Southampton? |
| *Mrs. Plummer*: | Because she was not treated properly. I am a very particular woman, although I do take a little brandy and water and sherry wine, and I should be very glad to give you some if you required it. (A laugh.) |

Surely Mrs Plummer had already partaken of more than a little brandy and water or sherry wine? In any event, she continued,

My daughter was at three different schools in Bath. There was a reason for her removal from each, and, besides, a change does her good. (Laughter.) She told me from the first that she did not like "the Hatches" and she was very anxious to get away. I swear that I did not hear outside that the gardener had been examined this morning. Mr. Plummer read a portion of the report in the newspaper last night. I cannot recollect whether Eugenia told her sister what had taken place during the day in court. I did not object to my child going to Mr. Hatch's bedroom, because I was anxious that there should not be any jealousy between the two children. My youngest child cannot read. I do not wish to hurry her into education, on account of her health being delicate. I do not go regularly to church or any other place of worship, but Mr. Plummer takes the children to church occasionally. I did not take my children to church during the year 1859, but I am as good as those that do go. I have had a bad foot, and my spirits have been failing since I lost one of my children...

The Plummers had had a daughter, Caroline, a year older than Eugenia, who died sometime after 1851. Nevertheless, Mrs Plummer's superposition of random thoughts indicates a fairly deranged state of mind. Mr James continued,

| *Mr. James*: | I ask you, without reference to any bodily function, was it your habit as a mother to take your children to chapel or church? |
| *Mrs. Plummer*: | No, it was not. |

This statement was also in direct conflict with what Stephana had deposed. Mrs Plummer continued to answer various questions:

I did not cause the great bell of our house to be rung upon my return home to celebrate the conviction of Mr. Hatch...I should say that both children had told their stories before we arrived at Paddington, but I am certain they had done so before we arrived home. My daughter was never removed from any school on account of misconduct. She was beloved by all. My children have been taught to say their prayers – the Lord's Prayer (not the belief), the prayer for their parents, and little hymns. My husband used to take the children to church, but he did not go every Sunday, because sometimes he was prevented by weather or some other cause.

This concluded the examination of Mrs Plummer, and the court was adjourned. No doubt Mr James was quite satisfied that he had shown Mrs Plummer (or rather she had shown herself) to be hysterical, unbalanced and a very poor parent. Eugenia, at the age of twelve, had already been to eight or ten schools – two for no longer than two weeks. Stephana, at eight years old, could neither read nor write (by contrast, Lucy Hatch, four months younger, *could* read and write – she and Eugenia used to play a spelling game in the Hatches' bed in the morning). Mr James had also shown that the Plummers, Caroline Plummer in particular, were guilty of two cardinal sins among respectable Victorian gentlefolk, they did not attend church – and took no care that their children should attend – but worse than that, they were fond of alcohol. And it was clear that Mrs Plummer was intoxicated while she was in the witness box.

The fourth day of the trial, Saturday, May 12th, opened with the examination of the hapless Thomas Plummer, husband of Caroline Plummer and father of Eugenia and Stephana. He provided his evidence in response to various questions from the defence:

I reside at Holcroft House, Wiltshire, and am possessed of considerable property. I am a member of the Church of England, and my daughter Eugenia used to attend before this. I took my daughter to Mr. Hatch's in consequence of an advertisement. I and my wife first took Eugenia on 11th August. While we were having lunch, something was said about my daughter being petted, and either Mr. or Mrs. Hatch said she should be treated the same way Lucy was. I went into Eugenia's bedroom, and my wife complained that it was very close and wished there should be a ventilator, but Mrs. Hatch said she thought the door being left open would be sufficient. I and my wife went again with the youngest child on 25th August, and I remarked that either Mr. or Mrs. Hatch was with us the whole day, and Mrs. Plummer had no opportunity of speaking alone to Eugenia, except by going to the closet. I observed this particularly at the time. I did not observe anything particular when they came out, but while we were walking on the front lawn Mrs. Plummer told me that my daughter said that Mr. Hatch was a disgusting man. Nothing more occurred until after we had got into the fly with the two children, [on the 26th August, the following day] when Eugenia gave a narrative of what had taken place during her stay at Mr. Hatch's. The children spoke to their mother, and not to me. It is not true that I and Mrs. Plummer drank porter with the cabman on our way to the Paddington station, or that we admitted him into any equality with us…I swear I did not…The moment we arrived at Swindon we sent a message to Mr. Gay, our medical man, and Mr. Pratt, our solicitor, requesting them to come to us immediately, and they both came in the course of the day, and my daughters repeated the same story they had told my wife in the cab on the previous evening…[The stories of the two children] did not differ in the slightest particular…I don't remember that the children complained of any other sort of unkindness. I consulted my solicitor as to what was best to be done and he gave me advice what course to adopt, and in consequence of what he said I consulted Messrs Humphreys and Morgan, the eminent solicitors, and discussed the matter with them, and I subsequently addressed a letter to the Bishop. Mr. Pratt wrote the letter, and I signed it. A day was subsequently appointed for an investigation by the magistrates at Wandsworth, but on the day it was to take place we were told that we need not attend, as Mr. Hatch had resigned his situation. I did go to London notwithstanding, and obtained a warrant for his apprehension…I never made it a habit, even in [Eugenia's] early days, to let her sleep in our bed. I never knew [the children] to surprise me whist I was dressing. I know they were not acquainted with children of vicious habits. I know they were never permitted to mix with the grooms or man-servants. The [children] never had a brother.

(This last evidence was provided to demonstrate that Eugenia and Stephana could not have learned about male sexuality at home; the most compelling argument of the prosecution in the first trial, and the defence in Eugenia's trial, was to question how the children could have known about the details of the charges they alleged, unless they had experienced them as deposed.) Mr Plummer was now cross-examined by Mr Giffard, and in answer to sundry questions:

Nothing had been told me to lead me to believe anything improper had been done to the children, except the expression, that Mr. Hatch was a disgusting man, down to the time when we left the house. We did not think there had been anything serious at this time, and did not consider it right to ask Eugenia for an explanation. I am quite certain I heard nothing else before the children were taken away.

Regarding the door from Eugenia's bedroom to the passageway – the door Eugenia had said was locked with a bath against it:

On the 26th August I cannot recollect whether the bolt was against the door. I will swear it was not open. I now recollect I did go through the door. I have made a mistake in saying it was closed.

(So the door was not locked or blocked with anything; and this was on a day when the Hatches could not have known that the Plummers were going to visit them.)

At this point, the newspaper reports of Thomas Plummer's evidence are confused. Among the other information regarding the Plummers' behaviour gleaned as a result of *The Detective's* investigations, one of the cab drivers who took them from Wandsworth to Paddington, either on 25th or 26th August, must have come forward with a story. More than once on the journey, the Plummers had stopped to get porter; Mrs Plummer had already been questioned on this and had implied that it was true, although Mr Plummer had denied drinking with the cab driver. The prosecution now questioned Mr Plummer on this. According to *The Times*, *The Morning Star* and *The Morning Post*, he said that

> We might have stopped twice while we were going from Mr. Hatch's to Paddington to get porter, both on the 25th and the 26th.

However, *The Observer* reported him saying,

> I will swear that we did not have porter brought to the cab. I will swear that Mrs. Plummer never stopped the cab at the Bayswater-road, or had porter brought to us.

The report in *Lloyds Weekly Newspaper* probably reflects what was actually said. It reported Mr Plummer saying,

> The cab might have been stopped twice to get porter as [we] were going from Mr. Hatch's to Paddington Station. [I] would not state that [my] wife did not stop the cab on both occasions, and order [me] to get beer.

The distance from Wandsworth to Paddington is around five miles. At the time, the journey by cab took no longer than an hour, so Mrs Plummer must have been very thirsty indeed to have insisted that they stop twice for refreshment on the way…

Mr Plummer continued with his evidence; in response to various questions from the prosecution:

> We had only one female servant at Holcroft, and she did not live in the house. A charwoman used to come occasionally. We employed a gardener but he did not live in the house. I should say that servants had not refused to live in the house with us, but I would not swear it was not the case. I paid £5 to one servant [Phoebe Easell] because she fancied she was ill-used… my wife used to beat her…but she used to steal things from us…She said that Mrs. Plummer struck her, and I believe that she did touch her. (A laugh.) My wife did not strike her with a poker – it was with a candlestick. (A laugh.) I paid the doctor's bill.

Poor old Thomas Plummer! Did he realize what a laughing-stock he had made of himself and his wife? A man of 'considerable property' had no live-in servants? And Mrs Plummer's weapon of choice was a candlestick rather than a poker? In addition to that, it was clear that Mrs Plummer had a drink problem.

The defence, however, were not finished with their witnesses; next on the stand was Mr John Gay. He was the Plummers' doctor, aged thirty-nine, whom Eugenia 'planned to marry' when she was seventeen. He went to the Plummers' residence in Wiltshire on 27th August. The elder child told him of the treatment she had received from Mr Hatch. She said that he had ill used her, and then went into 'a detail of the various acts of indecency that were the subject of enquiry'. The younger child made a similar statement to him. He had known Eugenia from birth, and he had 'frequently joked with her and called her his little wife', although he denied that they were ever formally betrothed. He never saw anything improper in her conduct, and he had not the slight-est reason for considering her otherwise than a truthful and a good child. He examined her and observed 'slight marks of violence...'

Under cross-examination by Mr James, he stated that he was not a trustee to Eugenia. He was on very intimate terms with the family (dealing with Mrs Plummer's victims?), but he had never dined at Mr Plummer's house. They did not keep a regular servant; the only domestic in the house was a charwoman. He said he was 'quite sure that he stated at the last trial that there were marks of violence'. Mr James was referring to the shorthand writer's notes and pressing Mr Gay on this point, when he (Mr Gay) fainted, and was removed from the court into the open air! This was all very interesting, because according to the records, Mr Gay was *not* called as a witness during the first trial. A key witness fainting in the middle of cross-examination could be construed as being somewhat suspicious (even though the judge commented upon the oppressive heat in the courtroom), and this was the doctor who had performed intimate examinations of the eleven-year-old Eugenia while calling her his 'little wife...'

While Mr Gay was being revived outside, Mr James Pratt, father and professional partner of Walters Freake Pratt (and presumably responsible for his son's name) was called. James Pratt deposed that he had been called to the Plummers' house on 27th August to find Mr and Mrs Plummer in a very distressed state. They told him that their children had been ill used by Mr Hatch, and Eugenia told him what had happened. He saw the younger child and she made a statement similar to that of her sister. Mr Plummer consulted him as to what should be done, and he (Mr Pratt) then went to London and saw Mr Humphries – another solicitor – following which he wrote the letter to the bishop.

Under cross-examination from Mr James, Mr Pratt said that he worked for the prosecution (of Henry) until Mr

Hatch resigned. After that he 'had nothing more to do with
the business.' (Perhaps seeking to distance himself from his
son's lucky escape at the Queen's Bench hearing in January…)
He had known Eugenia Plummer a good many years, and
never saw anything to induce him to think that she was an
ill-conducted girl.

Next on the stand was the by-now famous Walters Freake
Pratt himself (misnamed WB Pratt in the press report). He
deposed that he took up the matter in October after his father
had 'given it up' and after the letter had been received from
Mrs Hatch. He had two interviews with Mrs Hatch after
which an arrangement was made that Mr Hatch should come
to Ridler's Hotel. He continued,

> Mrs. Hatch came with him [Henry]. She afterwards
> left the room at my request. I believe Hatch knew I
> held a warrant for his apprehension. After she left I
> told him I thought I had the authority to state that
> it was the wish of the parents that the poor child
> should not be exposed, and as he had resigned his
> living, and involved himself in ruin, that the case had
> gone far enough and if he would confess his guilt and
> apologise to Mrs. Plummer there would be an end to
> the matter. He refused. We were all very much affected
> at the circumstance, and…[I was] so excited, that…I
> cannot recollect the precise order of the conversation.
> There, however, was an observation that he made
> that produced a great impression on my mind, and I
> recollect it perfectly. After we had been talking, Mr.
> Hatch said, "Well I hope you will deal as leniently as
> you can with me. I am mad" or "I was mad." I cannot
> swear positively whether it was "I am mad" or "I was
> mad. One or the other I am certain it was.

Mr Hatch was then given into custody. The officer had been

looking for Mr Hatch for about a fortnight before he was taken.

Under cross-examination, Mr Pratt declared that it was his 'sincere wish that Mr Hatch should be dealt with as leniently as possible, on account of his poor wife'. He also claimed that he had asked the constable whether it would be possible for Mr Hatch to remain at home, in Wandsworth, until the magistrates' hearing on the Monday morning. An apparent demonstration of concern, until it is remembered that it was Walters Freake Pratt who implied by denial to the Home Secretary, that Henry had made a confession; a fact which may well have decided the Home Secretary against granting the Queen's pardon. If anyone was responsible for Henry's extended stay in prison, it was Walters Freake Pratt.

The Reverend Mr Brighton was examined next. He was the proprietor of a school where Eugenia Plummer had formerly been a pupil. She was a 'very well conducted good child' while under his charge, and he considered her to be 'truthful and exceedingly simple-minded'. (Presumably he meant uncomplicated rather than of low intelligence.) She was at his school three years previously, and stayed for only five weeks. She was about eight years old at the time, and her education appeared to have been neglected, however, '…she never came into my bedroom. Certainly not.' He had heard that she had not been baptized until she was eight years old.

Rev Brighton was a witness for the defence and was called to prove that Eugenia was 'well conducted…and truthful'. But his experience of her behaviour was three years out of date and she only stayed at his school for five weeks. Was this really the best that the defence could do to affirm Eugenia's current good character? However, his evidence did establish that, contrary to Mrs Plummer's statement when she first brought Eugenia to Wandsworth, Eugenia had not been allowed even into the Rev Brighton's bedroom, never mind his bed…

Police Constable Taylor, 212, V Division, was now called

for the defence. In response to various questions:

> I had a warrant placed in my hands for the apprehension
> of Mr. Hatch on the 29th October. I heard nothing
> of him until the 12th November, when I found him
> at Ridler's hotel...In going to the Wandsworth police
> station he asked me the precise nature of the charge.
> I said the warrant was for an assault on a girl named
> Plummer, and there was another for assaulting her
> sister. He said, "Can I see that information?" I said,
> "No doubt it will be read to you on Monday." He
> said, "What is the punishment?" I said, if the case was
> proved, the magistrate could give him six months.

By now, Mr Gay had recovered sufficiently from his fainting
fit to go back to the witness box. He was asked about the
interview with the Plummers when Eugenia related what she
alleged was done to her. He said that Mrs Plummer had asked
questions like, 'What did Mr. Hatch do to you?' She did not
'ask questions that would convey their own answer.'

Responding to questions from Mr James, he 'persisted in
stating that he said on the former trial that there were slight
marks of violence on the child Eugenia's person'. However, he
also stated that the appearances that he observed 'might have
been occasioned by a variety of causes'.

In response to a question from Baron Channell, he said
that at the former trial he made the statement in a low tone to
the trial judge, and he thought it possible that the shorthand
writer did not hear him. He said that he was reading the
original trial notes, along with Mr Pratt, a few days previously,
and was aware of the omission. The judge accepted this
explanation, and this was very curious, because Mr Gay
certainly did not appear as a witness in the official shorthand
transcript of the evidence for the prosecution in the first trial,
nor was he mentioned as a witness in the press reports of the

trial. Since his evidence would have been significant, it seems remotely unlikely that had he been a witness, no report of it appeared in any of the newspaper accounts. One has to draw the conclusion, therefore, that Mr Gay did *not* give evidence in the first trial. In that case, it seems extraordinary that he, a professional man, should have made such a statement. However, it is also extraordinary that Baron Channell took his explanation at face value, apparently without checking it. In addition, it is strange that Mr James should not have sought to make capital out of it. Perhaps he felt that Mr Gay's evidence was not significant. Mr Gay was questioned about his fainting fit, and stated that he was frequently 'attacked' in a similar manner. This closed the case for the defence, and the court was adjourned for half an hour to allow the jury to take some refreshment.

It now fell to Mr Edwin James to sum up the prosecution case, addressing the jury 'in a most able and powerful speech, which was listened to with the utmost attention throughout...' With his theatrical talents, he knew how to spellbind an audience.[5] He said that the verdict the jury would now shortly have to pronounce would close one of the most remarkable and extraordinary cases that had perhaps ever been investigated in a court of justice. His learned friend had told them that Mr Hatch had stood at the bar of this court and was convicted by the jury of indecently assaulting these two girls, and that the learned judge who tried them had, as he was bound to do in such a case and under such circumstances, sentenced him to four years in prison and hard labour. Mr Hatch now came before another jury to complain that the former verdict had been obtained by false evidence, that in point of fact the '...stream of justice had been perverted by false testimony...' and on this ground, to ask the jury to reverse the decision that had formerly been come to. When Mr Hatch stood at

---

5    Direct quotations from Edwin James' speech have been transposed into the first person.

that bar on his former trial, and after his conviction, he made the remarkable statement that he was innocent and that he felt assured the day would come when God would prove the innocence of the crime laid to his charge. He believed the day had now come when their verdict would confirm his statement. He need not inform them that

> the effect of the former verdict was not only to destroy the immediate prospects of Mr. Hatch, but that, in point of fact, he might as well be deprived of existence...there was no appeal – he could not have the evidence of his wife...

Mr James stated that the object of the present prosecution was to show that Henry Hatch had been unjustly convicted, and to reverse the former decision. He went on to say that his learned friend had made a great many observations on the fact that the witnesses who had now been examined, were not called on the former occasion. He had the highest opinion of the ability of his learned friend, Serjeant Ballantine, who appeared for Mr Hatch on that occasion, and he had no doubt that he exercised a sound discretion upon the facts then before him, and the instructions he had received, in not calling witnesses. But was a man to be considered guilty of a crime because his counsel did not think it proper to call witnesses? The jury would also recollect that one scene of this foul conspiracy was the bedroom of Mr and Mrs Hatch, and that no witnesses could have been called to disprove this portion of the statement. The case of his learned friend (Serjeant Shee), as it appeared to him, was full of the most glaring inconsistencies:

> With one breath, Mrs. Hatch was represented to be a virtuous, respectable woman, against whom there did not rest the slightest suspicion, and with the next, she

was represented to have been the deepest accomplice of her husband, and she was charged with direct perjury...

He went on,

> The child [Stephana] was actually made to say that Mrs. Hatch, the wife of the accused, was present on one occasion when these abominations were going on, and that she actually saw what occurred...When a case rests upon such evidence as this, I ask you as reasonable and sensible men, whether you can rely on it, and whether the whole structure of this wretched story has not been completely shattered in the course of the investigation?

He continued,

> My learned friend has made a great many comments upon Mr. Hatch having adopted the course of procuring a number of statutory declarations, and his having submitted them to the Secretary of State with a view to obtain a pardon; but what was he to do? He had gone to his dungeon, he had no appeal allowed him by law, he could not call his wife as a witness, and what course was possibly open to him but to obtain the solemn declaration of every human being who was in his house at the time and who witnessed what occurred to show that he was not guilty of the crime of which he had been unjustly convicted? These witnesses, or the greater part of them at all events, had no interest in the matter. There were the servants, there was the governess, a highly respectable young lady, whose position entirely depended upon her character and her regard for veracity and honour; there were the two French ladies, also persons of great respectability;

and all these witnesses had given evidence which showed conclusively that Mr. Hatch could not have been guilty of the offence that was imputed to him by Eugenia Plummer upon the first occasion of her going to the school. Can you believe for a moment that these respectable witnesses are guilty of perjury? There is not the slightest foundation for such a suggestion, and I hope to be able to satisfy you that those witnesses have spoken the truth, and that the story that has been told by the children has been trumped up by their mother, and that from some trifling circumstance originally narrated by Eugenia Plummer, it had been swelled and magnified to the fearful accusations that have been ultimately made.

Mr James was declaiming to the gallery. As a large man, no doubt he had a large voice and was using it to best effect. Really getting into his stride, he now addressed the issue of the motive of the children for making the charge in the first place:

It has been asked by my learned friend what motive could have actuated these children to make such a charge? But I will show you presently, that there was ample motive for doing so, from the admission of one of the children herself. Serjeant Shee in his address to you, had said that this was not the first time on which it had been proved that a clergyman of the Church of England had been convicted of a crime of this description. This is undoubtedly true, but the observation applied equally to Roman Catholic ministers and to ministers of all religious denominations, and to all professions. Was this the first time, however, that you have heard of wicked, designing children making false charges, and do you not know that there have been instances in which men's lives have actually nearly been sacrificed upon the evidence of children which had been afterwards proved to be false? I believe that the statement of the children in this case is "a lie", "Guilt's offspring and its guard", and that the whole superstructure of the case against Mr. Hatch is based on falsehood, and this is the real history of this case.

The quotation, 'Guilt's offspring and its guard', comes from the melodramatic play of crime and detection, *The Iron Chest*, by George Coleman the younger, (1762 – 1836). No doubt Edwin James had performed in the play during his previous incarnation as an actor, and used quotations from it and other material in his repertoire to spice up his addresses in court. He continued,

As to motive, why, the girl herself, when she was examined at Wandsworth police court, let out the whole secret, "she did not like the Hatches," she wanted to get away, and she told her mother something likely to effect that object.

On Eugenia's character, Mr James pointed out that at the original trial she had sworn she had only been to two schools; now it transpired she had been to eight or nine. Mr Brighton had spoken favourably of her, but she was at his school three years ago, and

not a single schoolmaster or schoolmistress had been called to say how she had conducted herself while she was with them since that time...I ask you to look at the gross and glaring improbability of the story itself. We are asked to believe, that a gentleman who has for more than forty years enjoyed the esteem and respect of everyone who knew him [just a little exaggeration here, Henry was only forty-two years old...], a clergyman, had so far forgotten every principle of honour and decency as to commit an assault upon a child, a perfect stranger to him, just admitted under his roof, almost under the very shadow of her parents; and the innocent child Lucy Hatch, his adopted daughter, was actually represented to be a sharer in the abominable proceeding. Could such a thing be possible? It could not – it is unworthy of belief!

The learned Serjeant has told you that these two girls have been carefully and religiously brought up in the fear of God; but is this so? It is hardly reconcilable with the fact that [Eugenia] did not seem to have been baptized until she was eight years old, and her mother admitted that she was not in the habit of regularly attending church or of taking her children there, and made a frivolous excuse of having a bad leg, and not being able to get her stocking on...

He commented on the fact that Eugenia had been allowed into the Hatches' bed: '...this might have been an imprudent act; but it was quite clear from the evidence of both Mr. and Mrs. Plummer, that they had sanctioned it.' He continued,

With regard to Mrs. Plummer, you have seen her, and can judge what sort of woman she is, and I think you would agree with me that she is a most extraordinary sort of person, and her conduct in the witness-box can lead to no other conclusion than that she was either intoxicated or suffering from delirium tremens...At one moment she was crying, and the next she was laughing, and she actually forgot herself so far as to invite me while I was examining her to go to Holcroft House and have some brandy-and-water with her (a laugh). All this took place, too, during the investigation of a case in which the character and the future prospects of life for her daughter, a child 12 years old, were involved...

Mr James then commented at some length on the evidence and demeanour of Mrs Plummer, and to the contradictions and discrepancies in her testimony. He went on,

There can be very little doubt that it was at her instigation the children had been induced to make up the tale they have done. If the first accusation...was really too monstrous to be true, and you should come to that conclusion, it appears to me that there is an end to the case, for if you do not believe one portion of the story, how can you place reliance on any part of it? Then with regard to the evidence of the younger child, that Mrs. Hatch saw what was going on upon one occasion. Good God! Is it possible to place any reliance upon such a statement, is it not repugnant to human nature and manifestly false?

And on Henry's 'suspicious' behaviour after he had been accused:

No man can tell what course he would take under such circumstances...it was clear that his mind was borne down and that he was overwhelmed by his position and did not know what to do.

Mr James went on to make a slightly dubious point by saying that the outcome of the enquiry was of vital importance to Mr Hatch, whereas the defendant – should she be found guilty – would be liable to '...some trifling correctional punishment...'

He continued, by pointing out a similarly questionable consideration on the part of the defence:

> My learned friend has appealed to you on the defendant's behalf on the grounds that she is an heiress to £15,000 or £20,000; but what does it matter to you whether she is rich or poor? I am sure you will do your duty firmly, and the same justice will be done to her as to the poor creature who stood at that bar for having dashed his hand through a glittering shop window to save his famished offspring…You should do your duty firmly, and I pray to the God of justice and of truth, to whom perhaps you have already breathed the same prayer, to guide you aright in this great argument and direct you to a just conclusion.

It was a great performance and the court responded with a 'loud burst of applause', which was 'not repressed without some difficulty'. After some discussion between the judge and jury about carrying on, it being Saturday afternoon, the court adjourned until Monday for the judge's summing up. Once more, the court had been crowded for the whole day.

Monday, 14th May 1860, day five of the trial. The judge, Baron Channell, proceeded to sum up.[6] Baron Channell suffered from asthma and he spoke quietly. The court reporter heard him, and one hopes that the jury heard him – although they had probably already made up their minds. He said that the defendant, Mary Eugenia Plummer, was charged with the offence of wilful and corrupt perjury, and considering the very great importance of the case he was glad that he had postponed the summing up until this morning. His learned brother (Mr Justice Keating) would have had to have left on Saturday afternoon to perform various public duties, and he

6    Direct quotations from Baron Channell's speech have been transposed into the first person.

would have been deprived of his assistance. He continued, addressing the jury:

> The case is undoubtedly one of a most extraordinary character, and I thought I ought to state in the onset that it appears to me that there is no ground for complaint against Mr. Hatch by reason of his having instituted this prosecution, and he was justified in doing so under the circumstances. You ought, therefore, not to let the circumstances under which the case has come before you have any effect upon your minds; you should be guided solely by the evidence, and upon the evidence alone you should say whether the guilt of the defendant has been established to your satisfaction or not.
>
> The question you have to decide, undoubtedly involves another enquiry; but this cannot be avoided, and the real point for consideration is whether the guilt of the defendant has been established on this particular charge. It is hardly necessary for me to say, that in a charge of this kind it is impossible that positive or direct evidence can be laid before you, but if the evidence leaves any reasonable doubts in your minds, the defendant is entitled to an acquittal. In coming to a conclusion, I think it is right to say that you ought not to allow your minds to be warped in the slightest degree by considerations of what might possibly be the consequences of your verdict or the probability or possibility that in the event of a conviction a very slight punishment would be inflicted, while in the event of an acquittal the result to Mr. Hatch must be fatal. It is no part of your duty to enter into any such considerations – you must be bound by the evidence, and upon that evidence alone your verdict ought to

be given.

This was a direct instruction to ignore the comments made by Mr James in respect of the 'trifling correctional punishment' that Eugenia Plummer might expect following a conviction, against the effect on Henry's life should she be acquitted.

Baron Channell continued,

> The case has occupied four days, and the evidence is certainly of a most extraordinary kind...If the defendant had made the statements that she did, knowing they were false, there can be no doubt that she has committed the crime with which she is now charged. It is impossible to conceive a more important or extraordinary enquiry; there is contradiction on contradiction, and I confess that I feel utterly incapable of presenting to you any theory as to the probability of truth being on one side or the other.

The judge was being scrupulously honest. Based on the evidence at face value, it was one word against another. He went on,

> On the one hand there was positive evidence of the guilt of Mr. Hatch coming from young minds apparently without motive. There was the evidence of the parents, who also certainly did not appear to have any motive for making a false accusation...On the other hand, the charge involved improbabilities of the most extraordinary character. We are asked to believe that a clergyman – a gentleman who appeared to have all his life borne a most irreproachable character – had, on the very first night a young girl was placed under his charge, committed an act of gross indecency towards her, and that on the following night he

committed a still more atrocious act. Anything more startling or improbable could hardly be conceived; but these facts have been positively spoken to. Still, however improbable they might appear, such acts have undoubtedly been committed, and the annals of courts of justice show that men of high position, and bearing an irreproachable character, acting under the influence of a diseased mind, have been guilty of such offences... it is not, therefore, because the story was improbable alone that you should come to the conclusion that it is not true...

Baron Channell now turned to the evidence given by Eugenia at the previous trial – evidence that had been read out in court during the current trial, and which was the basis of the charge of perjury against Eugenia. He continued,

One very important matter for your consideration is whether the defendant at the time really meant to impute to Mrs. Hatch that she saw what occurred, and was, in point of fact, a party to the offence, or whether she merely meant to represent that she was present. If the latter was intended, then Mrs. Hatch's evidence was of the less importance, but if you should consider that the defendant charged her with being a party to the act, then her evidence was very important indeed, and the same observations also apply to the child Lucy Hatch.

Then relating to the evidence of what Eugenia said she told her mother in the water closet:

It is certainly difficult to account for the conduct of the parents afterwards, consistent with the supposition that they believed an offence of such an atrocious character had been committed.

Then the events in the Hatches' bed:

> The child Eugenia undoubtedly appeared to have
> sworn that Mrs. Hatch was in the bed at the time she
> was assaulted by Mr. Hatch, and that he hurt her, and
> it was certainly most extraordinary, if this was the
> case, that she did not cry or give some other indication
> of suffering.

The judge now dealt with the evidence given by Henry which
was 'an entire denial of the accusation made against him'. He
told the jury that they would have to consider whether they
ought to rely upon his evidence, and whether it had received such
confirmation as would justify them in coming to the conclusion
that the offence of wilful perjury had been established against
the defendant. He said that it did seem rather extraordinary
that he did not show the letter he had received from the bishop
to his wife the moment it came into his possession. The jury
had heard his explanation on the subject, and it was for them
to decide whether it was satisfactory or not.

He then commented upon Henry's resignation from
Wandsworth, his only source of income. His (Henry's)
explanation for this was that

> he acted upon the advice of Mr. Onslow, the governor
> of the gaol, who had told him that, whatever might be
> the result of the investigation, he could not retain his
> office with any satisfaction...It is very true that men's
> minds are differently constituted, and that some men
> would act differently under certain circumstances to
> others...It is certainly in Mr. Hatch's favour that he had
> an opportunity of escaping the consequences of the ac-
> cusation if he had have confessed that he was guilty,

and relieve the children from the imputation of having taken a false oath, and that he refused to do so.

And returning to Eugenia:

> It also appeared that when Eugenia Plummer was examined before the magistrate at Wandsworth she undoubtedly said that she did not like the Hatches, and that she told this tale to her mother in order that she might be taken away...This is a matter certainly for you to take into your serious consideration.

Then back to Henry:

> It is rather a remarkable fact [so many aspects of this case were remarkable...], that there did not appear to be any suggestion that Mr. Hatch had made any threats or promises to either of the children to induce them to be silent.

That was a very good point indeed, and it was indeed 'remarkable' that neither did Mr Edwin James spot it and make capital of it, nor did Serjeant Ballantine during the first trial.

The judge referred to the fact that it was Baron Bramwell, the original trial judge, who ordered that the charge of perjury against Eugenia Plummer be made. This action, he told the jury, could not be taken as any dissatisfaction on the part of Baron Bramwell with the outcome of the first trial, since he was bound by Act of Parliament to do what he did.

It was now the turn of the defence evidence to be examined. Baron Channell referred to the fact that Stephana, the younger child, swore that her mother took her to church every Sunday, whereas Mrs Plummer said that she did not do so, giving reasons why not. He also pointed out other contradictions in their testimony. And in strict fairness to Mrs Plummer, the Judge said that Mrs Plummer

> appears to have suffered a great deal of anxiety on account of her children...Although her conduct in the witness-box was certainly very extraordinary, you ought not to allow this to operate too much to her prejudice...You should weigh her evidence fairly and dispassionately, and allow it to have its due weight in influencing your decision.

In other words, even though Mrs Plummer appeared to be drunk and was sometimes given to violence, she too deserved justice, and to have her evidence fairly considered.

The judge then summed up his summing up; the defendant was on her trial, and if the evidence established her guilt, it was the duty of the jury to say so. But if the evidence left any reasonable doubt in their minds, she was entitled to the benefit of that doubt, and ought to be acquitted, although that result might involve very serious consequences so far as Mr Hatch was concerned. The jury, however, had nothing to do with that; they were bound to decide this case as they would any other, and if the guilt of the defendant was not satisfactorily established, they ought to say so by their verdict, without reference to the consequences to other parties.

If Edwin James' speech for the prosecution was a tour de force, the judge's summing up was a task of Herculean proportions, taxed as he was by asthma. Baron Channell had started summing up at ten o'clock in the morning. It was now a quarter to six in the evening, and he had spoken for seven and three-quarter hours without a break for himself or anyone else.

It was, therefore, early evening when the jury retired to consider their verdict. Whether or not the jury stopped for refreshment is not recorded, but it was eight o'clock before they returned, and the foreman of the jury handed the judge a written paper which the latter directed should be read out in court:

> We find the prisoner, Mary Eugenia Plummer, guilty, and while we recommend her to the utmost extent of mercy, we venture at the same time to express a hope that your Lordship, if you have the power to do so, will direct that any imprisonment to which she may be subjected may be accompanied by a proper course of training and education of which she has hitherto been deprived, and probably would still be deprived at home…

There was a burst of applause within the court, and the many people assembled outside who had been unable to gain entry were also heard cheering loudly. Henry was probably weeping. The judge said that he would consult his colleague Mr Justice Keating regarding the sentence, meanwhile the prisoner could be released to her father – who was found not to be in court! Eventually, William Hitchcock from Eugenia's defence team was able to 'enter into a recognizance of £500', and she left the court with him. Eugenia Plummer had been convicted, but it was her parents who had been found guilty. In their disgrace they had forgotten about her and fled. Henry was still a prisoner, and although he was, no doubt, thoroughly elated, he had to return to his cell in Newgate to await the slow evolution of justice.

This was Monday, and *The Times* of the *following* Monday, reprinted a story from *The Observer* to the effect that,

> The Secretary of State had advised Her Majesty to grant a free pardon to the Rev. Mr. Hatch…In the meantime, an order for the immediate release was despatched from the Home Office on Saturday afternoon…Baron Channell…has entirely concurred in the propriety of a

full pardon, upon being referred to for his opinion by
the Secretary of State.

The trial of Mary Eugenia Plummer had ended on the evening
of Monday, 14th May 1860, yet the order for Henry's release
was not sent to Newgate until the following Saturday. Since
the trial had taken five days – and the outcome was an odds-
on conviction – it cannot entirely have caught the Home
Office unawares. The probable truth is, that with such a high
profile case – and one involving the Royal Pardon – the Queen
had to be at least consulted, if not actually sign the official
document.

But the Queen was having a busy week, and considerations
of innocent clergymen held in her prisons naturally had to wait
their turn; it was her forty-first birthday in a few days' time,
and she had much to do. On Tuesday she held court, went on a
carriage drive with Prince Albert, and went to Covent Garden
in the evening for 'The Italian Opera'. On Wednesday, she went
horse riding in the morning, and had another carriage drive in
the afternoon, with a state ball in the evening at Buckingham
Palace attended by 1,800 people. On Thursday, she held court,
and went to 'Her Majesty's Theatre' in the evening. On Friday,
she held a 'Drawing Room' at St James' Palace in honour of
her birthday to which a vast number of people were invited.
Finally on Saturday, she managed to squeeze in an audience
with her Prime Minister before she, Albert, and the children
left for Osborne House on the Isle of Wight where she was to
celebrate her birthday.

And so it fell to Henry's namesake, Henry John Temple,
3rd Viscount Palmerston, to seek her Majesty's permission for
the release of Henry John Hatch. The Queen left for Osborne
at three o'clock in the afternoon, and the authority to release
Henry reached Newgate from the Home Office late on Saturday
evening. The authority consisted of a notification that,

> It [is] the intention of the Government, after the decision come to by the jury in the case of Eugenia Plummer, to grant Mr. Hatch a free pardon...

Mr Jones, the governor of Newgate, was empowered to release Henry. But with everything that had been done to get him out of prison, the petition to the Queen, the trial and conviction of Eugenia Plummer, and finally, the authority of Queen Victoria herself, Henry could not be released.

*The Law Times* described it as 'a detainer lodged in some civil matter'. It was, of course, just what Henry feared in the first place when he fled to Poplar during the previous November. The Chancery case against Henry regarding his shares and liability in the General Indemnity Insurance Company had been biding its time, and now it had him. Newgate doubled as a debtors' prison, and Henry was nicely secured. Nothing could be done until Monday.

The press reports do not indicate how the matter was settled, but settled it was. Probably, Henry's friends had no alternative other than to pay the £200, plus costs, needed to release him from the debt. By midday on Monday this had been done, and Joseph Gegg, Henry's assistant chaplain from Wandsworth, and Edward Wise, his friend from the Isle of Wight – Henry's unceasing champions for his liberty – came to the prison and took him home. Henry thanked Mr Jones, the governor, and the Rev Mr Davis, the Ordinary, who had allowed him 'every reasonable and proper facility' to prepare his defence and communicate with his friends, and left to spend his first night of liberty after 191 days of confinement.

# Lewis, Lewis, Lewis and (Sir George Cornewall) Lewis

Henry was free and vindicated; vindicated to a far greater extent than would have been the case had he been found innocent in the first trial, or even had the initial magistrates' hearing found that there was no case to answer. But freedom and his restored reputation were all that he had. He was penniless, he had no job, and he, Essie, and Lucy were living on charity. As he said some time later, it would take a year for him to recuperate physically. He was after all, a *gentle*man, quite unused to hard manual work and the enforced rigours of prison life. He would be unable to work for some time. His finances never recovered, and although that was not entirely due to his imprisonment, the latter had distinctly not helped his predicament.

Eugenia, of course, was worse off, at least in the short term. She was called to surrender on Tuesday, 15th May 1860, and placed at the bar for sentencing by Baron Channell. The press reports stated that 'she did not appear to exhibit any concern at her position', which was surprising, and was challenged a few days later by another letter to *The Times* from William Hitchcock. He, it was, who paid Eugenia's bail money after her conviction when her parents were found not to have been in court. He claimed to have been standing very close to Eugenia during sentencing, and said that she was in tears almost from the start. He added that he believed her to be innocent of the charge.

Baron Channell reminded Eugenia that she had been found guilty of the crime of perjury, but that the jury had recommended her to the fullest extent of mercy.[7] He said,

> ...it is lamentable to see a young child of your tender years standing at the bar of a court of criminal justice convicted of such an offence...but the jury were of the opinion that your position was in a great measure to be attributed to your want of moral and religious education. The crime of perjury is one of the most serious character, for it places in jeopardy not only the property but the liberty of Her Majesty's subjects... but I think in your case, you made a statement that was not true for a particular purpose...I will not enter into the question of whether your parents were justified in believing that statement, and in preferring the charges they subsequently did against Mr. Hatch...You are certainly not responsible for that proceeding, and there is good reason to believe that you are labouring under a want of education, both religious and moral, and have imbibed habits of untruthfulness which, if not checked, might lead to great mischief...

(Well actually, they *had* led to great mischief.) The judge continued,

> It is my impression that you told this story originally for the purpose of being taken away from Mr. Hatch's and not being sent back... afterwards you had been led to persist in it by interrogatories put to you by others...You did not scruple at last to make the same statement while under the sanction of an oath.

---

7    Baron Channell's address to Eugenia has been transposed into the first person.

He said that the court was desirous to deal with her as leniently as possible, so the sentence that would be passed upon her would be three weeks at Holloway, and thereafter she should be sent to a reformatory school. He went on to say, that he believed that a sentence had been proposed by her friends for her being 'placed in a position where she would receive a proper education'. If this was secured by sufficient guarantees which were, he believed, undertaken to be given, the latter part of the sentence would be a nominal one only. He had no powers to act judicially on the matter, which would have to be dealt with by the Secretary of State; the formal sentence he passed was three weeks imprisonment, followed by two years in a reformatory school – the lowest period allowed by the statute. If the guarantees he alluded to were not given, the original sentence would then be carried out. The prisoner, '...who did not evince any emotion', was then removed, and later taken to Holloway Gaol by Mr Weatherhead, the prison governor.

Less than three weeks later, on 4th June 1860, *The Times* announced:

> Mary Eugenia Plummer – we are requested to state that Her Majesty has been graciously pleased to grant a pardon to this child, on condition of her being placed in the care of a lady selected by her friends, and to add that she has been taken into that lady's care.

Henry John Hatch may have reflected ruefully on the ease with which Eugenia was able to get a free pardon, days after her conviction, and before she had even served her three weeks sentence in prison. The Home Secretary, acting in almost indecent haste, had taken the view that although Eugenia had been convicted, it was her parents, particularly her mother, who were primarily responsible, and thus a free pardon was appropriate. Mary Eugenia Plummer faded from public view, but not before extensive press reaction to the trial.

Many column inches were devoted to analyses of the two trials. It was a 'wonderful case', as *The Law Times* described it; unfortunately it was to be a wonder of the nine-day variety. But while it *was* still wonderful, the newspapers were determined to make the most of it. What they made of it differed widely, from a triumphal vindication of Henry Hatch (*The Morning Star*), a vilification of the Plummers and all their works (*The Morning Herald* and *The Daily Telegraph*), a criticism of both parties (*The Morning Chronicle* and *The Daily Telegraph*), a review of the facts with no comment on innocence or guilt (*The Times* and *The Daily News*), and a call for a Court of Criminal Appeal (*The Daily News*, *The Daily Telegraph* and *The Law Times*). Perhaps unsurprisingly, Henry did come in for some criticism. His actions in allowing Eugenia into his bed in the morning, in resigning his position, in appearing to abscond, even in asking the arresting officer what were the punishments for the offences were all considered to exhibit poor judgement.

*The Times* summed up the general view of the trial, having taken a day to consider what it was going to say (and having read everyone else's editorials of the previous day):

> We published yesterday the conclusion of a case regarded, by common consent, as one of the most extraordinary ever produced in a court of justice. Not only did the counsel on either side so describe it, but the very judge from the bench gave it the same character, and confessed himself incapable of presenting to the jury any theory including a determination of probabilities…Twice has the case been tried, and the decision was given first one way, and then another. Twice within the last week it has been stated and developed by rival advocates, and on each occasion the audience was carried away by the appeal.

The newspaper contented itself with a review of the history of the case, and an analysis of whether it was the Plummers or the Hatches who were more likely to have been telling the truth. It concluded that 'far less violence was done to reason and nature by absolving Mr Hatch than by believing Eugenia Plummer'. The newspaper made no comment on the perceived inadequacies of the law, or the need for an appeal court for criminal cases. *The Times* already had an established track record against a criminal appeal process. Considering that the editor had had the benefit of already reading the other leaders on the outcome of the case, it was a remarkably pedestrian offering.

*The Daily News* declined to comment on the probability either of Henry's innocence, or Eugenia's guilt, but was quite clear on the limitations of the law:

> Optimist lawyers and Home Secretaries may, perhaps, still maintain that no change in our present judicial system is required; but it will be difficult, after observing the course of the trial which closed yesterday, to persuade any man of common sense that the necessity of things does not require some authorized tribunal to reconsider verdicts in criminal cases.

Moreover, the 'Plummer' trial was really the 'Hatch' trial retried, so in fact, by suggesting that the indictment for perjury be made, the Home Secretary had effectively ordered a retrial. But such a circumstance would only work for cases where the evidence was of fact, so that a witness could be shown to have either answered true or false. Where the evidence was circumstantial, a trial for perjury against a witness or witnesses would be useless. Clearly, the law needed to be changed. *The Daily News* also pointed out that in a civil case, the parties 'should be placed in a position as like as possible to that which they originally occupied'. In the Hatch-Plummer case, the Hatches were unable to speak in the first trial, and Eugenia

Plummer, as defendant, could not speak in the second trial. The situation was untenable. Indeed, Eugenia Plummer was unable to respond to the evidence of Henry and Essie (and others) regarding exactly where in the garden, on the first afternoon, the alleged assaults took place, and was thus placed at a severe disadvantage. The newspaper observed,

> ...if the...spot where [Henry] played with the children [in the garden] on the 11th August, had been ascertained upon the first trial, the truth or falsity of the accusation made against him would have long ago been placed beyond question.

This point has already mentioned as having been overlooked by defence and prosecution teams in both trials. The newspaper continued,

> ...the conclusion is obvious...no time...should be lost...devising some means by which a new trial of the facts [in criminal trials] may be obtained.

*The Daily News* was firmly in favour of a Court of Criminal Appeal.

*The Morning Star* (the pre Communist Party newspaper), stated that the verdict had '...triumphantly vindicated the Rev. Henry John Hatch', and commented on Eugenia and her evidence as,

> ...utterly depraved...loathsome and baseless... endorsing the filthy details evolved by her own precociously prurient imagination... premature depravity [etc]...

The paper called for a Court of Criminal Appeal, finishing,

Thus ends the sad tale of wicked persecution and precocious crime; let us hope that our countrymen will show their appreciation of the moral which it inculcates, by demanding, without further delay, the accomplishment of the needful reform in the machinery of our criminal administration.

*The Morning Herald* called it, '...the horrible case of the wretched child Mary Eugenia Plummer', and in extravagant invective commented that,

In all the history of our courts of justice, and all the long and melancholy narratives of our criminal jurisprudence, we rejoice to say that no such case of revolting profligacy has ever before stained the annals even of trials for the utmost crime...[in] the case of this miserable child Plummer, and her equally miserable sister, the charges betrayed an amount of seething filth and ineffable iniquity for which even the patent conduct of the woman, their mother, could hardly account.

The paper went on to praise the open British legal system in providing justice, even in a case like this, and compared Henry's treatment as an Anglican cleric favourably with the 'tribunals to which Popish priests are amenable...' and the '...dungeons of St Angelo [Castel St Angelo in Rome] [which] tell no tales...' Having been somewhat carried away with Eugenia's iniquity, the paper, nevertheless, praised the extreme mercy requested for her by the jury. There was no call for an Appeal Court, but one interesting observation of the trial was made – not previously reported – that during the trial, Mrs Plummer had declared, on oath, that she was not in a state of drunkenness!

*The Morning Chronicle*, like *The Times*, provided a full account of the events leading up to the two trials and considered the evidence for and against. It commented in passing, '...unfortunately, there does not exist in Great Britain any Court of Criminal Appeal...', but made no plea for one. Mrs Plummer's behaviour in the witness box was mentioned, as was Henry's 'very serious imprudence', in allowing the children into his bed. After reflecting on what sort of life Eugenia could now look forward to, and hoping that Henry would soon be released from prison, the paper summed up the case thus: 'Turn which way we will, we see nothing but sin and misery in every act of this singular tragedy.'

Of all the London newspapers, it was *The Daily Telegraph* that provided the most comprehensive analysis of the case, while reining in, for the most part, its indignation. The editorial started,

> The trial of Eugenie Plummer will certainly become memorable in the history of English criminal jurisprudence as an illustration and a precedent. It establishes beyond all doubt the argument favourable to a Court of Criminal Appeal.

When this had last been suggested to Parliament, it said, the objection raised was that '...every indictment for felony might lead to a process longer and more irksome than a Chancery suit'. The newspaper then made the obvious comparison with civil law – which *did* have an appeal process:

> ...a question of property may be reasonably debated through all the Four Courts, and ultimately carried before the Lords [whereas] a question of life, death or personal liberty is at least of equivalent importance...

The paper did not question the '...supreme value [of the jury] in the sight of Englishmen', but asked whether twelve persons deliberating together and agreeing a verdict could be infallible:

If not, when degradation for life, if not a fearful expiation on the scaffold, must result from an adverse judgement, is it policy, is it justice to declare that no second investigation shall take place? When Dr Smethurst had been unjustly condemned, they clamoured at the doors of the Home Office, and were successful; but had Sir George Grey been Secretary of State instead of Sir Cornewall Lewis, the gallows might have read a lesson to the opponents of criminal appeal...

Sir George Grey had been Home Secretary on and off since 1846, and took the position over from Sir George Cornewall Lewis in 1861. He was in favour of the Separate prison system, and regarded prisoners as sinners needing redemption through religious instruction. He was a strong believer in capital punishment, and was 'unwilling to exercise the prerogative of mercy'. The paper had made a good point. Criminal justice in respect of unsafe verdicts should not function at the whim of whoever happened to be at the Home Office. Further: 'Sir Cornewall Lewis was...too perplexed to decide', recommending the course that was subsequently taken. The editorial continued,

> These indictments show that the actual state of legislation, instead of promoting celerity in the despatch of criminal business, tends to interminable confusion, and to perpetuate that frightful 'uncertainty of the law', which is unjust alike to prosecutors, prisoners, and to all classes of the public.

It went on to say that recent circumstances had shown the existence of two evils – the fact that a jury verdict can be reversed, and when the judge and jury had agreed in an 'unrighteous' verdict, the sole chance of justice lay in the isolated will and professional judgement of an official in Downing Street, counselled perhaps, by an officious lawyer or pedantic physician.

The paper concluded that there must be 'some intervening tribunal between the Old Bailey bench and the Old Bailey scaffold... penitentiary...hulks or penal settlement'.

Having provided convincing arguments in favour of a Court of Criminal Appeal, *The Daily Telegraph* addressed itself to the Hatch/Plummer case in detail:

> The Hatch affair...was surrounded with complications of inconsistency and ambiguity. They appear to have formed together a most eccentric group. Mr. Hatch was not entirely free from reproach; we don't like Mrs. Plummer; we don't like the children; indeed we like neither of the establishments. There is something ill-savoured about the story from its very beginning... [Most of all, however, the paper did not like the Plummers...] The Plummer people are living burlesques... the lady beats her servant over the head with a candle- stick; there is infinitely too much talk of brandy, sherry, bottled stout and porter; besides we are compelled to believe that hard swearing has been resorted to...

Henry, though, came in for some strong criticism too. In respect of the visits to his bed in the morning, he should not have 'adopt[ed] the maudlin suggestions of an ignorant mother...', indeed, '...the question still remains, whether he did not with his counsel do his worst to convict himself'. So the paper had a swipe at Serjeant Ballantine too, commenting later that he 'stifled...the testimony [in Henry's] favour...'

Whatever Henry's faults though, it was the Plummers who were in the firing line:

The second trial has handed the unhappy little girl Eugenie with the guilt of shameless, systematic, and unmitigated perjury. There was lying on the part of almost everyone who gave evidence for the defence… the Central Criminal Court…was a scene of such perjury as seldom or never has been exhibited before a British tribunal…

And on the subject of Eugenia,

It was not she, but her ignorant and ill-regulated parent who should have stood in the dock to stand trial, to receive a sentence, and to undergo an unsparing penalty…We trust that…this hapless child…the victim of a corrupt education, should be placed in a reformatory, and removed from the pernicious influence of an abandoned home…

*The Daily Telegraph* was clear that a 'vindictive punishment' for Eugenia was not appropriate, although

Charity would suggest that a nursery whipping and a week's conversation with a chaplain or with some parent who loved her offspring, would suffice for the correction of this child, morally desolate in the midst of her own family…

On Mrs Plummer, however, the paper was unmerciful:

If [Eugenia's] conviction be just, then Mrs. Plummer ought to be indicted by Mr. Hatch or his friends as a ringleader in an atrocious conspiracy. For her, there can be no compassion… Justice will not be satisfied, therefore, until that miserable woman has been put upon her trial, to answer for her own perjury.

After *The Daily Telegraph's* ringing condemnation of the Plummers, the final word on the trial ought to be given to *The Law Times* in order to assess the view of the legal establishment. Unsurprisingly, it was four-square behind the call for a court of criminal appeal: '...the hostility even of Sir Cornewall Lewis himself must yield to the arguments...' The editorial went on to condemn the weakness of the process followed in the Hatch case:

> Taking the precedent, henceforth...the prisoner and prosecutor will change places...evidence [will be] admissible to one [jury] and inadmissible to the other. This will be a criminal appeal in fact, only it will want the elements of justice and fair dealing...such a form of appeal is fraught with defects and mischiefs...

*The Law Times* went on to say that the evidence did not justify the conviction in the first trial:

> [The] contradictions and improbabilities even then were so many and monstrous, that the counsel for the defence were entirely justified in their conclusion that the case had broken down, and that they were not required to call witnesses, and so to give the prosecution the incalculable advantages of a reply...

So, Serjeant Ballantine had been right, and the jury were wrong. The paper went on,

> It is precisely such a case, wherein the jury convict on evidence not satisfactory to men more accustomed to measure its value, that needs a rehearing.

Having moved into the dangerous territory of criticizing trial by jury when the result is not 'correct', the newspaper then went on to congratulate itself on having declared, following the trials, that both the Smethurst and Hatch convictions were '...not justified by the evidence...' The important point was then made in the distinction between *belief* and *proof*, and the fact not whether the convicts were guilty or innocent, but whether they had been '...sufficiently proved guilty'. Finally, *The Law Times* made the observation,

> Here were two cases, occurring within a few months, of wrongful convictions confessed and proved. If two have been detected, how many more must there be wherein poverty and friendlessness find no vindication...

The Legislature was called upon to provide 'some means for the revision of errors of juries in the criminal courts'.

Although the newspaper reports were by no means unanimous in the call for a Court of Criminal Appeal, both *The Daily Telegraph* and *The Law Times* put forward strong arguments in favour of one. It would be nice to think that something good would come out of all of Henry Hatch's suffering and humiliation (which was sadly not over, but more of that later), his 191 days of unjust confinement, and the living hell of the previous two months before that. It was not to be. In civil cases, an appeal could be sought for cases even involving trifling sums. In cases of felony involving punishments of imprisonment or death, there was no appeal other than to the Home Secretary for a free pardon; and this was only granted under very exceptional circumstances as the Smethurst and Hatch cases had shown.

Parliament was aware of this anomaly, and starting in 1844, a number of bills for the formation of a Court of Criminal Appeal had been debated (and lost), the last one being as recently as February 1860. On that occasion, Sir George Cornewall Lewis had argued forcefully against the motion, which was again defeated. His speech covered three and a half columns of newsprint reportage. Some of his objections: a) mistrials happened very, very rarely, b) if the judge was unhappy with the verdict, he could refer it to the Home Secretary for a free pardon, c) most of the 'civilized' world did not have a criminal appeal system (in fact the majority seemed not even to have trial by jury), d) the process would be very expensive – and would inevitably have to be supported from public funds, e) it would be very difficult to assemble all the prosecution witnesses and evidence again for a second trial, f) it would be very time-consuming and the 'execution' of justice (where the appeal failed) would be delayed many months, thus diluting the deterrent effect, g) where criminal appeal *was* currently allowed, (for misdemeanours), it was hardly ever sought – out of 37,220 convictions for vagrancy, offences against the game laws or malicious trespass in England and Wales in 1858, only 26 individuals sought an appeal, h) the bill in question called for a right of appeal only by the defendant, whereas in civil law *either* the defendant *or* the plaintiff could appeal, i) it could make juries more likely to convict on doubtful evidence, since an appeal could always reverse the decision, and the second jury would be no more infallible than the first, j) more judges would be needed to deal with the extra cases; and so on. And he said all this two weeks before turning down Henry Hatch's appeal for a Royal Pardon.

*The Times* had an editorial on the debate, and once more some collusion is detected between Sir George Cornewall Lewis, and the editor John Thadeus Delane. As recently as 1853, the newspaper had been in favour of a criminal appeal process. Now, however, *The Times* was reaffirming, quite forcefully, what Sir George had said in the House, referring to the 'excellent arguments' of that gentleman. 'Our Houses of Legislature', it started, 'are generally understood to sit and deliberate in the interests of society, and not for the encouragement of offenders'. It dismissed the call for a criminal appeal process as a 'crotchet', (Crotchet – a whimsical fancy;

a perverse conceit; a peculiar notion on some point – usually considered unimportant – held by an individual in opposition to common opinion (OED)). It dismissed those who did favour such a move, as persons excited by, and sympathetic to, the criminal fraternity. Familiar arguments were presented. An experienced barrister, Mr Denman, claimed in the House that in many years of practice he had never seen anyone convicted whom he regarded as innocent, whereas many dozens had been cleared of whose guilt he had no doubt. The editorial finished by stating,

> A criminal appeal court would not aid innocent men; it would give fresh chances to guilty men; it would take away the promptitude of punishment, which now often deters hesitating men, and it would throw intolerable difficulties in the way of protecting honest men. Let us hear no more of it.

Well, they did hear more of it. Between 1844, and the passing of the Criminal Appeal Act of 1907, the issue was debated unsuccessfully in Parliament more than thirty times. However, as far as the Legislature of the 1860s was concerned, the law was already sufficiently biased in favour of the criminal, and did not require alteration any further in that direction.

One further item of discussion emerged following a letter to *The Times* from a Mr Pitt Taylor. He pointed out that many of the shortcomings in the Hatch and Plummer trials could have been avoided if the defendants had been allowed to give evidence on their own behalves. Cross-examination of the defendant would have allowed the rigorous testing of the evidence. *The Law Times* jumped on this idea, pointing out that it certainly used to hold the same view, but subsequently the problem it could not reconcile, was that if the defendant *declined* to give evidence on their own behalf, it would always 'tell against him terribly' in the minds of the judge and jury.

And if he did appear, there would always be the danger that he would convict himself. The same comments would apply to the defendant's wife, were she to refuse to testify on behalf of her husband. *The Law Times* suggested instead, that the lesson of the Hatch case was that judges and juries should not convict where there was reasonable doubt, and *never* convict on the basis of the evidence of one witness only. Surprisingly, there was no other direct comment on this point in any of the press stories. It certainly seems astonishing to a modern mind, that anyone in the dock be disallowed from speaking in his or her own defence. This anomaly too had to wait a long time before it was resolved by the Criminal Evidence Act of 1898.

Whether or not Henry's friends were exercised about the need for a criminal appeal court, or of the right of the defendant to give evidence, is not known. If they were in favour, any campaigning would have to wait until the legal bills of the case against Eugenia Plummer were settled. The petition to the Queen, and the case against Walters Freake Pratt had cost more than £400; the case against Eugenia Plummer cost 'upwards of £700', unsurprising for a case that had lasted five days in the Central Criminal Court. Following the publication of the Hatch manifesto in *The Times* on the 12th April 1860, the committee placed further advertisements in that newspaper between May and July, combining a specific appeal for funds with a listing of those who had already contributed. The first one started in messianic tone:

> Compensation to the Rev. Henry John Hatch – Truth is great, and has at last prevailed; while the light was shut out error had its temporary triumph, but an all-disposing Providence watches over innocence, and Mr. Hatch's prediction, that his would one day be established, has proved to be prophetic.

It continued, in more moderate language, to remind everyone that Eugenia's conviction constituted a virtual acquittal for Henry, who had spent five months in prison (it was actually more than six months altogether), and was now penniless. Reference was made to documentary evidence in the possession of the committee, not admissible in law, purporting to prove his innocence. Evidence was hinted at regarding a letter to the Bishop of London from a lady, '...the head of a collegiate establishment in Melbourne, Australia, a person wholly unacquainted with Mr Hatch...', a letter which, along with other proofs, would 'remove even the last faint shadow of a doubt of Mr. Hatch's innocence'. Henry had spent time in New South Wales fifteen years previously, but the fact that he was unknown to this mysterious lady suggests that she might have had evidence relating to the Plummers – possibly some previously unknown misdemeanour on the part of Eugenia.

The contributions to the appeals were many and varied: A.S. contributed one shilling and sixpence; several clergymen contributed five shillings each; 'A tribute of sympathy from a lady' was five shillings; a Kentish curate contributed ten shillings; 'A friend to truth and justice' contributed one pound; many people contributed a guinea; 'A friend to the oppressed' contributed five pounds; the Bishop of Winchester contributed twenty-five pounds and The Earl of Dudley contributed one hundred pounds. Seventy-seven clergymen and four bishops gave money to the cause, and the total published amount collected was more than six hundred and eighty-two pounds. Notable among the contributors were four eminent lawyers from Australia, of whom two were Edward Wise's sons and the third, his son-in-law. These were people, previously mentioned, whom Henry knew during his time in New South Wales.

The cost of Henry's legal actions had been underwritten by the generous British (and Australian) public. More than 250 people had contributed, and Henry, at least on that account, had no debts. He commented later that, of the funds collected, he personally, received no more than £5. Probably a private benefactor or benefactors provided the family with the means for his convalescence. In April 1861, Henry, Essie and Lucy were living in St Paul's Road Lambeth, near Crystal Palace, with a live-in servant, so even with their charitable status they were not too badly off.

The issue that Henry had to contend with was what to do next. He had lost his job, his only means of support. His reputation was somewhat rescued as a consequence of Eugenia's conviction, although he had been subject to considerable criticism for his questionable judgement. Mainly though, he had spent 191 days in prison for something he did not do. The architects of his misfortune were the Plummers, and *The Daily Telegraph* had suggested in its editorial that Mrs Plummer, at least, should be indicted for perjury and/or conspiracy. The Plummers had money; Thomas Plummer was a 'gentleman of fortune', and Eugenia was an heiress to £15,000, so if Henry Hatch was looking for financial compensation, the Plummers would seem to have been the obvious target. The fact that Eugenia had received the Royal Pardon, so soon after her conviction, makes it clear that in the view of the Establishment she was largely innocent. But if she were innocent, then one or other or both of her parents must be guilty. If they were guilty, then surely an action against them would succeed. It is odd, therefore, that it was not the Plummers, but James Lewis and his firm Lewis and Lewis that Henry decided to sue for damages. James Lewis was Henry's solicitor during his first trial.

There were, however, good reasons for this choice. How could any action *prove* that the Plummers had conspired to contrive the allegations against Henry for which he was convicted? Eugenia had been found guilty, so she was a convicted perjurer, but she was a child without financial resources. In any case, the call for extreme mercy in her sentencing by her jury, made it clear that they regarded her more as victim than the prime mover in the case. A further action against her – even if it were possible to move to sequester her anticipated legacy – would be unlikely to garner public sympathy. A jury might well find in her favour in such an event.

On what basis could an action be brought against Caroline Plummer? She had been shown in court to have been untruthful on a number of matters, and there were many inconsistencies and contradictions between her evidence and that of Eugenia and Stephana (and the letter written to the Bishop of Winchester by the Plummers); but Henry's legal team decided that these were not sufficiently strong grounds for a further action. The fact that Eugenia had been convicted of perjury proved only that she, and by implication her sister, had been lying. Mrs Plummer might simply have believed innocently (or naively) what they told her, and have become genuinely confused regarding the exact sequence of events. Her intoxication in the witness box would only have contributed to her confusion. They took the view that it would be very difficult to *prove* that she had conspired with Eugenia and Stephana unless one of them turned Queen's evidence, and that was remotely unlikely. On the other hand, there was no doubt that Henry's defence had been badly mishandled. Serjeant Ballantine had decided not to present material defence witnesses and *The Law Times* and others had sought to explain why, and approved of his decision. Ballantine had said that the prosecution counsel during Henry's trial had whispered to him that Henry had made a confession, but that he had made up his mind not to call witnesses *before* the trial had started. Ballantine's reasons had never been properly investigated or explained. As Henry's defence counsel, he received his brief from Henry's solicitors, Lewis and Lewis.

The basis of the new action was that their negligence and mismanagement had failed to provide Serjeant Ballantine with adequate information with which to construct a strong defence case. He had been given a very poor brief. The logic was straightforward. Henry had effectively been found innocent by two tribunals. First, by the statement of his original trial jury following publication of his petition to the Queen; secondly, by the jury in Eugenia's trial. Whatever Serjeant Ballantine had decided to do, he could not have called Henry or Essie as witnesses. But Henry's written material *could* have been used to lead the questioning of Martha Howe, Mrs Dillon and the two servants, Mary and Ellen, to bring out in court most, if not all, of Henry's evidence. For example, the point was made again and again, that what happened in the Hatches' bed in the mornings could only be sworn to by Eugenia, Henry and Essie. But since it was the servant Mary's job to get Eugenia up in the morning and get her washed and dressed, she (Mary) must have been able to give evidence of what side of the bed Eugenia was accustomed to occupy (Henry's or Essie's), and whether the child was only under the counterpane or in the bed. Similarly, other parts of Henry's evidence could have been aired, indirectly, in court.

If Eugenia was guilty, she must have lied about what she claimed Henry did to her. If she lied, then Henry must have been innocent. If he was innocent, then the defence in his trial must have been mismanaged.

Serjeant Ballantine had decided not to call witnesses for several reasons. It seemed to him that Henry had already incriminated himself by his various actions, and Essie's letter to the Plummers could be interpreted as acknowledging his guilt. He heard the rumour in court that Henry had made a confession. Then, after having heard the prosecution evidence, he decided that their case had broken down – following the major discrepancies between the evidence of Eugenia and her mother. Ballantine determined to prevent the prosecution from gaining any benefit from cross-examining his defence witnesses by sticking to his original strategy of calling character witnesses only. As a result, he had the benefit of having the last word in court.

The nub of the issue though, was the quality of the brief provided by the Lewises to Serjeant Ballantine. Henry had incriminated himself; but his notes of explanation together with sworn witness statements, should have been able to confirm his innocence as they had done following the petition to the Queen, and the verdict in Eugenia's trial. The Lewises had interviewed Henry in prison, and subsequently collected from him the written notes they had asked him to compile. They should then have examined Henry's witnesses to establish whether they could confirm the truth, or otherwise, of Henry's version of events. All of this material should have been organized into a brief for Serjeant Ballantine. When it was received by the Serjeant, the brief was found to be of no material benefit. If it was of no use in constructing a strong defence case, then the fault was quite clear: it was down to Lewis and Lewis.

When Henry was first arrested, Essie had contacted the firm of Lewis and Lewis on the basis that she had seen their names frequently in the pages of *The Times* in the reports of various court proceedings. It should have been a good choice. James Graham Lewis was from a Jewish family who had come to England from the Netherlands. In 1829 he established himself as a solicitor at 10 Ely Place, and when in 1834 his brother George Hamilton Coleman Lewis joined him in partnership, the firm became Lewis and Lewis. George Lewis, 'Uncle George', specialized in bankruptcy law, whereas James Lewis concentrated on criminal law. James Lewis was said to be the model for the lawyer, Mr Jaggers, in Dickens' *Great Expectations*. James Lewis' second son, George Henry Lewis, born in 1833, articled to his father in 1850, admitted to practice in 1857, and becoming a partner in 1858, was also a solicitor. George's youngest brother, the confusingly named Louis Lewis was a solicitor's clerk, probably also employed in the firm (Louis Lewis of Lewis and Lewis). Another brother, Frederick Henry Lewis, was a barrister at law, not employed by the firm but frequently retained by them. It was James Lewis, the senior partner, whom Essie had visited, and it was he who represented Henry as his solicitor, with his son Frederick Lewis retained as a junior barrister in court during Henry's trial.

James' son, George Lewis, who was twenty-four years old at the time of the trial, may or may not have participated in the Hatch case. He was called as a defence witness in the action against his father, but it is not clear how much he was involved in Henry's case. Nevertheless, he was to have a brilliant career. In later life, it was said of him that his 'knowledge of the law was not profound, but he was cool, keen and wily in court'. He was also 'meticulous in interviewing his witnesses before they testified', (ODNB), something which was clearly not done with Henry Hatch's witnesses. Years later, George Lewis became acquainted with the Prince of Wales and advised him over the Mordaunt divorce case – in which Serjeant Ballantine also acted. He was involved in a number of celebrated cases, including the Tranby Croft scandal over cheating at a game of Baccarat, and he represented Lord Alfred Douglas – at the request of Oscar Wilde – in a blackmail case. George Lewis subsequently campaigned against injustices in the criminal justice system including the Edalji case, an Indian solicitor who was imprisoned on spurious evidence, and he represented Adolphe Beck, who was famously convicted on the basis of a wrong identification. George Lewis was to become very much in favour of a criminal appeal court, as well as the right of the defendant and his wife to give evidence in criminal cases. In 1892, he was knighted and ten years later he became a baronet. He was the most famous solicitor in England when he died in 1911.

All of this was a long time in the future. George Lewis had only been admitted to practice two years before the Hatch trial; it was his father, James Lewis, who managed Henry Hatch's defence. It may be, though, that George Lewis' subsequent meticulousness in interviewing witnesses, his interests in injustices in the criminal court system, and his support for a criminal appeal court and the right of the defendant and his wife to give evidence owed much to the Hatch case…

The action against Lewis and Lewis was going to be expensive, and this time there was no question of seeking public subscription. Evidently, Henry's benefactors decided to put up the money for the case. If Henry won, he could expect to get compensation plus costs. If he lost, his benefactors would have to pay all costs. Having reviewed the evidence, and being advised by an 'eminent counsel', they decided that the risk was worth it. And it was risky. No one had previously attempted to sue their defence attorneys for negligence in a criminal defence case. Nevertheless, the team decided to aim high; the damages sought were £5,000, and the Bishop of Winchester and the Home Secretary were to be called to attend as witnesses for the plaintiff.

The case was due to be heard on 1ˢᵗ February 1861 in the Court of Exchequer, Westminster, before the Lord Chief Baron, Sir Frederick Pollock, in front of a special jury requested by the defendants. Henry John Hatch was the plaintiff, and 'Lewis and Others' (Lewis and Lewis) were the defendants.

Sir Frederick Pollock was seventy-eight years old at the time, and had been Lord Chief Baron for seventeen years. Serjeant Ballantine had a great regard for him. They lived opposite each other in Serjeant's Inn and he held him in 'much affectionate regard'. Pollock was 'upright and honourable…no stain ever found itself on his escutcheon'. He possessed 'firmness and decision [he was] solemn in manner…sometimes hasty [but] never harsh or discourteous'. In Ballantine's view, only Charles Dickens was a better after-dinner speaker. Elsewhere, the Lord Chief Baron was described as 'indefatigable, if sometimes sleepy' on the bench (ODNB). And although he was said to have hardly suffered a day's illness, he almost immediately stopped the case due to his indisposition. It was deferred for a week, and then for a further three months, finally recommencing on Friday, 10ᵗʰ May 1861.

A formidable team had been assembled to defend the Lewises. Serjeant Shee had led the unsuccessful defence of Eugenia Plummer in her trial. Mr Lush, QC, was also on the team. Mr Robert Lush (later, Sir Robert) had been called to the bar in 1840, and was to become a Queen's Bench judge in 1865. Lastly, there was Mr Charles Pollock (later Sir Charles), who happened to be the son of the Lord Chief Baron, the judge trying the case! Charles Pollock was to become a QC in 1866, and was raised to the Exchequer Bench in 1873 upon the retirement of Baron Channell.

The prosecution was led by Mr Montague Chambers, QC, who had more than twenty years experience before the bar. He was assisted by Mr Richard Garth, (Lord of the Manor of Morden, next door to Sutton). Mr Garth had been called to the bar in 1847, and as Sir Richard Garth was to become the chief justice of Bengal in 1875. Mr Gordon Allan completed the prosecution team.

The case continued over four days, and since much of it was a reiteration of evidence in the Hatch and Plummer cases, the entire press report was compressed into barely more than a column of newsprint. The material was summarized, and it was not clear what evidence was for the defence and what the prosecution. The defence and prosecution counsel summing up speeches were omitted, and what was printed of the judge's summing up seemed to be limited and biased. Fortunately, a report of the trial exists in a legal archive. Although this too, is much compressed and summarized, it does contain the essential legal arguments together with some material omitted from the press reports. Both sources have been used to assemble an account of the trial.

The press reports were heavily summarized, but the Lord Chief Baron could allow himself no such luxury. At the commencement of the case in February, he had stated,

I came here expressly to discharge the ordinary duties of a judge, to which I believed I was reasonably competent, but I must fairly tell you that I am physically incapable to take even the notes that would be required in a case of so much labour…

In view of this, the plaintiff and the defendants agreed to share the cost of a short-hand writer to take the evidence and provide the judge, at the end of each day, with a manuscript of the evidence taken. The cost came to £33 14s 8d. The judge recognized that it would be a long case, and rightly so, as he commented,

I quite agree that it is a question of considerable importance for the sake of the public and the profession, for the sake of the innocent and the guilty; it is a case which should be tried with the greatest patience and attention, and not disposed of in a summary way by any short view of the case.

Henry was to remember those words…

The case started with a reiteration of the events leading up to the magistrates' hearing – Henry's first appearance in court. The senior partner, Mr James Lewis, (hereafter, Mr Lewis) had agreed to represent Henry Hatch. He told Essie, having seen the letter from the bishop outlining the specific charges against Henry (and before the magistrates' hearing), that the case would have to go to trial. Mr Lewis promised to attend the court and to 'examine [Henry's] witnesses before the case came on'. In the event, he arrived late, and had to go straightway before the magistrates, who committed Henry for trial. Lucy, Mrs Dillon, and the two servants were present and gave evidence. Of this evidence, that given by Mrs Dillon and the two servants was to 'collateral matters [only]'. Only Lucy's evidence was considered to be of relevance, since she was present during the garden incident. Lucy also confirmed that Eugenia had been in Henry's bed in the morning when he was still in it. The magistrates determined to send Henry for trial, and in the absence of bail he was sent in the meantime to Horsemonger Lane Gaol. Mr Lewis was retained to defend him, and obtained a copy of the depositions made at the magistrates' hearing. He also received Henry's notes, 'a long statement', the key points of which were summarized thus:

> Eugenia had said that Mr. and Mrs. [Brighton] used to have [her] in their bed...

> We [Henry and the children] were rarely, if ever, in the garden without some others of the party, and mostly Mrs. Hatch; Miss Howe's window and Mrs. Dillon's, overlooked the garden...

> I used to go up...to wash my hands...when Lucy cried kiss me and Eugenie used to call out 'come into me too, Mr. Hatch'...at this time the doors were always wide open...

> Lucy Hatch can state that she was always in my room as I finished dressing, and that she was in the habit of dropping money, &c, into my pockets...

This summary was stated to be of the most material portions of Henry's notes; it did not state 'how far the charges were false', and implied that Eugenia had been in the bed when he was in it. This then was the 'significant' part of Henry's statement, prepared when he was in prison during the two weeks between the magistrates' hearing and his trial.

At this point, it is appropriate to cite some evidence from Henry himself that might or might not have been explicitly given in the action against the Lewises. Given the outcome and subsequent press comment, it was probably *not* included. Months later, Henry wrote to *The Times* – in response to a hostile editorial on the Hatch case – and among other things, revealed that after he had handed Mr Lewis the notes that he had made in prison about the case, they were given, 'uncorrected and un-commented upon', to a clerk to copy as Henry's brief. The clerk was unable to read much of Henry's writing (it was November, and prisons were not noted for their comfortable heating arrangements), and those parts were omitted; other parts, the clerk misunderstood. In Henry's words:

> My notes, poor as they were originally, were rendered absolute nonsense as copied by the said clerk. The blanks were never filled up, and remain blanks to this day, nor were the errors corrected, but in their mutilated state were handed to Mr. Serjeant Ballantine...

Comparing Henry's 'notes', with the material in the petition to the Queen, it is clear that the Lewises' clerk did indeed mutilate and/or misunderstand what Henry had written, which must have been much more comprehensive. Unfortunately, the last mentioned item about Lucy being in the habit of dropping money and other things in Henry's pocket, could have weighed heavily with both Serjeant Ballantine and the Lewises in consideration of Eugenia's first charge. That was, it will be remembered, that Henry caused her to put her hand into his pocket. A brief including the above material was prepared by the Lewises and given to Serjeant Ballantine. Given the so-called key points upon which that brief was constructed, the Serjeant's decision not to call defence witnesses looks even less inexplicable.

Continuing with the evidence, the Lewises did not examine the witnesses mentioned in Henry's brief – Lucy, Mrs Dillon, Martha Howe, the servants etc. Mr Lewis had said that Mrs Hatch was most anxious to have witnesses called, but that

Serjeant Ballantine was 'averse to that course being adopted'. This was the Serjeant's view initially, and was strengthened after he had read the brief, because he felt it was most important to get the last word. The witnesses were in attendance during the trial, but were not called. Serjeant Ballantine adhered to his original course of action after hearing the prosecution case, and 'the plaintiff [Henry] did not insist upon it, but submitted to his counsel's judgement'.

Details of Henry's trial and conviction, the petition to the Queen which was rejected by the Home Secretary, and the indictment of Eugenia for perjury and her conviction were read out. The latter was summarized thus:

> In April 1860, the girl Eugenie was indicted for perjury, on assignments, on such of which, as went to the substance of the charges, she could only be directly contradicted by the plaintiff himself; and, on such as related to collateral circumstances, chiefly by himself or his wife, partly confirmed by other witnesses...on this indictment, however, the girl was convicted.

(This court record, having been compiled and summarized by a lawyer, is saying that in fact, even in Eugenia's trial, the substantive evidence was only really Henry's word against Eugenia's. But this, then, must also have been true for Henry's trial. It was Eugenia's word against his – and his was not heard.)

The prosecution decided not to press the mishandling of the magistrates' trial (Mr Lewis arriving late and failing to examine the witnesses beforehand). The case against Lewis and Lewis was that they had not examined the inmates of the house who could bear witness in Henry's favour, and had not presented this material to Serjeant Ballantine to enable him to 'form a proper judgement as to the propriety of calling them'. Further, that it would have been proper to call them as witnesses, and that that is what counsel would have done, had their evidence been laid before him.

Henry, Essie and the other witnesses, Mrs Dillon, Martha Howe and the two servants were called and gave their evidence. Essie said that on the occasion of the Plummer trial, Mr Lewis told her that he had been telling everyone that it was Serjeant Ballantine's fault that defence witnesses were not called for Henry. Lucy's evidence was read out in deference to her age. It was pointed out that Henry and Essie could not have given evidence in the first trial, and that the 'significant' witness evidence was only in respect of the events in the garden and the fact of the door to Eugenia's room being open or closed.

Mr Chambers called Samuel T Keene, the foreman of Henry's trial jury. Mr Chambers proposed to ask him, having heard the evidence just presented by the witnesses, what his verdict would have been at the original trial. The Lord Chief Baron elected to consult his brother barons. Who's opinions he sought were not stated, but Barons Bramwell and Channell, at least, were elsewhere in the building on that day. Having taken advice, he ruled that the question could not be put. Mr Chambers then said that they were entitled to call the eleven jurymen who had signed the petition to the Secretary of State, and ask them the same question. The judge ruled that only the present jury were entitled to judge the testimony of the witnesses. Mr Chambers pressed the point. He wished to show that a petition had been presented to the Home Secretary, and he wished to ask him why a pardon had not been recommended and what his grounds for the decision were. Sir George Cornewall Lewis was in attendance in anticipation of being called. Again the Lord Chief Baron retired to consult his brother Barons, but again ruled that the question could not be put,

> ...even assuming that the Home Secretary would not, as probably he would, object to answer the question on the grounds of public policy...

In any case, his view could not affect the current action.

By declining to allow Henry's trial jury to give evidence, the judge had seriously undermined the prosecution case. Sir George Cornewall Lewis might have declined on grounds of 'public policy', to explain why he had denied the petition. Henry's defence team must have already spoken to him, and would have been unlikely to call him as a witness if he was going to refuse to answer their questions. However, since his decision was made after the very comprehensive petition to the Queen was presented to him, the actions or inactions of Lewis and Lewis in the first trial were hardly relevant to his decision. This may be the view that the judge took. The jury, on the other hand, would have affirmed in the strongest possible way that had the proper evidence been presented to them at the trial – as subsequently seen only in the petition – then they would have found Henry to be innocent. Serjeant Ballantine's defence had been based on his brief; having read the brief he elected to call no material witnesses, but the evidence of the jury would have confirmed a different result had he called witnesses. It is noteworthy, that Serjeant Ballantine himself was not called as a witness for the prosecution.

Serjeant Ballantine's clerk was, however, called, and proved that the Serjeant was retained on the 23rd November 1859 (seven days before Henry's trial), the brief was delivered on the 26th November, and there was a consultation on 29th November. This closed the case for the prosecution.

Serjeant Shee opened the defence case with a brief summary of the events leading up to Henry's trial and the outcome. The plaintiff was, he said, of the highest character,

> …and was well known to…the religious and benevolent societies of the metropolis for having taken a very active part in the concerns which those societies had in view…

He then outlined the details of the first trial and its outcome (How sick Henry must have been, of hearing this repeated endlessly). Serjeant Shee continued,

> By the conviction he was inevitably ruined, unless he should succeed in satisfying the Crown, as he had satisfied the country by the trial and conviction of the elder of the two girls for perjury, of his innocence... The plaintiff was ruined, and left with a very remote chance of re-establishing himself, unless he succeeded in obtaining a verdict in the case.

Serjeant Shee went on,

> In November 1860, and for the first time, he chose to impute to the defendant a charge of neglect as his professional advisor. No charge could be imagined more painful to meet, or more damaging to the reputation of a professional man...

Mr Lewis, had practised criminal law for 'the whole of his life', and had for twenty-seven years been the clerk of indictments on the Midland Circuit. Serjeant Shee continued,

> The object of the present action [is] to take money out of [Mr Lewis'] pocket and put it in the plaintiff's, and thereby, if possible, patch up the defects in his unfortunately damaged character.

Then, having said previously that he did not wish to 'tax the plaintiff with guilt or throw the slightest suspicion on his conduct', Serjeant Shee concluded by saying,

> If the plaintiff [Henry] did not commit the conduct imputed to him, still it must be admitted that he had

been guilty of the grossest indiscretion, for which he ought to bear the consequences, and not seek to throw them upon the defendants.

(That was not really the point. Whether Henry had been indiscreet or not – and he had – the fact that his defence was bungled was four-square down to the Lewises.)

Mr Lewis was now called. He stated that on Sunday, 13th November 1859 (the day after Henry had been arrested), Mrs Hatch and Lucy called upon him at his house in Euston Square and asked him to represent her husband the next day at the Wandsworth Magistrates' court. She gave him a copy of the letter from the Bishop of Winchester detailing the charges against Henry, together with a copy of the letter she had written to the Plummers 'directly implying the guilt of her husband'. Mr Lewis had said to Essie, 'Surely in writing this letter, you never intended to suggest your husband is guilty?' Essie had answered, 'No.' He said that he dismissed the relevance of Essie's letter when she told him that her husband was unaware of its being sent. He then examined Lucy, who assured him that Mr Hatch had never done anything wrong to the little girls. He agreed to represent Henry in the morning, for which his fee would be three guineas, and asked Essie to have the witnesses in attendance and to have a complete statement ready from her husband. The next day he did attend and received a statement from Henry, arriving too late to examine the witnesses. Henry was sent for trial, but was unable to raise bail. Then, referring to his diary, Mr Lewis stated that he visited Henry in prison on 15th, 17th and 21st November. He stated that during the visit of the 21st November, he spent half an hour with Henry going into all matters very fully, even making a partial sketch of the residence. (Subsequently, Henry insisted that they never exchanged one word about the details of the charges). He engaged a private detective, Mr Brennan, currently an agent to an inspector of prisons, to make enquiries about the

Plummers. Brennan was to be paid £5 for this service. Mr Lewis denied that he had ever asked Mrs Hatch about the guilt or innocence of her husband. He was then cross-examined, and conceded that his first visit to Henry in prison had been on the 21st November and he made only one other visit. He said that before the brief was delivered, he had a conference with Serjeant Ballantine at Westminster Hall, which resulted in a decision not to call witnesses except to character. Henry Hatch had said, '[I] must be guided by counsel,' on that question. Some notes from Henry to his counsel during his trial were presented to show that he did not insist that witnesses were called. (Ballantine may well have decided *before* he received the brief not to call witnesses. But that only reinforced the inadequacy of the brief when it was delivered, since in reading Henry's evidence Ballantine did not change his mind.)

Serjeant Ballantine was now called (for the defence). He had been a barrister for twenty-five years. He received a brief from Mr Lewis, and they had a consultation mainly 'as to the expediency of calling witnesses for the defence'. He (Ballantine) was strongly of the opinion that witnesses should not be called. Serjeant Shee then asked him to give his reasons. Serjeant Ballantine answered,

> Every counsel, of course, forms his reasons, and I consider these reasons Mr Hatch's property, even now. If Mr. Hatch desires it, I will give them.

Mr Chambers responded that certainly, Mr Hatch did not. (Undoubtedly, Ballantine had the very highest ethical code. As a defence witness, he could have seriously damaged the prosecution case at this point; he could have said that he had been told in court during Henry's trial that Henry had made a confession. The fact that he did not do so is infinitely to his credit.) Serjeant Ballantine went on to say that he knew the witnesses were in attendance, and that after he had cross-examined Eugenia and Stephana he decided not to call them. He added that in every case in which he was engaged, he took upon himself the responsibility whether or not to call witnesses; the Lord Chief Baron observed that in all cases, counsel were responsible for calling or not calling witnesses. Serjeant Ballantine then offered to state the impression he had formed at the conclusion of the trial, but Mr Chambers objected to him doing so.

It was proposed to call Mr Coulson Robinson, the junior counsel at the trial, but the judge thought it unnecessary to do so.

Mr Lewis was then recalled and said that,

> Out of the £75 [I] received for defending Hatch, [I] paid £44 out of pocket, and gave £5 towards a subscription for him, on account of his wife's unhappy situation.

(What he means here is that his costs were £44. The balance of £31 was his profit. By mentioning the £5 subscription – which does not appear in the published lists – he suggests that he was sympathetic to Henry's plight).

Mr George Lewis, 'Uncle George', James Lewis' brother and partner, was next called. He stated that he had visited Henry in prison the day after his committal in order to get the names of anyone who could stand bail. He also wanted Henry to make an 'elaborate statement', but reported that Henry had said that he wanted to see the depositions before doing so.

George Lewis junior, James Lewis' son, was called and asked to prove that his father had attended 'exclusively to the Hatch case'.

Mr Brennan, the private detective, was called to prove that he also visited Henry in prison, and swore, 'At Mr. Lewis's request, [I was to] spare no expense, nor leave a stone unturned'.

An attorney was called to prove that it was the 'duty and practice of attorneys retained for a prisoner to examine witnesses, and present their "proofs" to counsel'. However, he had 'never been engaged in criminal cases, and could only speak generally as to civil cases'. (If that were the case, one wonders why *he* was called, rather than call someone who *had* experience of criminal cases.)

Finally, the notes of the prosecution evidence in the first trial were read and this closed the case for the defence.

Mr Chambers, summing up for the prosecution, stated that the defendants had been 'wanting in due diligence, having failed in their duty to collect and arrange their evidence and examine the witnesses. Had they done this and laid the evidence before counsel, Serjeant Ballantine would have called witnesses and the trial jury would have acquitted Henry Hatch.

The basis of Serjeant Shee's case for the defence was that the current jury must be assured of Henry's innocence if they found for the plaintiff (Henry Hatch). It is interesting to note that Serjeant Shee adopted this slightly spurious tack, presumably on the basis that the actions of his clients, the Lewises, were indefensible. Whether Henry was guilty or not was not the point; what was at issue was whether the Lewises had acted with diligence in his defence. In any case, the verdict at Eugenia's trial effectively found that Henry was innocent.

The Lord Chief Baron's summing up was critical. It should have been an opportunity to summarize all the legal arguments in all of the actions involving Henry to that date. It should have been dealt with, with 'patience and attention', as the judge had stated at the commencement of the hearing. Effectively, Henry had now been tried three times. But until the current trial, some or other of the evidence had either been inadmissible, not presented, or not known. Here at last, might have been expected an informed, considered, balanced and complete legal assessment of the Hatch affair. Unfortunately, that is hardly what anyone got.

The judge began; addressing the jury he told them that there was no doubt that an attorney was liable in an action for any misconduct or miscarriage, which arises from his negligence. He went on,

> The present action is, so far as my knowledge goes, the very first that has ever been brought in a criminal case; and it raises great questions of gravity and difficulty.

He reviewed the dates of the events leading up to Henry's trial. The charge had been made on the 8th of October 1859 (the date Henry received the second letter from the Bishop). An enquiry before the visiting magistrates was due to be held on the 28th October, the same day that Henry absconded, having previously resigned. He remained away until a warrant was issued against him. The enquiry never took place. The judge continued,

> The effect of the absconding was very strong, insomuch that within living memory it was a question to be tried on indictment, whether the prisoner had 'fled from justice'…

Then there was the fact that Henry's friends did not bail him, and he was, therefore, in prison until his trial. (Henry justified his 'absconding' by reference to the Chancery case and the insurance shares, and concern about being arrested for debt. The fact that this was not brought out and shown to have been true, either in the perjury trial or the current action, must question either its accuracy, or the competence of the prosecution team. It seems tough on Henry though, that the fact that no one would (or could) bail him counted against him.)

The judge now commenced to dissect the detail of the evidence in the perjury trial, and from his tone, he seemed to be questioning the outcome. The first 'assignment' (allegation) in the perjury action, was that Eugenia had said initially (in the magistrates' hearing), that the indecency in the garden had *not* taken place on the first day. In her original deposition, apparently, she did not state that it had, but under cross-examination in Henry's trial, she did fix it on the first day – a day on which several witnesses were able to give contradictory evidence, and 'that assignment went merely on the precise time'. (In other words, the judge was questioning the relevance of the allegation.) The second assignment related to the hole in Henry's pocket, for which witness could also be called. (Presumably the witness was Lucy, who gave evidence that neither she nor Eugenia put their hands in Henry's pockets). The judge pointed out that the perjury trial took place nine months after the events in the garden, implying that such a level of detail could not reliably be remembered, particularly by an eight year old child. The third assignment related to whether the outer door of the plaintiff's bedroom was shut or fastened. Eugenia swore that it was, but 'not that it was always so; and it may have been so at some particular time'. (Surely this was incorrect; Eugenia had said that the outer door to her room was fastened with a bath in front of it – this was clear from the transcript of the first trial.) The judge said that witnesses could be called to contradict her evidence. On the more serious matters

> involving the substance of the charges, it [is] not possible to call witnesses to contradict her, as they were alleged to have occurred when she and the plaintiff were by themselves, and it seems strange that there should have been assignments of perjury on such matters.

By way of example, he instanced the fourth assignment, in the bedroom on the night of the party (but Lucy was present then...), the fifth and sixth, when Henry was supposed to have visited Eugenia in her bedroom, and the seventh:

…as to whether he was a quarter of an hour with her engaged as described…on all of these and the other similar charges she could have been contradicted only by the plaintiff, who could not have been examined at his own trial…And it is strange that a child of eleven or twelve should have been indicted for perjury on such a matter as whether a man was engaged with her a quarter of an hour or ten minutes, a few minutes more or less; or whether he hurt her. How could she be contradicted on such a point as that?

He went on to say, with regard to the allegations of what took place in the Hatches' bed, 'too disgusting to mention', that those allegations could only be refuted by Henry and Essie who could not be examined at Henry's trial. The judge then stated that the verdict on Eugenia at her trial had been on an indictment containing many assignments of perjury, for which there were one or two witnesses only to contradict her – as well as Henry's word on oath – so it was not possible to determine 'on what assignments her conviction went'. On that basis, the judge felt that Eugenia's conviction had 'little bearing on the present action', particularly in respect of calling witnesses. In relation to Henry's trial, the defendant (Lewis) had told the plaintiff (Henry) the Serjeant's opinion and his reasons; the plaintiff had said he was sorry for it but that he must be guided by counsel.

The lord Chief Baron was saying that the perjury trial proved nothing; it was still Henry's word against Eugenia's with a few collateral witnesses. As far as Henry's legal team were concerned, Eugenia's trial had *proved* that Henry was innocent. Given the general approbation with which the verdict in Eugenia's trial was received, the judge seemed to be in the minority in his view of its importance or relevance. In addition to that, he was clearly biased in regard of the original trial. He had stressed the incriminating effect of Henry's absconding; he even suggested that Henry's failure to get bail was suspicious, and made no comment to the effect that if Eugenia's trial was her word against Henry's then so must have been Henry's trial. He seemed to be suggesting that Henry was, after all, guilty. Finally, he pointed out that Henry had acquiesced in the decision not to call witnesses.

Next, the judge referred to a letter from Henry to a friend, offered as prosecution evidence, in which he stated that the charges against him being so difficult to refute, his 'escape' depended upon having a number of witnesses. The judge then conceded that *Henry probably would have been acquitted, had the so-called collateral witnesses been called at the original trial*, but qualifies that statement by saying,

> The plaintiff himself does not appear to have a very strong opinion [on the subject] having been convicted in December 1859, and released in May 1860, he did not bring this action until November 1860...nor up to that time does it appear that he made any complaint of the conduct of the defendants.

The judge said that the present action consisted of two complaints: first, regarding the magistrates' hearing; second, the trial itself. He was of the opinion that there was no ground for the first complaint, since the depositions from Eugenia indicated that 'the case must go for trial'. He added that the defendants were not responsible for the plaintiff's inability to get bail (but surely, the prosecution had never suggested that they were...) On the second complaint, it was that the defendants

> did not get up the case with sufficient care and diligence, especially in examining witnesses, so as to lay their proofs before counsel. [The answer was, he said, that the plaintiff] by his own conduct, had placed

313

himself in such a position, that any course was full of peril, and that everything was done which could be done, with any reasonable hope of doing good.

He went on, addressing the jury,

You will have to consider, in substance, whether all was done which could have been done for any useful purpose, and whether the not doing of anything which might have been done was the cause of the plaintiff's conviction...The declaration alleges, that by reason of the defendants' negligence, [Henry] was convicted.

The judge said that the charge was divided into two parts: first, not calling witnesses; second, not examining witnesses in order to instruct counsel effectively and allow him to exercise the best judgement in the calling of witnesses. He continued,

With regard to the first, the question of calling or not calling witnesses is entirely for counsel...The plaintiff's counsel took the entire responsibility on himself...and the plaintiff himself said 'he must be guided by his counsel'...He did not insist that his witnesses should be called, and his counsel at the time stated to him the reasons why he did not call them; reasons in which he appeared to acquiesce, and which the counsel was ready to state on this trial.

This does seem a bit hard on Henry; he was not a lawyer and was entirely dependent on Serjeant Ballantine's professional judgement. Now, however, the judge's bias started to show clearly; he went on,

There were...the most grave and weighty reasons [why witnesses were not called]...Justice had been evaded;

the accused had absconded. When apprehended, he had asked the officer what punishment could be awarded for such offences (the last question one can suppose an innocent man to ask), there was the evidence of not one girl only, but of two – and two of such tender age that it is impossible to suppose they would have invented the disgusting circumstances to which they deposed…on the main charge their testimony could not have been contradicted…Under such circumstances it is not to be wondered at that Mr. Serjeant Ballantine advised his client not to call witnesses, who would have opened up a perilous cross-examination and given a reply; nor is it to be wondered at that the plaintiff acquiesced in that decision, nor can he now complain of it.

However, having said all of that, he then observed,

I should wish with the clearest, the firmest, and strongest voice to say that I honestly mean to throw no doubt on Mr. Hatch's innocence – I again say, in my judgement, he ought to have been acquitted, from the contrast between that improbable story and the position he occupied…

The jury might have been forgiven for being confused at this point; the judge thought that Henry was innocent, although he strongly appeared to be guilty! Serjeant Ballantine had been absolutely correct in not calling witnesses, given Henry's self-incriminating actions. But surely that point was never in doubt. What was at issue was the fact that Lewis et al had entirely failed to brief him with the extenuating circumstances.

Now, however, the judge *did* concentrate on the point at issue; did the defendants make the best of the defence material at hand? He continued,

315

> The charge against the defendants...resolves itself into
> this: that [they] did not make such enquiries as [they]
> might have done, nor make the best or most for a
> defence at [their] disposal...

He advised the jury that they would have to use their judgement
to decide whether further enquiries would have made it
advisable to call Lucy Hatch and the other witnesses. The
judge reminded them that the defendants had the witnesses
ready in court should counsel, at the last minute, have decided
to call them.

He now commented on Essie's evidence:

> Mrs. Hatch states that the defendants did not examine
> Lucy Hatch, the principal of the witnesses, who might
> have been called, and yet she had been examined at
> the hearing [at the magistrates' court]...Mrs. Hatch
> says, she told the defendants that witnesses were in the
> house at the time, who could contradict all that was
> said against her husband. But from the nature of the
> charges that was impossible; the main charges could
> not be contradicted, but only some of the details on
> collateral points, and then on such points the witnesses
> who might have been called might have contradicted
> each other, as two of them actually did on the trial for
> perjury.

The judge was ignoring the point that three of the charges
– what happened in the garden, the incident of the story, and
Henry's alleged visits to Eugenia in her bedroom – *could be*
contradicted by several witnesses, and their evidence hardly
related to 'collateral points' only. However, the judge insisted
that the witnesses would only be able to speak to collateral
issues, and be 'hazarded' to hostile cross-examination from the

prosecution while being unable to contradict the main charges. This was the decision for counsel. The judge went on,

> The great question is, whether the plaintiff's conviction was owing to the want of care and skill in the defendants, or was the result rather of his own conduct in placing himself in such a position...You must consider, also, the position in which the defendants found the case, when it was put in their hands. The plaintiff had absconded after resigning his situation; and his wife put into their hands a copy of a letter she had written to the prosecutrix, imploring her not to press the charge. You must consider what effect at the outset these things must have had upon their minds, as to the hopefulness of a defence...Nor was this all, the plaintiff admitted that the girl was accustomed to be in his bed in the morning while he was still in it, that was admitted; and it is impossible not to say that it was highly improper that a girl twelve years old should be in or on a man's bed while he and she were both undressed...Above all, the plaintiff had absconded... that was a fatal step, and it had been taken some time before the defendants were retained in the case...

And if there were still any doubt of the judge's view:

> Even if you should find for the plaintiff [even?] these things must all be considered with reference to the question of damages, for you must take into consideration how far the plaintiff himself contributed to the injury, if any [if any?], which he may have sustained, and how far his own conduct caused the mischief which is ascribed to the defendants' negligence.

Henry Hatch commented later that the judge was biased; this was not bias, this was blind prejudice. Sir Frederick Pollock had made up his mind; Henry had incriminated himself, and the evidence of his witnesses was irrelevant.

The judge's summing up of the summing up:

> The declaration alleges, that by reason of their [Lewis and Lewis] negligence [Henry] was convicted. The plaintiff is not bound to prove that, in order to maintain his action. If the defendants' negligence largely contributed to the result, they would be answerable for such damages as you might think just under all circumstances. But if you think that either it would not have been wise to call witnesses, and that, under all the circumstances as they then appeared, it would have been useless or perilous to do so, then find for the defendants.

This was to have been the final instruction from the judge to the jury. It should have summarized the key points upon which they had to deliberate and the questions they had to answer, and the judge got it wrong! Virtually everyone who had expressed an opinion on the subject had already agreed that Serjeant Ballantine had been right, *given what he knew*, not to call witnesses at Henry's trial. That was never really at issue. The point of this action was that messrs Lewis had failed, through negligence, to prepare an adequate brief for the Serjeant; a brief which would have made it clear that Henry's defence witnesses would be critical in getting him an acquittal.

Mr Chambers pointed out the error – no doubt very tactfully – declaring that the proper question that the jury should consider was, 'whether the defendants had used due care and diligence in preparing and conducting the case for the defence'. The Lord Chief Baron agreed that he had been deficient in his summing up, and he then directed the jury to consider whether the defendants' negligence had caused 'mischief', adding that,

> Negligence is nothing without damage…was there any good that could have been done by examining witnesses? If not, then the negligence was immaterial, at all events for more than merely nominal damages.

The sting was in the final comment, and evidently the jury took it to heart.

To sum up the summing up of the summing up, the judge was saying that even if the jury found that Lewis and Lewis had been negligent, unless that negligence had caused damage – Henry's conviction – then the jury should find for nominal damages only. But the damage – Henry's conviction – was self-inflicted as a consequence of his own actions! It was a clear direction to find the defendants guilty, but award nominal damages only.

The jury retired, and returned after one hour. The verdict, 'We find for the plaintiff', was greeted with cheers in the court, cheers that turned to hisses when the amount of damages was announced – forty shillings!

It was a total and unmitigated disaster. After the all the expectation – and the very clear hostility of the Lord Chief Baron – to have, nevertheless, won a judgement against 'Lewis and others', and then to be slapped in the face with peppercorn damages, must have brought Henry closer to despair than he had ever been before. And that was not all. The jury had found for the plaintiff, and the defendants had to pay their costs; but the Lord Chief Baron refused to grant Henry *his* costs on a technicality. For damages below £5, there was no justification for bringing the action in a superior court, and therefore, costs could not be claimed.

*The Law Times* damned the verdict and damages as 'an absurd conclusion which the defendants may claim as a practical acquittal'. If Lewis and Lewis were guilty, then Mr Hatch should have been awarded several hundred pounds. If not guilty, they should have been acquitted. The Lord Chief Baron's summing up was, *The Law Times* said, very fair, (however, *The Law Times* based its comments on the report of the trial that appeared in *The Times* newspaper, and that article had failed to report the Lord Chief Baron's blunder at the end of the summing up.) The article continued by saying that at one point, the defendant's counsel had told the jury that they were effectively trying Mr Hatch again, and that the jury seem to have been saying,

> We think that Mr Hatch ought to have been acquitted...
> and therefore we give him the verdict; but we think
> also that it was not negligence in messrs Lewis...

(But the jury had simply been following the judge's direction. He had said, 'was there any good that could have been done by examining witnesses? If not, then the negligence was immaterial, at all events for more than merely nominal damages') Nevertheless, *The Law Times* insisted that Lewis and Lewis were blameless, since they had, effectively, only been charged with failing to call witnesses, and that was still the correct decision given the state of the prosecution case in Henry's trial.

There were very few options left. Henry's legal team could move for a mistrial; the judge's bias had been very evident, he had confused the jury during the summing up, and the damages awarded were absurd and clearly at odds with the verdict reached, notwithstanding the judge's direction. However, that course of action was problematic. It would cost as much again as had already been spent with no guarantee of success; the financial liability could be doubled. The only other option open was damage limitation, in that Henry's lawyers could move to be awarded costs by challenging the criteria used for rejection.

Whoever was providing the financial resources for the action would have to decide how far they were prepared to go.

Mr Montague Chambers received his instructions, and the new hearing commenced two weeks later on 25th May 1861, there having already been some consultation with the judge in chambers. Once more, press reports and legal notes have been used to reconstruct the proceedings. The hearing was again in the Court of Exchequer, presided over by the Lord Chief Baron, but this time, joined on the bench by Barons Martin, Bramwell and Channell, with no jury.

Barons Bramwell and Channell, Henry had met already. No doubt Henry regarded Baron Bramwell with mixed feelings. He was the judge who had condemned Henry to four years' hard labour with such harsh words, but he had also approved the indictment against Eugenia Plummer. Baron Channell had presided over Eugenia Plummer's trial. Both of these judges, therefore, had intimate knowledge of Henry's case, although one of them had pronounced him guilty, and the other had effectively found him innocent. Baron Martin, Henry had not seen before. Sir Samuel Martin was sixty years old and Liberal MP for Pontefract. He had been both a QC and Serjeant-at-law before being appointed to the Court of Exchequer. He had also been a pupil of Sir Frederick Pollock, (the Lord Chief Baron) and in 1838 married his eldest daughter. It was said of Sir Frederick Pollock that,

> in his prime, his only shortcomings were a tendency to make his mind up early in a case and an apparent partiality to the arguments of his son-in-law Samuel Martin…[ODNB]

Since the hearing was presided over by the same judge who had 'misdirected' the jury in the first place, who had already refused costs, and whose bias was very clear, Mr Chambers and his colleagues, Messrs Garth and Allen were evidently optimists. The proceedings did not start well. Mr Chambers moved to be allowed the full costs of the action, as well as a rule to set aside the verdict on the grounds that the damages were inadequate, together with misdirection and the improper rejection of evidence. To this broadside, the court '...intimated that it was not competent to the learned counsel to move as he proposed'. Mr Chambers tried again. He said that he was entitled to do so, and the court was under an obligation to hear him (he was on dangerous ground; that sounded like a threat). The judge, the Lord Chief Baron, replied,

> If you choose to move for a new trial, you can do so; or if on the other part of your rule [for costs], you can do so; but you cannot mix the two together.

Mr Chambers responded that there was no rule against it; the judge said that it had never been the practice. Mr Chambers stated that he hoped that he might be heard before the Court decided against him. The judge started to get testy:

| | |
|---|---|
| *The Lord Chief Baron*: | If you choose to move for a new trial you may do so, but you cannot move in the alternative. |
| *Mr. Chambers:* | I move for both. |
| *The Lord Chief Baron*: | Then we will not hear you. |

Mr Chambers had to think quickly:

| | |
|---|---|
| *Mr. Chambers*: | Then I move on the question of costs. |

At this point Baron Bramwell chimed in and asked Mr Chambers whether he insisted that it was the practice of the court to hear both questions together. Mr Chambers explained his position, in the course of which what had happened with the Lord Chief Baron in chambers came out:

> Your Lordships will see why I move in this way. If I split the motion in two I shall have to go twice over the same ground. Application has been made to the Lord Chief Baron to certify that this was a proper case to be tried in a superior Court and not in a County Court, and the Lord Chief Baron then said, 'I will do nothing until the first four days of the term are over, and I see whether either party will move for a new trial'.

(Lewis and Lewis might also have moved for a new trial to preserve their reputation.) To this the judge responded,

> You have a perfect right to move for a new trial and a perfect right to move for the costs, but they have no connexion with one another.

To which Mr Chambers replied,

> The course taken by my Lord Chief Baron has driven us into this perplexity, to split the present rule into two motions would put the plaintiff to unnecessary expense.

(It would double the cost, since much of the same evidence would have to be presented in the two actions.) Mr Chambers then described what had happened in the judge's chambers when Mr Garth had presented a motion to the judge for costs:

> If the costs had been refused upon an application made after the four days had elapsed he would have lost his right to move for a new trial. He thought it fair to his client that he should not be put to the expense of two motions, and fairer to the Court to come with the

motion in the alternative, and had so determined after consultation with his learned friends, as they could find no rule against it.

Unfortunately, Mr Garth had managed to irritate the Lord Chief Baron; the latter commented,

> One of the reasons why I paused and refused to grant the certificate [for costs] was that it was held out to me that if I would grant it there would not be any motion for a new trial. I would not enter into any compromise. I thought the observation one that was most improper. I call it a most improper mode of endeavouring to awe a judge in the exercise of his discretion…

Mr Garth had overplayed his hand, and the judge felt he was being blackmailed. Mr Garth responded,

> As soon as I had made the application, your Lordship asked, 'Did any of the parties intend to move for a new trial?' I then said that that would depend upon whether the certificate was granted or not.

This does seem to be an odd response from Mr Garth. He seemed to be suggesting that if he could secure costs in the case of Hatch v Lewis, he would not move for a new trial. But if they could secure costs, they would be no worse off (financially) than they had been at the commencement of the action, and opting for a retrial would give them the chance of a successful verdict and sensible damages. Nevertheless, the judge was not having any of it:

> That was not the way in which the mention of a new trial was first made; at least it certainly reached my ears before…

Mr Chambers sought to calm troubled waters:

> [There was no] intention to attempt to awe the judge or say
> anything offensive…there was no thought of stipulating
> [presenting a demand]. Had there been, his Lordship's
> indignation would have been most properly founded…[I]
> was informed that his Lordship had asked whether either
> of the parties would move for a new trial.

Baron Channell then observed that he had himself in several
instances made such an enquiry when applied to, to certify.

Following this exchange, it appears that Henry's legal team
decided to try for both courses – retrial, and costs in the previous
action, but one after the other. Mr Chambers now elected to
move first for a retrial on the basis of inadequate damages,
misdirection and the improper rejection of evidence.

Once more, details of the first two trials were repeated,
joined this time by the third trial (Hatch v Lewis), and in the
process more information began to emerge. Mr James Lewis
had cross-examined the witnesses for the prosecution in the
initial magistrates' hearing (Eugenia, Stephana and Caroline
Plummer) without any previous discussion with Henry. He
had, it will be remembered, arrived for the hearing too late
to interview Henry's witnesses. Essie 'entreated' Mr Lewis
to represent Henry, and his brother, 'Uncle George' Lewis,
went to see Henry to establish whether he would retain James
Lewis for his defence, and took away Henry's memoranda
regarding his side of what had happened. Essie did not sit at
home wringing her hands but visited Mr Lewis several times
asking him to see her husband and interview their witnesses.
She wanted to see Serjeant Ballantine, but was told that that
would be 'irregular', and that the Serjeant would not see her.
Mr Lewis never personally interviewed Henry's witnesses. The
day before the trial, Mr Lewis went to see Henry and told him
of Serjeant Ballantine's intention not to call witnesses except

to character. Henry said that he was sorry for it, but deferred to counsel's experience and judgement.

Mr Chambers continued. Under the circumstances, and with the information that he had to hand, his friend Serjeant Ballantine would have been a madman to have called defence witnesses. He described the brief as prepared by Mr Lewis as a 'ragged brief [and a] thieves' brief'. Mr Hatch was, he said, in bad circumstances financially, and it was Richard Onslow the governor of Wandsworth Prison, who had set up a defence sum to the value of £75. Mr Lewis had agreed to do the work for that sum, but had already admitted that the total cost of doing so was £44. That left the balance as fees for himself and his brother for visiting the prison on three occasions for no more than ten minutes or half an hour, the preparation of the 'shabby' briefs, and seeing Mrs Hatch and telling her to get 'as many bishops &c. as she could' as character witnesses. Mr Chambers observed that 'The highest attorney in the land could not have charged more than ten guineas for what was done…' He went on,

> If, as was said, the case was difficult and perplexing, there was the more reason for care and diligent inquiry…If Mr. Lewis had not time to bestow, he should not have undertaken so grave a responsibility…He should have examined the witnesses of the plaintiff, and consulted with Mr. Serjeant Ballantine and Mr. Robinson whether anything further could be done… Had the testimony of these witnesses been laid before counsel, they would, no doubt, have been called.

And that, of course, was undeniably true.

Then there was the putative evidence of the private detective, Mr Brennan. He had been sent to Wiltshire to make enquiries regarding the Plummers. On his return, he told Mr Lewis that he had 'discovered a clue' to one of the servants who had lived with the Plummers, and this servant could provide some evidence of the previous character of the child and other circumstances. Brennan was paid off, and told that the information would not be necessary as they were not calling witnesses.

Mr Chambers now addressed the central issue of who had made the decision not to call witnesses. Mr Serjeant Ballantine had, in a 'manly' way which the Lord Chief Baron had commended, said, 'It was all my own act not calling witnesses; I used my discretion, and I always will.' Mr Lewis had given the Serjeant information on which he was to form his judgement – the 'ragged brief' – but,

> [Mr Lewis] had not informed his own mind, and therefore could not inform that of Mr Ballantine... Had [Ballantine] known at the first trial all that the witnesses could say who were examined on the trial for perjury, there could be no doubt that he would have called them; but the carelessness which led to the committal of the plaintiff operated also on the subsequent proceedings.

(The whole ghastly ineptitude of James Lewis in conducting Henry's defence was now clear. He arrived late for the magistrates' hearing and had to go straight in without examining Henry's witnesses; and having done that, he then failed to examine them before the Old Bailey trial. His clerk took no care in transcribing Henry's memoranda, and so the brief as presented to Serjeant Ballantine was ragged indeed. He ignored the evidence from the private detective which might have provided crucial character evidence against Eugenia Plummer – and possibly her mother also. He cross-examined Eugenia, Stephana, and Caroline Plummer during the magistrates' hearing, and probably took the view that the case was unwinnable. Having done so, he decided that there was no benefit to be gained from any further investigation, particularly since it was clear that Henry had no financial resources of his own, and he would have to do the work for a fixed fee. And having done all of that, he pocketed upwards of £30 of pure profit for a few hours' work. It was now apparent why Lewis and Lewis did not seek a retrial. James Lewis had got off lightly. Admittedly, he had the judgement against him and had to pay his defence costs, but the damages were derisory – less than his initial fee for representing Henry at the magistrates' hearing. More importantly, had there been a retrial he could well have been facing damages of £5000; a sum which could well have bankrupted him and his firm.)

Mr Chambers, meanwhile, was still seeking a retrial, and now commented on what he regarded as misdirection on the part of the Lord Chief Baron. His Lordship had, he said, treated the action as one of tort instead of contract, simply because the plea was 'not guilty'. (Tort is the breach of a duty imposed by law, whereby some person acquires a right of action for damages; (OED)). The judge observed that he thought that the technical form adopted for convenience would not alter the legal obligation of the parties. Mr Chambers continued,

> His Lordship had excluded the petition [Henry's jury who had petitioned the Queen, were refused leave to appear as witnesses] and questions to Sir George Cornewall Lewis as to his refusing to recommend [Henry] to the clemency of the Queen.

Mr Chambers then accused the judge of confusing the court, by observing following Serjeant Ballantine's avowal of responsibility in not calling witnesses, 'then there is an end of the case'.

*The Judge*:　　　　I said, 'an end to the case as to the not calling witnesses', but

|              | that did not touch the question you particularly urged against Mr. Lewis. |
| Mr. Chambers: | I wish your Lordship had said so, particularly at the end of the case. |
| The Judge: | I wish that you would hand up a short-hand copy of the summing up. I think you are bound in candour to do so. |
| Mr. Chambers: | I have every wish to be candid, but the Court is in the habit of trusting to the honour and truthfulness of counsel, and I protest against the old practice which used to be resorted to in cases where a counsel was of evil reputation being adopted. |
| The Judge: | The practice was growing into disuse when I came into this court, but is still the regular course in the Courts of Chancery, and it is well now and then to resort to it in Courts of Law. |

This was an argument about what the judge had actually said and the nuance of meaning that might have been understood by the jury. A transcript of the proceedings would have proved what was and was not said, and surely one existed – Henry and the Lewises had agreed to share the costs of providing it. Nevertheless, Mr Chambers was, perhaps, pushing his luck in telling the judge what he did or did not say.

Mr Chambers continued, commenting on other parts of the summing up as tending to protect the defendant and give undue weight to the conduct of Mr. Hatch when first charged with the assault...Mr. Hatch's conduct could not be urged to excuse Mr. Lewis's negligence, and rather increased his responsibility.

That was no less than the truth. The judge replied,

I thought the story of Eugenia Plummer so incredible as to amount almost to an impossibility, and that the jury found their verdict on account of some of the other circumstances that had come to their knowledge, and that the best course that Mr. Serjeant Ballantine could have pursued, even had he known all the circumstances afterwards proved, was that which he did pursue...

Mr Chambers responded,

The point to which your Lordship's mind was directed seemed to be the calling of the witnesses, not the being prepared with them, which it was Mr. Lewis's duty to have been.

The damages were, he said, inadequate, and this resulted from his Lordship treating the action as one of tort instead of contract. He concluded by expressing the hope that,

...the Court would excuse any undue warmth of expression into which a warm interest for [my] client might have betrayed [me], trusting that nothing that [I have] said has given pain...

The judge responded that so far as he was concerned, certainly it had not.

Baron Martin asked whether there was any case in which, where a plaintiff had gained the verdict, an action for negligence against his attorney had been maintained. Mr Chambers was unable to say, but finished with a perhaps ill-advised snipe at the court, by saying that on the Monday following, he would move for a certificate that the case was one fit to be tried in the Superior Court, and he trusted he should not be required to go over the same statements in support of it.

A few days later, on 30th May 1861, their Lordships 'having taken time to consider the application, now gave judgement, declining to grant the rule.' No explanation was given. The move for a new trial was refused. It was the inevitable consequence of asking the same judge who had presided over the previous trial, for leave to call a new trial on the basis of his misdirection. For Henry, it was his last chance to get any financial compensation for the wrongs he had suffered, and he might have been excused for feeling very bitter. The action now reduced to getting the prosecution costs out of Lewis and Lewis. The costs of the current action, Henry's financial backers would have to bear themselves.

The next sitting was on Tuesday, 11th June 1861. Again, it was before the Lord Chief Baron, accompanied by Barons Martin, Bramwell and Channell. Mr Chambers moved upon an affidavit for a rule nisi for a certificate for costs, founded on the Statute of Parliament, 15th & 16th Victoria, chapter 54, section 4, which gave power to the court or a judge in chambers to make an order for the plaintiff to recover his costs. The question was, he said, not whether the action was fit to have been brought at all, but whether it was a 'fit and proper case', to be tried in a superior court.

Baron Bramwell commented, 'This is not an appeal from the judge's decision, but an original application', to which Mr Chambers replied in the affirmative. (Perhaps this was esoteric legalese. Clearly, the original decision at the close of the trial was that a certificate for costs should *not* be granted. So how was this not an appeal against that decision?)

Mr Chambers moved for the rule to be returned – ie a decision made – on the next day, which was the last day of the legal term. In the event it was not, because the court ran out of time, and unaccountably, there was now a five month delay until the case was heard again on Monday, 4th November 1861. The usual team presided, with Baron Martin being replaced by Baron Wilde. The Lewises' defence team were also present – Serjeant Shee, Mr Lush and Mr Pollock. Mr Chambers, Mr Garth and Mr J P Murphy were for the plaintiff (Henry Hatch).

The first day was spent arguing the plaintiff's case that the rule should be made absolute, and costs granted. The second day, Wednesday, 6th November, the defence team argued against. They contended that the application should be considered an appeal against the decision of the Lord Chief Baron,

> whose decision in refusing costs ought not to be interfered with lightly…Assuming the application to be an original motion, there were no grounds for certifying that there was no sufficient reason for bringing the action in a superior court, and that in judging the importance of the cause the court ought to be governed by the amount of damages awarded by the jury.

(The court reporter appears to have got his double-negative wrong here; surely, 'there were no grounds for certifying that there *was* sufficient reason for bringing the action in a superior court…')

Mr Chambers now advanced a most telling argument, one that unfortunately fell on stony ground. He pointed out that it would have been unwise and absurd to have brought the action in a County Court, where only sums less than £20 in contract and £5 in tort could be obtained. He continued,

...no counsel of any position or knowledge, called upon to advise Mr. Hatch upon the evidence obtained previous to bringing the action, could have discredited himself by recommending the plaintiff sue in the County Court. Trouble and inconvenience has been put forward on the other side as an objection to this motion, although the Legislature has cast a duty upon the superior courts that they cannot retire from on that account; and if in this case it could be said that the plaintiff was not entitled to his costs, the result must be that the County Courts would become a curse instead of a blessing to the community...

He continued, citing his colleague Mr Garth's arguments made earlier,

A man having a right to 40s had a right to bring an action for it. The plaintiff had brought an action for a larger sum, and the jury had awarded him 40s, which verdict had been confirmed by the court. Had a judge a right to say that in his opinion, either morally or in equity, such an action ought not to have been brought? Every action that would lie [was admissible] was fit to be brought. The meaning of the words of the statute, 'Sufficient reason for bringing the action in the superior court', could not be whether there was sufficient reason for bringing the action at all; the real question was, whether a plaintiff had sufficient reason with reference to his own particular case – whether he had sufficient reason for bringing it in the superior instead of the County Court. The judge had no right to go into the motive for bringing the action. It by no means followed that because a man only recovered 40s, he had not a good reason for bringing an action for a larger sum [this, surely, was the crux of the argument].

The importance of the right of action cannot be said to depend on the right of the case. When the cause is difficult to be tried, as it was admitted this case was, then there was good reason for bringing it in the superior court. The case was treated throughout as one of importance by the judge, as well as by the defendants, who made it a special jury case.

Mr Chambers had done his best; it was now down to the four judges to rule. Rule they did, and the outcome was a foregone conclusion. The legal notes pertaining to the judgement occupy seven and a half A4 pages, and are understandable only to a legally trained mind – possibly, only a nineteenth century one. No attempt will be made to analyse them except to reproduce the Lord Chief Baron's conclusion. Barons Bramwell, Channell, and Wilde gave their judgements first. All were in favour of discharging the rule – that is, disallowing costs.

Then the Lord Chief Baron:

> I abstained from giving judgement in this case until my learned brothers had expressed their opinion, because, although not actually an appeal from my judgement, substantially, it is so…the argument was, that the plaintiff had a right to 40s, and therefore, he had a right to sue for it in this court. That would apply to a farthing – he had a right to a farthing, therefore he had a right to recover that farthing in this Court, at the expense of several hundred pounds. That, in my judgement, is so contrary to all sense of equity, and natural sense of justice, of which no lawyer, in spite of technicalities, can entirely divest himself, that it never can be the rule by which the judges should exercise the power given by this Act of Parliament.

Reviewing the facts of the case, he went on,

> The defendants never heard any remonstrance against
> their mode of conducting the case till a year after the
> trial...and Mr. Hatch himself said that if he could have
> brought an action against the prosecutor he should
> not have proceeded against Mr. Lewis, thus plainly
> showing that it was not his object to recover damages
> against Mr. Lewis, but by some medium or other to
> give effect to the pardon which he had received from
> the Crown...It occurs to me that we were right in
> deciding the question of damages in enquiring what
> Mr. Hatch's real object was.

(If Henry had said this, and presumably he had, it was a fatal
error, and one his legal team should have been aware of and
have warned him against.) The Lord Chief Baron continued,

> It has been urged that this is a case, which from its
> novelty and importance, ought to be tried in this Court
> – a case which was considered by the defendants so
> important, that they moved for a special jury, and to
> change the venue...

(Originally, the action was to take place in Hertfordshire but
was changed to Middlesex at the request of the defendants.
Possibly, Henry's main financial benefactor resided in
Hertfordshire.) The judge went on,

> But the distinction that occurs to my mind is this – you
> must look, not merely to the novelty of the case, or
> the amount claimed, because any unheard of demand
> might possibly require the attention of the learned
> Judges, or the intelligence of a special jury, but you
> must look at the particular instance and the kind of

action before the Court. It is not because a plaintiff claims £10,000 he is to have his costs if he recovers 40s. Or one farthing. It must be seen whether the real ground of claim is such as justified the bringing the action in a superior Court. Here that is settled, and conclusively settled, by the verdict of the jury. For these reasons, I concur with my learned brothers, that the rule ought to be discharged.

And, of course, the rule was discharged.

That was that. All legal avenues explored. Henry forty shillings better off, and his financial supporter(s) many hundreds of pounds the poorer. It was Wednesday, 6th November 1861, two years and a week since he fled to Poplar.

# The Essex Marshes

It is difficult not to conclude that Henry John Hatch was very grievously wronged in the Hatch v Lewis trials. Indeed it was the verdict of the jury – as directed by the judge – in awarding Henry only forty shillings that was at the heart of the problem. He was denied real damages for the substantial wrongs he had suffered, and the value of damages awarded was central to the argument of the Lord Chief Baron and his colleagues in denying costs.

*The Times* commented on the case, but before considering that, it is instructive to see what *The Law Times* had to say, and its support was, as before, unequivocally for Lewis and Lewis:

> We congratulate Messrs Lewis on their final release from their ungrateful client…The full court has supported the very just refusal of the presiding judge to certify for costs in an action which should never have been brought, and in which the jury ought not to have found for the plaintiff. Their verdict stultified themselves. If Messrs Lewis had been guilty of the negligence with which they were charged, £500 would not have compensated Mr. Hatch for the damage thereby done to him. If not guilty, they were entitled to an entire dismissal. Damages to the amount of 40s were simply an absurdity and in singular keeping with the entire history of this remarkable case…A wrongful conviction against evidence, only set aside

by the prosecution of the principal witness, whose lips were sealed in her turn, resulting in an action against the solicitors for the defendant, against whom a wrongful and ridiculous verdict was given, and to which the court afterwards refused to attach costs, is a complication of miscarriages of justice such as we should not have conceived to be possible in these days of reformed law, had we not witnessed them.

At least *The Law Times* had admitted to a series of miscarriages of justice.

*The Times* offered a very spiteful piece:

Once more we have been obliged to report law proceedings about the Rev. Mr. Hatch. If it had been Mr. Smith...or Mr. Jones...or Mr. Robinson...we probably should not have noticed the frequency of the recurrence of these truly British names, or have been struck with the immense prolixity of the litigation. [So even Henry's surname was against him]...this case of the Rev. Mr. Hatch is a disagreeable case; it was disagreeable in the characters of the parties implicated, in the circumstances of the charge, in the conviction of a clergyman, in the after-conviction of a child for perjury, in the mistiness of all the principal facts, and in the indelicacy of some of the circumstances upon which no decision hung, but which were admitted on all hands...

And in relation to the frequency of recurrence of reports of the Hatch case in *The Times'* columns:

It is like looking out upon a river, where a hundred waifs and strays are daily oscillating up and down upon the tidal waters before they at last get down to the sea...old tubs and stumps of trees, and even expired kittens, make their daily journey, and attract no notice. But if some inflated carcass of a dead dog should return in periodical transit every twenty four hours, offending the nostrils at every passage, then the philosophical reflection would come strong upon us that these vain repetitions are neither useful nor pleasant... Litigation in this country is still absurdly protracted...Here is this Mr. Hatch. Are we never to hear the last of him?

*The Times'* view was that Henry, having secured his free pardon, should at that point, have held his peace:

If the Rev. Mr. Hatch had any enthusiastic admirers they might have shown their sympathy in a silver tea-pot; or the magistrates of the county might have restored him to his chaplaincy...surely the law had done with the transaction [but] no sooner had Mr. Hatch got the royal pardon in his pocket than he started up a new career of litigation.

That at least was not true. It was nine months from his release that the action against Lewis and Lewis was started – Henry had even been criticized for the period of time he waited. However, the rhetoric of *The Times* was not to be moderated by details of fact:

Again we find the Rev. Mr. Hatch taking possession of our columns, and again we find all the nasty evidence sifted and screened every morning before a nauseated public, up whose nostrils all the dust of the once more ventilated mass of corruption ascended...

One might conclude that the editor of *The Times* had no control over the material appearing in his columns. Now, however, he starts to reveal his motives in this nasty editorial:

> He [Henry] could not bring against the judge who tried him, nor the jury who convicted him, nor the witnesses who had deposed against him. Generous as the Law is to persons desirous of putting her in motion, she is not tolerant of attacks upon her ministers…

So, Henry's sin was daring to challenge the legal establishment; can one detect, yet again, the influence of the Home Secretary? The editorial continued,

> The action was unprecedented, unexpected and took everyone by surprise [but] if the law gave Mr. Hatch an action against his attorneys, Mr. Hatch had a right to avail himself of it…How long that action went on, with its many delays and its ever-recurring motions, we cannot recollect…To and fro with every tide the dead dog was again floating before the public eye, making the atmosphere unsavoury…

Continuing with an irony reminiscent of Mark Anthony's eulogy on the dead Caesar:

> We do not mean to pretend, if Mr. Hatch had a right of action against his solicitors or against anyone else, that he had not a perfect right to bring that action… During the action, some of the judges took a distinction between 'an action that will lie and an action which is fit to be brought', and the Lord Chief Baron said, 'There are circumstances which will confer a legal right, but on which it would be disgraceful to bring an action.' But these observations could hardly apply to Mr. Hatch…

And after summarizing the outcomes of the four actions, the newspaper concluded,

> What may be the real mind of the English law upon all these matters can hardly be even vaguely guessed at, but these decisions when brought together, however proper each may be separately, scarcely sound rational in sequence. All this has been evolved with the greatest difficulty after much delay, enormous expense and reiterated trials...As to Mr. Hatch's case, we hope never to hear of it again in any shape, but we must confess that its notoriety, its multifariousness, its continual iteration, and its long endurance make it valuable as an example of the low state of judicial art in this country.

The editorial was quite indifferent to the detailed facts, making little attempt to get to the real truth of the situation, and seeking only to impress with invective. At least it was critical of the law, as well as having a most unfair swipe at Henry Hatch.

However, one other newspaper thought that *The Times* editorial was most unjust. *The Morning Chronicle* took it to task, commenting the following day, that the piece contained, 'not one spark of generous feeling in the column of heavy cynicism and irrelevant attempts at ridicule...' The paper went on to say that although it agreed with the decision of the Court of Exchequer, Mr Hatch had, nevertheless, been perfectly justified in pursuing the course that he did in order to clear his name. It ended,

> It is surely enough that a clergyman occupying a responsible and useful position, known for his efforts in the cause of philanthropy, a scholar, a gentleman, a man of accomplishments, and of respectable antecedents

and good connection should be robbed of his good name, deprived of his income, stripped of all worldly advantages, and indeed totally ruined, without, in addition to all this, being subjected to the arrogant comments and contemptuous sneers of the Thunderer in one of its most unamiable and intolerant moods.

It was a fair summary of Henry's position, although the fact that *The Chronicle*, too, agreed with the court's decision was a little surprising.

As far as Henry was concerned, the outcome of the Court of Exchequer hearing was the end of the road, and he no longer had any need to keep silent in respect of the newspapers. On the second anniversary of his arrest, Henry wrote to *The Times* to set the record straight following its editorial. His letter was published the following day.

Naturally, the editor could not resist some further mocking; he headlined Henry's letter 'Ecce Iterum!' – Here he is again! – a quotation from the Roman satirist Juvenal, who used it to introduce Crispinus, a sycophantic courtier to the emperor Domitian. The first few lines in a translation by Peter Green:

> Here's Crispinus again... a monster without one redeeming virtue, a sick voluptuary strong only in his lusts, which draw the line at nothing except unmarried girls...

This really was a bit close to the mark. As a classical scholar, the source and meaning of the quotation was quite clear to Henry, and he might even have considered a libel action if he had not completely done with legal proceedings. His letter began,

> My attention has been drawn to a leading article in The Times of the 7th inst., wherein you state with a feeling I can fully appreciate, that 'you hope never to hear

of my case again in any shape.' Nevertheless, relying upon the common justice which I am bound to believe regulates your pages, I venture to ask the insertion of some observations upon remarks in that leader. I have hitherto scrupulously abstained from addressing my observations to the public press, and, though I think the tone of your article somewhat ungenerous to me, after all I have suffered, I should still have considered it more consistent with my duty to have remained silent, but for one or two points therein, which, if permitted to pass unexplained, would be further injurious to me.

Henry pointed out that the year that passed from his release, to the commencement of the action against Lewis and Lewis, was because he was 'so worn down by distress of mind, and so enfeebled in health', that he could do nothing until after a long period of recuperation, even though he had rigorously objected to Lewis and Lewis being paid following his conviction.

He continued, 'The graver imputation…was that [the action against Lewis and Lewis] was a vexatious and unnecessary proceeding.' He said that he would have been glad to let the matter drop, had he not felt that he owed it to himself and the public to take the action he did, which was always under the advice of 'the most eminent counsel'. It is worth reproducing his version of events in their entirety:

In the first instance, I placed myself with every confidence in the hands of Mr. Lewis, sen., who by his own admission, never saw one of the numerous witnesses who could have proved my case, and, as I deposed, never exchanged one word with me on the details of the charges against me. The memoranda made by me, and which, as it afterwards appeared, were valueless without other information, Mr. Lewis handed, uncorrected, and uncommented upon, to a clerk to copy as my brief; much of my writing the clerk evidently could not read, and thus it was omitted altogether; much more he mistook; so that my notes, poor as they were originally, were rendered absolute nonsense as copied by the said clerk. The blanks were never filled up, and remain blanks to this day, nor were the errors corrected, but in their mutilated state were handed to Mr. Serjeant Ballantine, with a report from an inspector who had made some preliminary enquiries in the neighbourhood where my persecutors resided. These materials formed the whole ground of information upon which my leading counsel was to prove my innocence in so important a case, involving consequences to me as dreadful as can well be imagined. Under such circumstances, I could not but feel I had been cruelly neglected, and that such fact should be proved by public investigation, and the reasons why my innocence was not fully established in the first instance clearly manifested. It was on these grounds the action was commenced – not to gratify a feeling of revenge, but to prove to the world that the non-production of witnesses was not only not my fault, but was against my expressed desire; and that had Messrs Lewis done their duty to me in December 1859, by ascertaining, for my counsel's guidance and discretion, the facts to which the various witnesses could testify, and which they afterwards proved, I should have been spared the unspeakable infamy, degradation, and misery of a conviction.

The action against the Messrs Lewis came on for hearing on 1st February last, before the Lord Chief Baron and a special jury (nominated at the insistence of the defendants), when it was suddenly stopped by the judge in consequence of indisposition, and deferred for a week, and then to 9th May, thereby inflicting upon me an additional cost of £200. On the last day appointed the cause again came on, and occupied four days. Three times during the trial did the Lord Chief Baron retire from the court to consult the judges on difficult points of law submitted for his consideration; and after his summing up – at the end of which Mr. Chambers reminded his Lordship that he had not left to the jury the question whether or not the defendants had been guilty of negligence (the very pith of the action) – the jury in his Lordship's absence, returned a verdict in my favour. Only those present can understand the burst of approbation of a crowded court, which thus signified its approval of the result, or the hisses with which the assessment of the damages at 40s was unanimously received. On application being made to the Lord Chief Baron, on the first day of the following Trinity Term, for a certificate to entitle me to my costs, his Lordship delayed his decision thereon so late as to prevent my applying to the Court until the last day but one of the term for a rule; the consequences whereof was that the case was thrown over until the present term.

The question then, for the consideration of the full Court was whether, in the terms of the 4th section of the 15th and 16th Victoria, cap 54, 'I had sufficient reason for bringing my said action in the superior court.' Barons Bramwell, Channell and Wilde, while admitting that the said statute gave them an original jurisdiction, expressly refused to exercise it, on the ground that the facts then before the Court were identical with those before the Lord Chief Baron when he refused to certify; and the Lord Chief Baron simply declared that he adhered to his original opinion. By this refusal to "administer the law", I was denied the advantage the Act of Parliament in question was expressly intended to confer, and my case left solely to the Lord Chief Baron, whose bias throughout the whole proceedings had been painfully manifest.

Thus in the teeth of the fact that it was an action against attorneys for negligence in a criminal case – the first ever attempted; that it was made a special jury by the defendants themselves; that it was adjourned in February last by the Lord Chief Baron on account of his indisposition, at an expense to me of £200; that in the May following I was put to the further expense of £13 7s 4d, merely to supply the learned judge, at his express request, with short-hand written notes of the evidence; that the cause lasted four days and involved many difficult points of the law; yet because the jury limited the damages to 40s, the Lord Chief Baron refused to certify that there was 'reasonable ground for my bringing the cause in a superior court;' and that in the face of his own remarks when he commenced the cause in February, on which occasion he said, 'I came here expressly to discharge the ordinary duties of a Judge, to which I believed I was reasonably competent, but I must fairly tell you that I am physically incapable to take even the notes that would be required in a case of so much labour.' I quite agree that it is a question of considerable importance for the sake of the public and the profession, for the sake of the innocent and the guilty; it is a case which should be tried with the greatest patience and attention, and not be disposed of in a summary way by any short view of the case.

Surely I cannot be blamed for believing that, after such observations, there could be no doubt that I had "reasonable ground for bringing my action in a superior court." The fact of the jury finding a verdict in my favour limiting the damages to 40s has often been a subject of astonishment, and to many is to this moment incomprehensible.

The circumstances which led to it have, however, since been detailed to me by one of the jurymen, and from him I learnt that the desire of the majority on retiring was to award me £500, but that one member resisted, and declared he would only consent to such a verdict as would give me my costs. Some one said 40s would do that, and that sum was accordingly ultimately agreed to. On entering the jury-box the dissident juryman said to my informant, 'You think 40s will give the plaintiff his costs, but it won't.' It was, however, then too late to remedy the error; the 40s were awarded, and the avowed intention of the jury thereby defeated.

It must not be overlooked that the proceedings which were forced upon me in order to effect my liberation by an indictment for perjury against my accusers, was brought to a conclusion while I was languishing in prison, and the expenses were such as to prevent my receiving any portion of the fund afterwards raised for my benefit beyond the sum of £5. Notwithstanding my sufferings, I have the satisfaction of knowing and feeling that throughout the whole proceeding I have abstained from either word or deed which should even have the appearance of vindictiveness, or be inconsistent with the character of a clergyman and gentleman.

I have been unjustly accused, and have proved it. My character was unblemished to the moment the charge was made against me. I have been thereby cruelly driven from a position of usefulness and respectability to one of want and the deepest distress, and the result of the whole has proved that for one so situated legal difficulties exist which preclude any possible redress, unless at a risk which few would face, and at a cost which none but the wealthy could sustain. I am, sir, your obedient servant, Henry J Hatch, 19 Arundel St, Strand, Nov 12.

Henry had shown himself to be no mean advocate, but he knew when he was beaten.

However, *The Times* with all its cruel mocking had done Henry a favour in printing his letter in full together with his address. The fair-minded British public no doubt showered him with correspondence, much of which must have contained financial contributions.

For the next five or six years, Henry had a variety of jobs. In 1862 he was curate of Pennington in Lancashire, although that did not last very long. The Clergy list shows him unemployed in 1863, but in 1864 he became curate of St Peter's Church, Molash, in rural Kent, a post he held for two or three years. All the time, of course, the Chancery cases against him, Cochrane v Hatch and the action of his solicitor George Annesley, were grinding on inexorably. Henry was now effectively bankrupt, and would have been unable to offer any material defence.

There was also the question of the advowson of Sutton and the living, vacant now that Uncle Henry had been removed. But there was a problem. Under normal circumstances, and with Uncle Charles' agreement, surely not withheld given Henry's situation, Henry could immediately have become rector at £350 a year. But he didn't; or rather he couldn't. The Sutton advowson was the one remaining tangible asset of his father's estate. Cochrane was after it, since the will provided for a portion of the sale proceeds to go to Henry's sister Eleanora, Alexander Durnford's wife. Naturally, any incumbent of the living would have devalued the advowson – the younger the incumbent, the lower the value. Henry was in his forties. If he proposed himself and the bishop accepted, the advowson could have been unusable for another thirty years or more. Cochrane had to keep him out at all costs, and unfortunately he succeeded. Henry must have been truly heartbroken after all he had been through and with the living vacant, to see the advowson advertised for sale in *The Times* of February and March 1866, and sold by order of the Court of Chancery to Hertford College, Oxford, for £5,500.

That was absolutely, completely and irrevocably that. At least Henry's father's will provided Essie with the interest on one third of the sale proceeds of the advowson. By the time that the costs of the Chancery case had been paid, this amounted to the interest on only £1000 – around thirty pounds a year. Still, thirty pounds was thirty pounds more than Henry and Essie had otherwise, and later on they were able to take a mortgage out using it as security. One trusts that Cochrane was satisfied with the £330 – less his costs – which Eleanora received as a result of the sale of the advowson. After all the misery and suffering that Henry had endured, to have had the Sutton rectory within his grasp, and to be cheated of it at the very last moment for a miserable £330 must have been a very bitter pill to swallow.

But life had to go on. Evidently, the curacy of Molash was not satisfactory – or very poorly remunerated – so when the Maidstone Union advertised for a chaplain to the workhouse at a salary of £100, Henry applied for the position and was appointed. The duties must have been difficult; ministering to the sick, the unrelenting poor and miserable, trying to educate the children and holding services. Henry did not stay longer than a year.

It would be nice to think that his next situation resulted from someone in Government who thought that Henry had been badly treated by the legal establishment, and decided to provide him with a viable living. The rectory of Little Stambridge in Essex had become vacant upon the death of the incumbent, the Rev John Robert Barber DD, and Henry was appointed rector in 1867. The living was worth £177 per annum and was in the gift of the Lord Chancellor. It was ironic that the sponsor of the living was the same person who would have ruled over the Cochrane v Hatch case, thereby depriving Henry of the much more lucrative parish of Sutton. And in a further irony, one of the parishes adjacent to Little Stambridge was called Sutton! Nevertheless, Henry and Essie spent the next twenty-one years of their lives together in the tiny parish of Little Stambridge, tucked away in the Essex marshes on the estuary of the river Roach.

Only Henry and Essie, because as if they had not suffered enough, there was a schism with Lucy. In researching the life of Henry John Hatch and his 'trials', this writer consoled himself with a picture of Henry and Essie in picturesque old age, surrounded by Lucy's children in a Victorian sunset of happy and fulfilled family life. It was not to be. In 1871, when she was nineteen, Lucy was a pupil, possibly a pupil-teacher, at a school in Sandown on the Isle of Wight, not far from Newport where she had lived with her family before the death of her parents. Her name was recorded incorrectly as Lucy H Butcher – clearly a mistake for 'Buckler', her original family name. In any event, she had discarded the 'Hatch' name. She was certainly in contact with her blood-siblings, because most of them were present when she married James Staniland Stocks, a leather-tanner in Bushbury, in the county of Stafford, in 1876. Bushbury was not very far from where Henry and Essie had lived when Henry had been a curate following his return from Australia. That was long before Lucy came into the family, but it is possible that Lucy was acquainted with friends from that period, and in that way met her future husband – a well-to-do employer in the leather business.

There is no direct evidence of Lucy's break with the Hatches, but she does not figure in Henry's will or on the death certificates of either Henry or Essie. It would seem highly unlikely that Henry would have made no mention of a loved and loving daughter in his will, no matter that she was adopted and he had virtually nothing to leave her. But more telling than that, Lucy had changed her maiden name from 'Hatch' back to 'Buckler'.

Some might conclude that Lucy's estrangement from the Hatches was highly suspicious. If Henry *had* interfered with Eugenia Plummer, then according to Eugenia, it had happened at least once in Lucy's presence when she too was abused. Younger children can be awed by adults, and will not 'tell' if told by adults not to. If Lucy had been abused, then as she grew up, she would have realized what had happened and would have wanted nothing further to do with the Hatches. However if the substantial arguments – detailed below – *against* the likelihood of Henry having abused the Plummer girls are to be believed, then there is no reason to think that Henry treated Lucy in any way other than as a much loved daughter.

Such a circumstance as losing Lucy must have tested Henry's faith to breaking point. But he still had his life-long companion, the loyal Essie, and together they made the best of life in the east of England, where the land falls into the sea.

That part of Essex hosts tidal river estuaries characterized by mud-flats and saltings. The river Roach is a tributary of the river Crouch, which is the next river north from the Thames. Little Stambridge was largely agricultural, growing wheat, barley, peas and beans. There was a tide mill dating from 1762 at the head of the river, although shortly after Henry arrived this was replaced by a steam-powered mill. The river was navigable at high tide, and there was wharfage allowing the shipment of produce. Adjacent to Little Stambridge was Great Stambridge, with Paglesham close by. The church of St Mary's at Little Stambridge (= Stone Bridge), very close to Little Stambridge Hall, was described as of 'brick and stone in the early English style, with a chancel, nave, vestry, south porch, small wooden tower, spire and one bell'. Little Stambridge was appropriately named. In 1871 the population was 136. Ten years later, it had increased by just eight, entirely consistent with the number of baptisms and burials in the intervening period. There was quite a decent sized rectory about half a mile north of the church, and 36 acres of glebe land, although whether Henry and Essie ever lived there is not clear.

When Henry arrived in 1867 the church was in a very poor state of repair, and he set about encouraging a subscription for renovation. Eventually, around £280 was raised, to which he contributed the cost of repairing the chancel whose floor had deteriorated badly – as had the floor elsewhere in the church. Henry's sister, Augusta, contributed a 'handsome new altar cloth', and Mr Allen of Little Stambridge Hall, made the gift of some new windows. Following the restoration work, the church was reopened on 6th May 1870, being described as a 'neat, plain and pretty place of worship'. Four local clergymen participated in the opening ceremony, including the Reverend John Harris of Paglesham. The Venite, Gloria and Kyrie Eleison were performed, set to music composed by the Reverend Henry John Hatch, and accompanied on the harmonium by Miss Jeannie Brean. Subsequently, Henry also organized a concert at the Corn Exchange, Rochford (the nearest town), to support the church building fund. In 1869, Henry and Essie had taken out a mortgage with the University Life Assurance Society using Essie's income from the advowson sale as collateral. The total amount borrowed was £400, and some of the money probably paid for the repairs to the chancel.

Despite the size of the parish, Henry had engaged in his new work with enthusiasm. It cannot have been easy to persuade his meagre flock to part company with the amount of money he managed to raise, and one can imagine that the events he organized and the knocking on doors made him well-known in the area. Apart from that, the parish work was not onerous. In the twenty-one years of his residence, Henry conducted just 71 baptisms, 39 burials and 7 marriages; an average of three baptisms and two burials a year and a marriage every three years. At times, he and Essie must have thought they had been buried alive. Still, at least it was a living, and they were able to live comfortably enough to afford to keep two servants. They also had a live-in (male) student, whom Henry was tutoring to help to balance the books. The limited calls upon Henry's time enabled him to boost his income by also taking on the curacy of Little Wakering, just across the estuary from Little Stambridge, a post he held for at least ten years.

By around 1880, Henry and Essie had had enough of residing in Little Stambridge, and moved into accommodation in Southend, accessible via the railway. Between 1881 and 1886 they had at least three residences there, one of which they named Illawarra Lodge, after the area near Sydney near where they had lived so many years previously.

Henry's letter to *The Times*, and his articles in *The Philanthropist*, make it clear that he was perfectly capable of writing good English, and with what must have been plenty of time on his hands in Essex, writing would have been a natural pastime. It is a pity that he did not write his life story; he certainly had far more to tell than most rural parsons. Instead, he contributed stories and music to a whimsical collection of curiosities called *The Paglesham Oyster*. *The Paglesham Oyster* was published in Rochford in 1870, co-authored with the Rev James Harris, the rector of Paglesham, and James Wiseman a local landowner. James Harris, the same age as Henry, was living with his wife, several children and three servants in the new and spacious rectory at Paglesham. He had been rector for ten years. James Foster Turner Wiseman kept oyster beds, and subsequently he was a farmer also. He came from a well-established local family, and lived at The Chase in Paglesham, also with a wife, children and three servants. He was a great sportsman, poet, sailor and later a painter too. He was younger than Henry – thirty-five years old when the book was published. The two Jameses knew each other well, and James Wiseman's eldest daughter was to marry one of James Harris' sons. However, they took Henry into their circle, and it was James Wiseman's main occupation – the laying and harvesting of oyster beds – that was the inspiration for the name of the book. The preface had puns on oysters and fish sufficient to do credit to a Cambridge Footlights Review sketch. The 'pearls' of the book consisted of stories, some of fact some of fantasy, poems, some quadrilles, a song (music by Henry), charades, riddles, anagrams etc. Henry's contributions are of most interest to the current narrative, although one has to question one of the contributions from the Rev Harris in such a light-hearted compendium. He described in the most graphic detail, the guillotining of a criminal in Rome – an event he personally witnessed.

Of the pieces that Henry wrote, including a ghost story, the clever epilogue in verse, and the music for a ballad called A Mother's Love, it is the story of James Thrayle that most attracts attention. The story, founded as it says on fact, occupies a quarter of the book, and is taken from the 'journal of a prison chaplain'. Henry used the opportunity to affirm his charitable views on the causes of crime and the reform of prisoners, noting the effect of evil influences and lack of education, and that 'circumstances make the man'. He contrasted the attitude of people to ex-prisoners as more like the Old-Testament Pharaoh who demanded that the Israelites make bricks for his buildings but gather the straw themselves, than St Paul, who advocated 'Proof of love'. He spoke about the difficulty of discharged prisoners in finding employment, and commented on a society formed in 1824, in Surrey, to provide material assistance to discharged prisoners in respect of food clothing and training. Here was Henry, after all he had been through, still proselytising his basic Christian values and attitude towards a section of society that most people would prefer did not exist.

The *Oyster* was followed six years later by a more ambitious book penned by the same trio, *Logs for the Christmas Fire*. The format was as before but this book was twice as long – nearly 300 pages. Once more, among Henry's stories, was an account of a refuge for discharged prisoners, taken almost certainly, from his own experiences.

By 1881, the population of Little Stambridge had increased to 164, but it was a struggle to maintain enthusiasm in such limited circumstances. It must have been clear to Henry, even then, that the parish was unsustainable. In addition, the church restoration of 1870 had obviously been a half-hearted affair – possibly because of the difficulty of raising money – and the church had become more and more dilapidated. In 1889 the decision was taken to combine the parishes of Great and Little Stambridge and pull down the church of Little Stambridge. It was in a poor state of repair, and it had no architectural feature worth preserving and no monuments or mural tablets. All that now remains of the church, apart from a few gravestones in the grounds of Little Stambridge Hall, is its single seventeenth century bell, made by Peter Hawkes, which was taken to the rectory of Great Stambridge.

Poor old Henry Hatch! After all his trials and tribulations, to have had the parish of which he struggled to make a success for twenty-one years abolished, and the very fabric of the church unceremoniously demolished because it had 'no architectural feature worth preserving' must have been beyond endurance. And he didn't endure it. He would have seen such a decision coming, and in 1888 he and Essie were on the move again, this time to Little Linford in Buckinghamshire. Only on this occasion, the move must have been difficult; Essie was sixty-three, Henry was seventy. He should have been retiring, but of course, he could not afford to.

If Henry's last parish had been small, the even more aptly named Little Linford was microscopic. It had only seventy occupants in 1891, but at least the living had a house and a net income of £126 per year. The church of St Leonard's dated from the 14th century and was a similar size to that at Little Stambridge. Here it was that Henry and Essie lived out the rest of their lives together. Henry did no more writing, or if he did, it was not published. They were distant from their circle of friends in Essex, but no doubt as they had done so many times before, Henry and Essie made the best of it, starting yet again in unknown territory.

# *Epilogue*

What is one to make of the Hatch affair? Was Henry, after all, guilty? Was his indiscretion his downfall? Were his persecutors (and prosecutors), the Plummers, guilty of conspiracy? Or was he just a victim of a perfidious legal system? Discounting the possibility that he *was* guilty, it was probably a combination of all of those factors that led to his imprisonment and subsequent failure to win any sort of compensation.

Eugenia Plummer had provided a quite detailed description of the alleged offences; far more detailed than a girl of her age ought to have known about unless the incidents had happened as described. She was also able to withstand cross-examination by an experienced barrister – and judge – in the intimidating surroundings of the Old Bailey. There is, however, the most telling piece of circumstantial evidence that casts serious doubt over the truth of Eugenia's (and her sister's) allegations. With all of the detailed descriptions of what Henry did to her provided by Eugenia, together with similar allegations from Stephana, *neither of them ever claimed that Henry told them not to tell*. It seems utterly inconceivable that had Henry done what was alleged – every day that Eugenia was at the Hatches' – he would not have told her not to tell anyone. Even assuming the most unlikely collusion between Henry and his wife, as Eugenia had implied, there was Martha Howe the governess, Mrs Dillon, the servants, and of course, her parents who could have been told what was going on.

There was a further piece of evidence, albeit indirect, in Henry's favour. Henry had been chaplain of Wandsworth prison for eight years. At any one time, Wandsworth had upwards of seventy female prisoners between the ages of seven and seventeen confined in the Separate System and seen only by the (female) prison guards and the chaplain. If Henry's leanings were in the direction alleged by Eugenia, he was in a position only slightly less convenient than that of a middle-eastern prince with a harem. He had seventy female children to choose from. Although they were prisoners, and any allegations they made would have been treated with the utmost scepticism, after eight years and so many children, *something* would have come out. The fact that nothing did, suggests that there was nothing *to* come out.

Was Henry his own worst enemy, incriminating himself time after time by his actions? Some of the newspaper reports following Eugenia's trial, as well as the Lord Chief Baron in the Hatch v Lewis action, took the view that Henry bore a significant burden of guilt. His agreement to let Eugenia into the family bed, his resignation from Wandsworth, his flight to Poplar, what he said to Walters Freake Pratt when he surrendered and the questions he asked the arresting officer, all exhibited very poor judgement. Allowing the child into his bed was, as he and Essie maintained, acceding to a direct request by Caroline Plummer. But this point was never pursued in detail in any of the trials. His resignation followed advice, affirmed under oath, from Mr Onslow the prison governor. His flight, Henry insisted, was prompted by an imminent fear of being arrested and imprisoned for debt; no one from his defence thought to check his story about the call against the insurance company shares and the date when the demand was received and offer it as evidence. If it were not true, it would certainly have been odd to include a deliberate falsehood in the petition to the Queen – one that could easily have been checked. As for what he said to Walters Freake Pratt, and his questions to the policeman, his mind must have been in such a turmoil he probably hardly knew what he was saying. In Henry's favour, was the fact that at the time of his arrest, Pratt had offered to drop the case if Henry agreed to admit guilt and make an apology. It must have been obvious that he was facing a prison sentence if found guilty, and the fact that he declined to take the easy way out and confront the awfulness of possible imprisonment, suggests that he really was innocent.

It is tempting to conclude that Caroline Plummer was the real villain of the piece. Her eccentric behaviour at the Hatches', her intoxicated performance as a witness during her daughter's trial, and the information on her background dredged up by *The Detective* suggests that she was at best emotionally unstable, and at worst verging on the psychotic. She was certainly far from being a good mother, and life at Holcroft House appeared to have been dissipated, Godless, and occasionally violent. Probably what really happened, was that Eugenia was unhappy with the sober, proper, and disciplined life at the Hatches' after enjoying a dissolute time with her parents, and told the story as a ruse to be taken home. There may have been a fleeting and accidental glimpse of Henry 'undressed' during the morning visits to the bedroom which gave her the idea – perhaps when she was resisting getting out of bed. Her hysterical mother was unable to distinguish fiction from reality, and subsequently coached her daughter to get the story consistent, embellishing it to make it more credible. This seems the most likely explanation for events. It is a great pity that Henry did not sue the Plummers and get compensation from them for all the pain, misery, and loss he had suffered directly and indirectly at their hands.

How should we consider the behaviour of the various legal personalities involved in the Hatch case? Serjeant Ballantine had made a creditable enough effort at Henry's defence, given the criminally deficient brief provided to him by Lewis and

Lewis. He acted with great integrity when he was called as a defence witness in the Hatch v Lewis action.

Lewis and Lewis, surely, should have been properly called to account. Henry's letter to *The Times* completes the story of James Lewis' criminal incompetence. He arrived late to the magistrates' hearing and failed to examine the defence witnesses; he asked for a memorandum of events from Henry – claiming initially that he had visited Henry three times, then admitting it had only been twice, and Henry denied that they ever discussed the details of his case; he allowed his clerk to mangle Henry's efforts, leaving parts out that he could not read, and misunderstanding others, and then allowed this 'ragged brief' to be presented to Serjeant Ballantine, ignoring also the report from the investigator Brennan; he ignored Essie's entreaties to examine the defence witnesses and put pressure on Ballantine to call them in the trial, and for this few hours of grossly incompetent work, he pocketed £31 of pure profit out of a £75 fee. And after all this, he was telling everyone at the Hatch v Lewis hearings that the whole thing was Serjeant Ballantine's fault for deciding not to call witnesses! If James Lewis had applied the attention to detail that Essie was entitled to expect having retained him because of his eminent reputation, then Henry would almost certainly have been acquitted, and would have had to have served only two weeks rather than six months in prison.

Then there was the highly questionable behaviour of Walters Freake Pratt. He had a lucky escape when he suggested to Essie and Henry that the case could be dropped if Henry confessed. But in his economy with the truth under questioning from the Home Secretary, Pratt bore a large measure of responsibility for the decision to deny the Royal Pardon.

It is a moot point whether or not Henry's legal team could have won any action against Walters Freake Pratt, given the biased opinions of their lordships Cockburn, Crompton, Hill, and Wightman on the case. They considered that Mr Pratt was simply being 'humane' when he visited Essie, and that his offer to withdraw charges was just an error of judgement. They even doubted that his ambiguity with the Home Secretary was misconduct.

The actions, or rather inactions, of the Home Secretary were also highly questionable. He was the final arbiter of the success or otherwise of petitions for mercy, and as such, the ultimate judicial appeal rested with him. His possible motives for not granting Henry's petition have been examined earlier, but there was still the simple fact that he told Mr Gegg that Walters Freake Pratt had implied to him that Henry had confessed; but the outcome of the Pratt hearing established unequivocally that Henry had *not* confessed. Given the wealth of evidence presented in the petition to the Queen and its associated sworn affidavits, why did the Home Secretary still decline to recommend mercy?

There was the considerably biased attitude of *The Times* newspaper. Mr Holt, Henry's new solicitor, had circulated copies of the petition to the newspapers. A number of them, including *The Detective*, published either extracts or the full text with some comment. It seems astonishing, given the coverage *The Times* gave to the Smethurst case, that there was no published correspondence or editorial coverage of the Hatch case until the reports of Eugenia's trial in mid May. In addition to which, there was the very unpleasant and mocking editorial following the failure to get costs in Hatch v Lewis. The suspicion of collusion between the editor and the Home Secretary has already been mentioned.

In Eugenia's trial, Henry's team won a complete victory, but still there were questions to ponder. Mrs Plummer could have been asked to confirm that it was at her wish that Eugenia was allowed in the bed (rather than just agreeing to it, as she said in her evidence), and Essie and Martha Howe, at least, could have been called upon to confirm that fact. According to the Hatches and Martha Howe, Caroline Plummer had stated that it was while at the school of the Rev Brighton that Eugenia had got used to going in his bed in the morning. He was called as a defence witness, and denied emphatically that Eugenia was even allowed into his bedroom. The prosecution, apparently, never thought to pursue that point with Caroline Plummer.

The prosecution team also failed to analyse the garden to confirm what could and could not be seen. Perhaps what was more surprising, was that they failed to establish from Essie, Mrs Dillon, Mary Ann Reed or Ellen Farr the status of the passage door to Eugenia's room. She had claimed in her evidence in Henry's trial that it was locked with a bath against it, whereas Henry had claimed earlier – as had Mrs Dillon – that the door was always open. Thomas Plummer, also, deposed that it was not locked. Lucy had claimed that she always went into the bed next to Henry, whereas Eugenia had said that *she* was next to Henry. This point was not clarified, and neither was Lucy asked to confirm that she only went under the counterpane and not the blankets.

Then there was the mystery of John Gay, the Plummers' medical man. He fainted under cross-examination when Edwin James was referring to the previous trial record, trying to establish whether Mr Gay had or had not given evidence regarding 'marks of violence' upon Eugenia. And yet Mr Gay was not mentioned as a witness in the press reports of that trial, and he was certainly not included in the court reporter's transcript of the prosecution evidence. He could not possibly have been overlooked, since medical evidence of interference would have been central to the prosecution case. John Gay was thirty-nine years old, unmarried, and living with his father, a retired doctor. His behaviour was quite suspicious, and yet the facts were never followed up. His relationship with Eugenia, his 'little wife', was decidedly inappropriate. Why did the prosecution team not follow that point up if only to discredit one of the defence's witnesses? There was also the questionable behaviour of the trial judge in accepting Gay's explanation that his previous evidence did not appear on the record because he spoke in a 'low voice', when the totality of evidence points to him not having been called at all during the first trial.

Finally, there was the question of Caroline Plummer's insistence that the doors to Eugenia's bedroom be left wide open – even removed from their hinges. Was this really out of a wish for Eugenia to be well ventilated, or did Mrs Plummer want to prevent, at all costs, any chance of her being in a closed bedroom unobserved? Perhaps something had already happened to Eugenia in one of the many schools she had attended and this raised Caroline Plummer's suspicions. Perhaps, given the lax and dissipated environment at the Plummers' home, something had happened there. If that were the case, then Eugenia might be far from the innocent she was assumed to be, and this would explain her knowledge of matters about which she should have been ignorant.

All of these matters could have been investigated and used in an action for damages against the Plummers. On the face of it and individually, none of them were particularly damning. Taken together, and with some private detective work on the Plummers' background, a clever lawyer could have made a winnable case. At the very least, some research on these points would have helped to guarantee a guilty verdict. The more decisive the guilty verdict was on Eugenia, the easier it would be, subsequently, to win a case against her mother. If Caroline Plummer could be proved to have been substantially lying in her evidence, then that would have enabled Henry to sue her for damages with a good chance of success. It was clear from the press reports of the trial that Mrs Plummer was generally regarded as the villain, and a jury would have found against her with little persuasion. Yet Henry had observed in the Hatch v Lewis trial, that had he been able to have sued the Plummers, he would not have pursued the Lewises. It was yet another lost opportunity, and he was, yet again, badly let down by his legal team.

One cannot entirely blame Edwin James, Henry's chief barrister, for this series of oversights. The strategy adopted for Eugenia's prosecution should have been the result of a team effort involving Henry's new solicitor and Edwin James' brother barristers as well as James himself. Edwin James was, after all, worried about his indebtedness, a state of affairs that would have him bankrupt the following year for the sum of £100,000. And even that fact throws doubt on the judgement of Henry's new solicitor in instructing him. One does not become bankrupt for such an enormous sum overnight. The legal cognoscenti must have been aware of his precarious financial position. Any man with such an issue hanging over him cannot give of his best.

The bias of the Lord Chief Baron in the action against Lewis and Lewis was palpable. Sir Frederick Pollock lost no opportunity to emphasize, time and time again, that Henry had incriminated himself by his various actions. At the same time, he dismissed the relevance of the prosecution evidence in Eugenia's trial since for the most part her counter-evidence (from Henry's trial), by its nature, could not be contradicted. His clear direction to the jury (and his bungling of the summing up) was effectively followed to the letter in finding for Henry, while awarding him absurd damages and completely negating the purpose of the action. There was also the questionable fact that Charles Pollock, Sir Frederick's son was appearing for the defence, and Sir Samuel Martin, Sir Frederick's son-in-law, was one of his brother judges on the bench. Perhaps the concept of 'conflict of interest' was unknown in the nineteenth century.

Interestingly, in the contemporary legal notes on Hatch v Lewis, there is a footnote detailing what might have happened if Henry had been awarded substantial damages, and Lewis et al had moved for a retrial. The note makes very interesting reading:

[Since misdirection regarding the 40s damages was refused]…it did not become necessary…to enter into the grave and serious questions which would have arisen had the plaintiff [Henry] recovered substantial damages, and had the defendants moved for misdirection, on the ground that no such action would lie, [be admissible] in a criminal case, where the accused had his witnesses in Court, acquiesced in the decision of counsel not to call them…and, finally, sued, without alleging his innocence of the offence of which he had been convicted. Had he averred [proved or justified] his innocence, then supposing the allegation [against him] to have been material [significant] – as, it is submitted, it would have been – it might have been traversed, [contradicted formally] and both the girls might have been examined, as well as the plaintiff and his wife, and the jury would at least have had a fairer opportunity of judging of the matter than the jury who convicted Eugenie of perjury. And it is conceived that the omission of the averment was fatal, because on grounds of public policy it would be dangerous to allow a guilty person, duly convicted, to sue anyone either for malice in the prosecution or negligence in his defence. He cannot sue for malice, and it seems a strange ground of action for a guilty man, that, by some industry in dealing with witnesses, or taking legal objections, he might have escaped conviction, and thus defeated justice. Beyond all doubt a guilty man may be convicted through negligence, and, perhaps, to hold such an action to lie would be to open a very wide door.

How is one to understand this legal doublethink? 'Beyond all doubt a guilty man may be convicted through negligence'? Does not his very guilt or innocence *depend* on a properly conducted prosecution and defence? If negligence is present in the process that *defines* his guilt or innocence – in the prosecution *or* the defence – who can say whether he is guilty or innocent? Specifically, in Henry's action against the Lewises, the case notes appear to be saying that his legal team had failed to *prove* that Henry was innocent of the charge for which he was imprisoned. The rationale, presumably, was that although he had received the Royal Pardon, he was only 'pardoned' from the sentence; it did not quash the conviction, and thus Henry was still technically guilty. As such, and for the reasons given, the action against James Lewis should not have been admissible. In the process of suing the Lewises successfully, Henry would have had to have first *proved* his innocence – effectively by a full retrial of his case, with Eugenia and Stephana, Henry and Essie all giving evidence. If this opinion is correct, it seems that Henry's legal team even bungled the case against Lewis and Lewis on a technicality.

Of course it was the action for costs and a retrial that revealed the Kafkaesque nightmare of the whole legal process. Mr Chambers had moved for a retrial on the basis of misdirection and inappropriate damages. Unsurprisingly, this had been rejected. After all, would the Lord Chief Baron really have accepted that he, himself, had misdirected the jury just days after the event? He had refused costs on the basis that although Henry had won the case, the amount awarded – forty shillings – did not justify bringing the case in a superior court, since amounts not exceeding £20 in contract and £5 in tort could be claimed in County Court actions. Mr Chambers presented comprehensive arguments detailing why bringing the case in a County Court would have been absurd, citing the Lord Chief Baron's own words on the importance of the case. Nevertheless, the judge and his 'brothers' refused costs citing arguments so circular and tortuous, they must have made Henry's head spin.

Unfortunately, Henry himself might have unwittingly contributed to the failure of the move for a retrial and the case for costs. He admitted, in court, that if he could have sued the Plummers, he would not have brought the action against the Lewises. It was a most unwise statement, since a successful action against the Plummers would not have changed the Lewises' negligence or otherwise. The comment allowed the action against the Lewises to be interpreted as vindictive and vexatious, giving the judges further grounds for dismissing it. It was yet another failure by his defence team.

Finally, there were fatal defects existing in the law at that time. If Henry and Essie had been able to give evidence in the first trial (and Serjeant Ballantine had called them), an innocent verdict would almost certainly have been the outcome. And if Henry had still been found guilty, due to some quirk in the jury, surely a Court of Criminal Appeal would have cleared him, given the evidence – even if Lewis and Lewis had bungled the defence the first time round. The inability of the defendant or his wife to give evidence in criminal cases conspired to turn a relatively straightforward criminal action into a two-year nightmare for Henry. It cost the various players in the drama thousands of pounds, and did no-one's reputation any good. And it is an indictment of the Legislature at the time, that given the facts of the Hatch affair, the ability of the defendant to give evidence in a criminal case was not introduced for another forty years, and a Court of Criminal Appeal was not introduced until another ten years after that.

From all of this, three things seem to be abundantly clear. Firstly, Henry John Hatch fell victim to a malicious, highly damaging, and almost certainly baseless series of allegations by two children, materially exaggerated by the children's mother. Secondly, he was let down by almost everyone in the various legal teams acting supposedly in his interests. Thirdly, in the behaviour of the Home Secretary, the Lord Chief Justice, and the Lord Chief Baron and their various chums, the administration of the Law, as a means to achieve Justice, was a shambles. To paraphrase Mr Bumble, the Law really was an Ass...

In Henry's financial and personal affairs too, he was extraordinarily unfortunate. He had been given several thousand pounds by his father, and stood to inherit the Sutton parish living as well. His investment in *The Philanthropist* was effectively demolished when the Surrey magistrates forced him to give up his ownership, although that was largely self-inflicted. What was left of his inheritance was then dissipated in the various Chancery cases – his own unsuccessful action against his uncle, and the actions of Cochrane and Annesley against the indebtedness of his sister and her husband. The claim on the insurance company shares caused him to appear to flee from justice in order to avoid being arrested for debt. Then, he had to watch the Sutton living snatched away from him for the sake of a few hundred pounds benefit to the litigant. After Henry had managed to claw back his reputation and become established as rector in Little Stambridge, he had to watch the parish deteriorate to the extent that they pulled the church down the year after he left and abolished the parish! And then there was the split with his adopted and beloved daughter Lucy. No doubt the Reverend Henry John Hatch turned to the Book of Job and read about Job's suffering when his property and children were taken from him; Henry might well have reflected on the parallels between the two of them. Unlike Job though, good fortune and another child were not restored to Henry in his old age.

Six years after moving to Little Linford, Essie died at the vicarage. She was sixty-eight, and among other things, the cause of death was given as exhaustion. Finally, Henry had lost his soul mate. Essie had been Henry's loyal companion and champion during the dark days of Newgate, and his best and most constant friend for forty-nine years. It was a blow from which he could never recover. A year later, in October 1895 at the age of seventy-seven, Henry died alone in the Northampton General Infirmary, the house surgeon registering his death.

Reading Henry's will, this writer was saddened, heartened and then saddened again. Saddened at the lack of any reference to Lucy and the realization that there must have been a break-up; heartened that the value of Henry's estate at his death was just under £1200, he having finally managed to reverse some of his losses. But that too turned to sadness when it became clear that his debts exceeded his assets by £65. His executors were a local farmer and friend George Taylor, and a nephew, Herbert Bayley Dillon, son of Henry's youngest sister Adelaide and her first husband Thomas Dillon – who was probably related to Essie. Herbert, born in India, was in the Royal Navy, a lieutenant serving on HMS Edinburgh, a 10,000-ton ironclad boasting twelve-inch guns. Of all of Henry's sisters and their husbands and children, it was Herbert, frequently away at sea, who was the relative Henry could trust as his executor. Henry's death was briefly reported in *St James' Gazette* with no obituary.

Henry John Hatch had lived an extraordinary life for an Anglican clergyman. Coming from a genteel and well-to-do background, he travelled half way round the world, lived and married in Australia, owned and edited at least two journals, became a clergyman in the industrial north of England, was chaplain for eight years at a brand new prison operating the Separate System of confinement, and regularly saw his name in the newspapers doing good works. He spent six months incarcerated in Newgate, and was for two years in the public gaze in what was one of the most notorious series of court cases of the period. With all of that he still had the energy and enthusiasm to make a new, and for a time successful, life in Little Stambridge, retaining his good humour and charitable outlook. If the final thirty-four years of his life were relatively uneventful, then that is probably what he would have wanted. The great pity is that he never found the time or inclination to write his memoirs, because they would have been truly fascinating.

And what of the other players in our little Victorian melodrama? Lucy and her husband, James Stocks, had no children, but she lived to be ninety, dying in 1943, and leaving over £8000 to a friend. In later life she became an inventor, and registered at least two patents for cooking apparatuses – one for poaching eggs and one for frying fish – which were granted in 1902 and 1903 respectively.

Naturally, the judges lived out their lives in great wealth and comfort. On their deaths, their honours Bramwell, Channell, Cockburn, Keating, and Pollock left between them over £240,000. Lewis and Lewis went from strength to strength. James Lewis died in 1873, but his son George was knighted, and became the richest and most famous solicitor in England. Sir George Cornewall Lewis, the Home Secretary who initially denied Henry his Royal Pardon, died in 1863, but not before he suffered the 'scholastic embarrassment' of having his translations of some Greek fables rejected on account of the originals being fakes (ODNB). Serjeant Ballantine published two books in later life; the first one, *Some Experiences of a Barrister's Life*, was eagerly analysed for any mention of the Hatch case. Naturally there was none, although the book is interesting as a record of life in and out of court at the time. As reported in *The Law Times*, Ballantine died 'very poor indeed'. Edwin James became bankrupt owing £100,000, was found guilty of obtaining money by misrepresentation, disbarred and struck off. Walters Freake Pratt died quite young at the age of 43; his first name *was* Walters (rather than 'Walter'), as confirmed by his gravestone in Wootton Bassett churchyard, although his middle name was spelled 'Freak' without the final 'e'.

Eugenia Plummer does not appear in the 1861 census. She was probably living under an assumed name in order to protect her from unwelcome attention. By that time, the Plummers had moved out of Holcroft House and were living in Imperial Square in Cheltenham. Perhaps the expenses of defending Eugenia had forced them to sell. Possibly they were compelled to leave, having received too much unwelcome post or too many unpleasant callers. Some time later, they moved to Weston Super Mare where Thomas Plummer died in November 1870. If he intended to leave Eugenia £15,000 then he failed in his endeavour. His gross estate was valued at only £16,000 split between his wife and the two girls. First, though, it all passed to Caroline Plummer.

Following Thomas's death, Caroline, Eugenia, and Stephana moved from Weston Super Mare into rented accommodation at Westbury on Trym – now a suburb of Bristol. In 1871 they were residing at a boarding house in a select area, among professional people and persons of independent means. Eugenia, now 23, evidently had survived her time spent 'where she would receive a proper education'.

However, years of dissipation told on Caroline Plummer. Soon afterwards, she died from chronic liver disease, liver cancer, stomach disease, and heart hypertrophy. At last, her drinking had caught up with her. Her death certificate was signed by a local doctor, and neighbour, Rice Wasbrough. By this time, Stephana had married Edward Coleman, a prosperous maltster and hop merchant from Bristol; they had a daughter, Stephanie, born in 1889. Edward died in 1892, and two years later Stephana married an estate agent, Louis Edward De Ridder by whom she had a son the following year, also named Louis Edward, who became a clergyman. Stephana died in 1926 at the age of seventy-six.

With her mother dead, Eugenia, now of independent means, moved in with the Wasbroughs. In 1886, one year after Rice's wife Frances died, when Eugenia was thirty-eight and Rice was seventy-one, she married him! It was, no doubt, a mutually convenient arrangement. Rice was able to exchange a woman of seventy-seven for one of half that age, and one not without her own financial resources. From Eugenia's standpoint, Rice's bank balance and advanced years may have been too much of a temptation. No doubt events had scuppered any chance of marrying John Gay – if that was ever seriously in the offing – and Eugenia had remained obstinately single. It is ironic though that she did, in the end, marry her medical man. Rice proved to be remarkably durable, lasting until 1898, at which point he bowed out leaving Eugenia the best part of £9,500.

But Mary Eugenia or was it Eugenie – even her solicitor when seeking probate was not sure – outlived everyone except Lucy. When Rice Wasbrough died, Eugenia was fifty. She had enough money in the bank to live the rest of her life in luxury, and since she does not appear in either the 1901 or 1911 census returns, it is likely that she was living abroad. When she finally died in 1937, aged eighty-nine, she was worth £30,000, making her a millionaire in today's money. The cause of death was intestinal obstruction, just like her father sixty-seven years earlier. The fact that Eugenia was able to double her money in forty years, suggests that either she lived a relatively frugal life, or she was a shrewd money-manager. Perhaps both. She left the bulk of her estate to her nephew and niece, the son and daughter of her sister Stephana.

Henry and Essie died effectively penniless, but at least so close to one another that each was able to comfort the other for most of their lives together. Lucy lived a very long life in relative comfort and financial security. Caroline Plummer reaped what she had sown in respect of her lifestyle. Stephana prospered, and her children had the benefit of Eugenia's wealth in the end. Eugenia Plummer, in terms of material wealth, did best of all. In the end though, she died, apparently friendless, with sufficient distrust in those around her that she appointed the public trustee to be the executor of her will.

# *Appendix 1*

## COURTS OF LAW IN MID NINETEENTH CENTURY BRITAIN

(These notes were compiled mostly from J H Baker's *An Introduction to English Legal History*; direct quotations are from that work.)

The legal and court system in England and Wales in the mid nineteenth century was nothing if not complex. Criminal cases were generally taken first before a Magistrates' Court, also known as a Police Court or Petty Session. Cases beyond the jurisdiction of Magistrates, but of a less serious nature, were then sent to the Quarter Sessions. The most serious crimes would be sent for trial at the Assizes in the provinces, or the Central Criminal Court (the Old Bailey) in London and the surrounding metropolitan area. There was no Court of Criminal Appeal, and neither the Defendant (the person charged with the offence) nor his or her spouse could give evidence in the trial. The Plaintiff in an action was the person bringing the action (usually the Crown in criminal cases). Indictable crimes requiring to be heard before a jury could be subjected to a preliminary Grand Jury hearing rather than a Magistrates' Court. If the Grand Jury 'found that there was a case to answer', by a majority of 12 (Grand Juries usually had around 23 members), they found the bill 'true', and the case was sent for trial by a 'petty' jury, that is, a conventional jury of 12 persons, at the Assizes or the Old Bailey.

Civil cases involving common law, that is to say, unwritten law, 'derived from ancient and universal usage', could be heard in the Court of the Queen's Bench, the Court of Exchequer or the Court of Common Pleas. These three 'Superior Courts of Common Law', derived originally from the King's court, the Curia Regis. Initially, the three courts had different functions. The Court of Queen's Bench (or King's Bench) had a supervisory role and dealt with actions of trespass, and suits to correct 'courts of record'. The Court of Common Pleas had exclusive jurisdiction over actions to recover property or debt, with a special guild of barristers called Serjeants-at-Law. They were identified by the 'Coif', initially a silk skull cap, which by Victorian times had degenerated into a round patch sewn into the wig. The importance of Serjeants-at-Law came to be superseded by Queen's Counsel (QC) in the nineteenth century, and in 1846, the Serjeants lost their exclusive rights in the Court of Common Pleas. The Court of Exchequer, dealt initially with Crown revenue and litigation. Eventually, other litigants were attracted to it also. Judges in the Court of Exchequer, the oldest of the common law courts, were called Barons; the title arose because barons of the realm were originally employed in that office. These three courts, along with Chancery, were based in Westminster Hall.

Initially, each court had a specific and specialist function with different processes (and costs), but more and more they dealt interchangeably with the same actions, competing with each other for business. In the 1850s and 1860s, '...the choice [of which court to use] more often depended on the sphere of practice of the attorney consulted, on subtle differences in costs, and procedural advantages'. In 1832 the three courts were made procedurally uniform, and in 1873 the Judicature Act abolished the lot and transferred their function to the High Court. In addition to the civil courts already mentioned, County Courts existed for modest claims not exceeding £20.

One more court needs to be mentioned. The court of Chancery was the real villain in *Bleak House*, but, '...two centuries before Bleak House, Chancery became synonymous with expense, delay and despair'. In Chancery, the Lord Chancellor's '...transcendental form of justice acquired the name equity'. Initially it was called a court of conscience. It existed, as explained by Lord Ellesmere in 1615, because,

> ...men's actions are so diverse and infinite, that it is impossible to make a general law which may aptly meet with every particular, and not fail in some circumstance. The office of the chancellor is to correct men's consciences for frauds, breaches of trust, wrongs and oppressions of what nature soever [sic] they be, and to soften and mollify the extremity of the law...

Chancery was a court of equity, or natural justice, and was the refuge of a wronged litigant when he had no recourse either to Statute or Common Law. If natural justice was to be had though, great patience (and financial resource) was required. In the current narrative, it can be seen that although Henry Hatch's Chancery action over the conflict between his father's and grandmother's wills was concluded after only a few months, his grandfather's suit over the Sutton advowson took four years. Baker observes that in the eighteenth century, cases could take thirty years to resolve. The Court of Chancery was also abolished by the Judicature Act, although a Chancery division still exists in the High Court.

# *Appendix 2*

## POUNDS, SHILLINGS AND PENCE

Prior to 1971, the monetary system in use in Britain consisted of Pounds, Shillings and Pence. The Pound Sterling was made up of twenty shillings; a shilling being equal to twelve (old) pence, two sixpences or four threepenny bits. Each penny was divisible into two halfpence (ha'pence or ha'pennies) or four farthings. Five shillings was written 5/- and seven shillings and sixpence ha'penny was written 7s 6½d or 7/6½d. Three pounds, ten shillings, and tenpence, three farthings, was written £3 10s 10¾d. Sometimes quantities in small numbers of Pounds were written in the equivalent number of shillings: 20/- = 20 shillings = £1 or, 30/- = 30 shillings = £1 10s. A guinea was £1 1s, 21s, or 21/-. The descriptors were £ = Libra, a Roman pound, s = Solidus, originally a Roman gold coin, and d = Denarius, originally a small Roman silver coin. The equivalent value today of money from Georgian and Victorian times, has been calculated using a routine on the National Archives web site. Thus £1 in 1840 would have the purchasing power of £44.10 today. £1 in 1760 would purchase the equivalent of £74.79 today.

# Family Tree of the Hatches

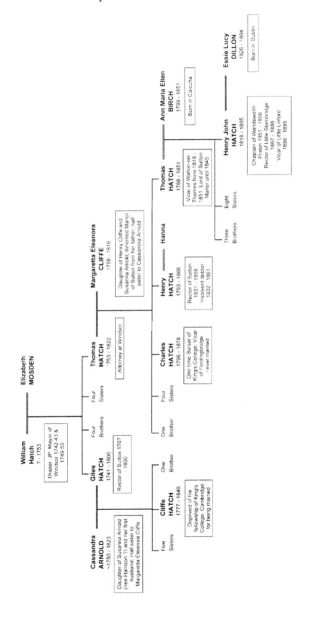

377

# Family Tree of the Cliffes

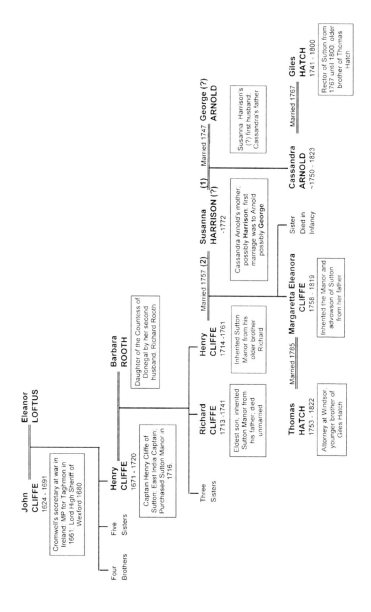

**John CLIFFE** 1624 - 1691
Cromwell's secretary at war in Ireland; MP for Taghmon in 1661; Lord High Sheriff of Wexford 1680

**Eleanor LOFTUS**

Four Brothers

Five Sisters

**Henry CLIFFE** 1671 - 1720
Captain Henry Cliffe of Sutton; East India Captain; Purchased Sutton Manor in 1716.

**Barbara ROOTH**
Daughter of the Countess of Donegal by her second husband, Richard Rooth

Three Sisters

**Richard CLIFFE** 1713 - 1741
Eldest son, inherited Sutton Manor from his father; died unmarried

**Henry CLIFFE** 1714 - 1761
Inherited Sutton Manor from his older brother Richard

Married 1757 (2)

**Susanna HARRISON (?)** -1772
Cassandra Arnold's mother; possibly Harrison; first marriage was to Arnold possibly George

Married 1747 (1)

**George (?) ARNOLD**
Susanna Harrison's (?) first husband; Cassandra's father

Sister Died in Infancy

**Margaretta Eleanora CLIFFE** 1758 - 1819
Inherited the Manor and advowson of Sutton from her father

**Cassandra ARNOLD** ~1750 - 1823

**Giles HATCH** 1741 - 1800
Rector of Sutton from 1767 until 1800; older brother of Thomas Hatch

Married 1785

**Thomas HATCH** 1753 - 1822
Attorney at Windsor; younger brother of Giles Hatch

Married 1767

# SOURCES

*Alumni Cantabrienses 1752 - 1900*, J A Venn, Cambridge University Press 1922 - 1954

*Alumni Oxonienses 1715 - 1886*, University of Oxford, Oxford & London 1887

*Convicts and the Colonies*, A G L Shaw, Melbourne University Press, 1966

*Crockford's Clerical Directory*, Church House Publishing, 1858 - 1896

*A Concise History of Australia*, Stuart Macintyre, Cambridge University Press, 1999

*The Clergy List*, various, 1851 - 1890

*The Criminal Prisons of London*, Henry Mayhew and John Binny, Frank Cass, 1862

*English Criminal Appeals 1844 - 1944*, Rosemary Pattenden, Clarendon Press, 1996

*Final report of the House of Correction at Wandsworth*, Committee of Justices, David Batten, 1852

*History of the Commoners, Vol 4*, Various, Burke, 1862

*A History of the English Clergy 1800-1900*, C K Francis Brown, The Faith Press, 1953

*A History of English Criminal Law*, Leo Radzinowicz, Stevens & Sons, London, 1948 et sec

*A History of the English Parish*, N J G Pounds, Cambridge University Press, 2000

*A History of Eton College*, Sir H C Maxwell Lyte, Macmillan & Co, 1911

*A History of Sutton*, Robert P Smith, Derek W James, 1970

*A History of Solicitors in New South Wales*, J M Bennett, Sydney: Legal Books , 1984

*An Introduction to English Legal History*, J H Baker, Butterworths, 2002

*Justis – Legal archive database*, Various, Justis, Current

*John Mildred, or Love One Another*, 'H J H', William Tweedie, 1860

*Juvenal, the Sixteen Satires*, Translated by Peter Green, Penguin, 1998

*John Thadeus Delane - His Life and Correspondence*, Irwen Dasent & John Murray, John Murray, 1908

*Logs for the Christmas Fire*, J Harris, H J Hatch & J Wiseman, Simpkin, Marshall & Co    1876

*Lewis and Lewis*, John Juxon, Collins, 1983

*London Labour and the London Poor*, Henry Mayhew, Constable, 1968

*LexisNexis – Legal archive database*, Various, LexisNexis, Current

*The Life and Times of Sir George Cornewall Lewis*, R W D Fenn, Logaston Books, 2005

*The Oxford Dictionary of National Biography - On Line*, Various, Oxford University Press, Current

*The Oxford English Dictionary - On Line*, Various, Oxford University Press, Current

*The Oxford History of the Prison*, Edited by Norval Morris and David J Rothman, Oxford University Press, 1995

*Paglesham Natives*, Mark & Rosemary Roberts, M A & R Roberts, 2006

*The Paglesham Oyster*, J Harris, H J Hatch & J Wiseman, Arthur Harrington Jun., 1870

*Some Experiences of a Barrister's Life*, William Ballantine, Richard Bentley & Son, 1890

*Sydney and Melbourne...*, Charles John Baker, Smith, Elder & Co, 1845

*The State of the Prisons in England and Wales...*, John Howard, Reprinted Routlage 2000, 1789

*Victorian London*, Liza Picard, Weidenfield & Nicolson, 2005

*Victorian Prison Lives*, Philip Priestley, Pimlico, 1999

*Wandsworth Prison A History*, Stewart McLaughlin, HMP
Wandsworth, 2001

Archives of the following newspapers and journals have been
consulted:

*The Times*
*The Daily Telegraph*
*The Manchester Guardian*
*The Observer*
*The Morning Star*
*The Morning Post*
*The Morning Chronicle*
*The Morning Herald*
*The Daily News*
*Lloyd's Weekly Newspaper*
*The Law Times*
*St James' Gazette*
*The New South Wales Magazine*
*The Detective*
*The Philanthropist*

# Picture Credits

Nos 1, 2, 3, 4 & 6, from The Criminal Prisons of London, by Henry Mayhew and John Binny, Frank Cass, London, 1862

No 5, photograph by the author

No 7, from John Mildred, by H, H. J., William Tweedie, London 1860, reproduced by kind permission of the British Library, © British Library Board. All Rights Reserved, 12807.f.5.

No 8, Reproduced by courtesy of Essex Record Office

No 9, photograph by the author

# *Index*

**A**

Abbiss, Mr 212
Advowson 44, 45, 46, 52, 53, 54,
    55, 56, 57, 64, 65, 348, 349,
    352, 375
Alcock, Thomas 41
Alexandria 37
Allan, George 43, 44
Allan, Mr Gordon 298
Allen, Gordon 15, 212
Allen, Mr 352
America 34
Annesley, George 65, 144, 348
Aristophanes 38
Aristotle 38
Arnold, Cassandra 53
Arundel St 348
Asia 37
Australia 20, 34, 37, 38, 39, 41, 42,
    44, 66, 291, 350, 369, 379
Australian Club, The 36
Avignon 37

**B**

Baccarat 296
Baker, Charles John 35, 36, 37, 39,
    373, 375, 380
Ballantine, Serjeant 15, 85, 86, 87,
        102, 103, 104, 105, 106, 107,
        108, 109, 110, 111, 112, 113,
        114, 115, 116, 118, 120, 122,
        127, 128, 129, 130, 132, 138,
        139, 141, 142, 143, 144, 178,
        181, 182, 192, 193, 195, 213,
        233, 259, 270, 284, 286, 293,
        294, 295, 296, 297, 301, 302,

303, 304, 307, 308, 309, 314,
315, 325, 326, 327, 328, 330,
344, 359, 360, 367, 370, 380
Banks, Isabella 195, 196, 197
Banks, Sir Joseph 34
Barber, Reverend John Robert 350
Barnard, Mr 213
Barnes, Richard 53
Bates, Theodore 152
Bath 176, 180, 247, 372
Bathford 175
Battle of the Boyne 31
Beck, Adolphe 296
Bedlam 21
Bellingham, John 57
Bengal 30, 32, 182, 298
Best, Captain 63, 206
Bethlehem Hospital for the Insane,
    The 21
Binny, John 23, 379
Birch, Lady 201
Birch, Richard Comyns 30
Birch, Sir Richard James Holwell 30
Blair, William T 180
Bleak House 10, 52, 87, 374
Bombay 37
Booth, Dr James 144
Botany Bay 34
Boyle, Richard 31
Braim, Thomas Henry 38
Bramwell, Baron 15, 85, 87, 89, 93,
        95, 96, 97, 98, 99, 106, 110,
        111, 112, 113, 114, 116, 117,
        124, 125, 126, 127, 144, 145,
        165, 199, 209, 210, 270, 321,
        322, 331, 334, 345, 370

383

Brean, Jeannie 352
Bridge, Captain Robert 144
Bridge, Mrs Robert 144
Brighton, Reverend 66, 154, 159, 171, 256, 262, 300, 362
Briscoe, John, MP 144
Bristol 371
Brixton House of Correction 43
Brixton prison 22
Buckingham Palace 273
Buckler, Anne 62
Buckler, Buckler, Martha 62
Buckler, Buckler, Mary 62
Buckler, Cass 62
Buckler, Cass, Senior 62
Buckler, John 62
Bullock, Reverend Thomas 144
Bumble, Mr 367
Bushbury 350
Byron, Lady 51

C

Cairo 37
Calcutta 30
Cambridge 30, 32, 33, 37, 38, 41, 47, 64, 214, 354, 379
Cape of Good Hope 37
Carden, Sir Robert Walter 212
Carter, Rt Hon John 212
Castel St Angelo 281
Ceylon 64
Challoner, Colonel 63, 206
Chambers, Montague 15, 208, 298, 303, 307, 308, 309, 318, 321, 322, 323, 325, 326, 327, 328, 329, 330, 331, 332, 334, 345, 366
Chancery 10, 52, 54, 55, 58, 64, 65, 75, 142, 144, 162, 163, 201, 274, 282, 310, 329, 348, 349, 368, 374, 375
Channell, Baron 15, 211, 230, 241, 242, 257, 258, 265, 267, 268, 270, 271, 272, 275, 276, 321, 334, 345, 370
Chapel Chorlton 41, 42
Chapman, WIlliam 53
Chertsey 29
China 30
Cliffe, Captain Henry 30
Cliffe, Henry 30
Cliffe, Margaretta Eleanora 30, 41, 52, 53, 54, 55, 56, 57, 58
Cochrane, John 63, 64, 65, 163, 348, 349, 350, 368
Cockburn, Sir Alexander 15, 182, 183, 187, 188, 189, 190, 360, 370
Coghlan, Francis 156
Coldbath Fields Prison 19
Coldbath Fields prison 25
Coleman, Edward 371
Coleman, George, the younger 262
Colombo 64
Conder, Mr 212
Cook, Captain 34
Cooper, Mr 15, 85, 87, 122, 123, 124, 125, 126, 127, 128, 181, 187, 192, 212
Cooper, William 43
Copeland, Mr, MP 212
Cotterell, Reverend George 144
Court of Criminal Appeal 9, 148, 166, 180, 202, 213, 278, 280, 281, 282, 284, 287, 367, 373
Court of Exchequer 297, 321, 341, 342, 374
Covent Garden 273
Coward, Walter 184
Cragie, Mrs Mary 201
Crawford, WIlliam 19
Cricklade 175
Crimea 10, 51, 59, 62
Crimean War 62

Criminal Appeal Act 289
Criminal Evidence Act 290
Crispinus 342
Crockford's Clerical Directory 39, 60, 379
Crompton, Sir Charles 182
Crouch, River 351
Crystal Palace 62, 292
Crystal Palace, The 62
Cumberland county 37

**D**

Daily News, The 278, 279, 280, 381
Daily Telegraph, The 166, 176, 195, 278, 282, 284, 285, 286, 287, 292, 381
Danks, Thomas 167
Davis, Reverend John 59, 146
Delane, John Thadeus 17, 199, 288, 380
Dent, Marmaduke 152
De Ridder, Louis Edward 371
Detective, The 167, 168, 174, 176, 177, 179, 192, 194, 195, 198, 202, 204, 209, 211, 231, 232, 252, 359, 361, 381
Dickens, Charles 10, 52, 85, 86, 87, 146, 295, 297
Dillon, Dr Thomas 201
Dillon, John 39, 40
Dillon, Mrs Esther 39, 66, 143, 168, 210, 227
Dixon, Hepworth 146
Domitian 342
Donegal, Countess of 43
Douglas, Lord Alfred 296
Downing Street 284
Dublin 39
Dudley, The Earl of 291
Dupuis, Reverend Henry 144
Durham, Mary 196, 197

Durnford, Alexander Hamilton Earle 64
Durnford, Colonel 64

**E**

Easell, Phoebe 175, 253
Edalji, George 296
Edwards, John Passmore 192
Elizabeth I 21
Escher 24
Eton 30, 32, 33, 34, 182, 193, 214, 379
Europe 37, 60

**F**

Farnham Castle 85
Farr, Ellen 29, 30, 143, 230, 362
Florence 31
Fordingbridge 57
France 34
Francis, Charles 144

**G**

Gardiner, Charles 57
Garrick Club 85
Garth, Mr Richard 15, 182, 183, 189, 298, 321, 323, 324, 332, 333
Gay, John 17, 68, 108, 216, 239, 240, 241, 250, 253, 254, 257, 258, 362, 372
Gegg, Joseph 144, 164, 180, 181, 185, 192, 203, 210, 274, 361
General Indemnity Insurance Company, The 75, 162, 274
Genoa 37
George III 34
Gifford, Mr 15
Glebe 40, 41
Gordon Riots 146
Gray, Eliza Gordon 176
Great Blunsdon 66
Great Ormond Street 59

Great Stambridge  351, 355
Great Western Railway  68
Grey, Sir George  283
Gridwood, Dr  180
Grove, Amelia  183
Guardian, The  166
Guildford  43

## H

Hale, Mr  212
Halley's Comet  38
Harker, Mr  213
Harris, Reverend John  352
Hart, William  152
Hatch, Ann  9, 10
Hatch, Charles  10, 15, 16, 17, 33, 36, 37, 39, 41, 47, 52, 57, 58, 64, 84, 86, 201, 297, 348, 364, 380
Hatch, Cliffe  33, 46, 53, 55
Hatch, Eleanora  32
Hatch, Eleanora Wingfield  30, 41, 52, 53, 64, 65, 201, 348, 349
Hatch, Essie  39, 40, 41, 42, 50, 62, 64, 65, 66, 67, 68, 69, 73, 75, 77, 99, 143, 149, 153, 168, 169, 177, 180, 181, 183, 184, 185, 187, 189, 190, 191, 192, 201, 202, 210, 218, 220, 221, 222, 223, 224, 227, 231, 232, 235, 237, 275, 280, 292, 295, 296, 299, 303, 306, 312, 316, 325, 349, 350, 351, 352, 353, 355, 356, 358, 360, 361, 362, 366, 367, 368, 369, 372
Hatch, George Cliffe  32
Hatch, Giles  30, 45, 47, 53, 54, 55, 56, 57
Hatch, Henry  13, 46, 47, 48, 49
Hatch, Henry John  3, 9, 10, 11, 12, 13, 14, 16, 17, 28, 29, 30, 31, 32, 33, 34, 35, 36, 37, 38, 39, 40, 41, 42, 43, 44, 45, 49, 50, 51, 52, 53, 57, 58, 59, 60, 61, 62, 63, 64, 65, 66, 67, 68, 69, 73, 74, 75, 76, 77, 78, 84, 85, 86, 87, 90, 100, 105, 118, 130, 132, 138, 141, 142, 143, 144, 145, 146, 147, 148, 149, 150, 151, 152, 153, 155, 156, 157, 158, 160, 161, 162, 163, 164, 165, 166, 167, 168, 169, 170, 171, 172, 173, 174, 176, 177, 178, 179, 180, 181, 182, 183, 184, 185, 187, 188, 190, 191, 192, 193, 194, 195, 196, 198, 199, 200, 201, 202, 204, 206, 209, 210, 211, 212, 213, 214, 215, 216, 217, 218, 219, 220, 222, 224, 225, 228, 231, 232, 234, 235, 236, 237, 241, 242, 254, 255, 256, 259, 263, 264, 267, 269, 270, 272, 273, 274, 275, 277, 278, 279, 280, 281, 282, 284, 287, 288, 290, 291, 292, 293, 295, 296, 297, 299, 300, 301, 302, 303, 304, 305, 306, 307, 308, 309, 310, 311, 312, 313, 314, 315, 316, 318, 319, 320, 321, 325, 326, 327, 328, 329, 331, 332, 335, 336, 337, 338, 339, 340, 341, 342, 343, 348, 349, 350, 351, 352, 353, 354, 355, 356, 357, 358, 359, 360, 361, 362, 363, 364, 365, 366, 367, 368, 369, 370, 372, 375, 379, 380
Hatch, Lucy Harriet  10, 40, 62, 63, 65, 66, 67, 68, 73, 89, 97, 98, 99, 100, 112, 113, 133, 141, 143, 144, 154, 155, 156, 157, 158, 159, 161, 168, 169, 171, 172, 173, 194, 200, 202, 210, 212, 215, 216, 217, 218, 221,

223, 224, 225, 226, 227, 228, 229, 230, 232, 238, 239, 240, 241, 243, 244, 249, 263, 268, 275, 292, 299, 300, 301, 303, 306, 311, 316, 350, 351, 362, 368, 369, 370, 372

Hatch, Richard 31, 32

Hatch, Thomas 10, 13, 29, 30, 39, 41, 42, 44, 45, 46, 50, 52, 57, 64

Hatch, Thomas, Senior 13, 52, 53, 54, 55, 56, 57

Hatch, Thomas, The Younger 32

Hatch, William 30

Hawkes, Peter 355

Head, William 152

Heath, Walter 152

Helsdon, Robert 152

Henry VIII 21

Hereford House 40

Hertford College 349

Highworth 73

Hill, Sir Hugh 16, 182

Hitchcock, Mr 16, 209, 210, 272, 275

Holborn 78, 141, 163, 184, 222

Holcroft House 73, 176, 249, 264, 359, 370

Holt, Mr 16, 166, 210, 225, 226, 227, 361

Holwell, John Zephiniah 30

Home Secretary, The 9, 17, 34, 147, 166, 180, 181, 182, 186, 188, 189, 191, 192, 194, 198, 199, 203, 208, 256, 277, 279, 283, 287, 288, 297, 302, 303, 340, 360, 361, 367, 370

Horsemonger Lane Prison 13, 21, 43, 84, 85, 86, 196, 300

Hortense 87

House of correction 22, 23

Howe, Martha 66, 67, 68, 143, 144,

153, 155, 159, 160, 168, 169, 170, 171, 172, 173, 210, 225, 226, 228, 229, 231, 232, 235, 300, 301, 303, 357, 361

Hue and Cry 77, 184

Humphreys and Morgan 250

Humphries, Mr 16, 254

Hunt, Alfred H 152

Hyde, William 151

**I**

Illawarra 37, 353

India 30, 31, 35, 37, 41, 44, 63, 369

Indian Mutiny 30

Insolvent Debtor's Court 46

Isle of Wight 62, 144, 172, 273, 274, 350

Israelites 354

Italy 34

**J**

Jaggers, Mr 295

James, Edwin, QC 10, 16, 182, 183, 185, 186, 188, 189, 193, 212, 213, 220, 232, 233, 239, 244, 245, 246, 247, 248, 249, 254, 257, 258, 259, 261, 262, 264, 267, 270, 271, 292, 299, 306, 308, 325, 327, 328, 354, 360, 362, 364, 366, 369, 370, 379, 381

James Chilman 10

James Thrayle 354

Jarndyce v Jarndyce 10, 52

Jessop, Reverend 63

Jesus College 37

John Mildred 200, 201, 202, 380

Johnson 196

Juvenal 342

**K**

Keate, Dr 32, 33

Keating, Mr Justice 16, 211, 265, 272, 370

Keene, Samuel T 151

Kemp, Mr 213

Kennett, Martha 175, 176

King's College 32, 33, 46

Knatchbull, Sir Edward 33

**L**

Labour machines 24, 26

Laidley, Eliza Jane 40

Laidley, James 40

Lambeth 292

Laporte 197

Law Times, The 176, 177, 191, 192, 274, 278, 286, 287, 289, 290, 293, 337, 338, 370, 381

Le Havre 37

Leichhardt Street 41

Lewis, Frederick Henry 85, 295

Lewis, George, Junior 16, 295, 296, 308

Lewis, George Hamilton Coleman 295

Lewis, James Graham 295, 296, 297

Lewis, Louis 295

Lewis, Sir George Cornewall 17, 180, 181, 182, 183, 185, 188, 191, 193, 194, 196, 197, 198, 199, 200, 275, 283, 286, 287, 288, 303, 304, 328, 370, 380

Lewis and Lewis 227, 292, 293, 295, 297, 302, 318, 323, 328, 331, 337, 339, 343, 360, 364, 366, 367, 370, 380

Lichfield 41

Lichfield, Bishop of 201, 214

Lincoln's Inn 85, 144

Little Linford 355, 356, 368

Little Stambridge 350, 351, 353, 355, 356, 368, 369

Little Stambridge Hall 352

Little Wakering 353

Lloyds Weekly Newspaper 252

Logs for the Christmas Fire 355, 380

London Sacred Harmonic Society 51

London Zoo 62

Lovatt, James 175

Lucy 351

Lush, Mr, QC 16, 298, 332

Lyon 37

**M**

Macaulay, Mr 16, 187, 190

Magdalene College 33

Maidstone Union 349

Malta 37

Manchester Examiner and Times, The 179

Manchester Guardian, The 381

Manning, Emily 62

Manning, Frederick George 86

Manning, Marie 86, 87

Manning, Sir William M 37

Mark Anthony 340

Marseilles 37

Martin, Sir Samuel 16, 321, 331, 332, 364

May, Charles 25

Mayhew, Henry 23

McLellan, Samuel 152

Melbourne 35, 291, 379, 380

Merino wool 34

Metcalfe, Mr 16, 79, 80, 81, 83, 85, 87, 88, 89, 90, 91, 92, 93, 94, 95, 96, 97, 98, 99, 100, 101, 102, 116, 117, 118, 119, 120, 121, 130, 131, 133, 134, 135, 136, 137, 139, 140, 212

Middle Temple 43, 194

Millbank Penitentiary 29

Molash 348, 349

Moon, Sir Francis Graham 212
Mordaunt 86, 296
Morning Chronicle, The 281, 341, 381
Morning Herald, The 278, 281, 381
Morning Post, The 147, 166, 252, 381
Morning Star, The 166, 252, 278, 280, 381
Morris, Mr 47

N

Naples 37
Napoleonic War 31
National Association for the Advancement of Social Science in Birmingham 51
National Orphan Home 51
National Society for Promoting the Education of the Poor, The 48
Newcastle under Lyme 41
Newgate Prison 9, 59, 86, 145, 146, 147, 148, 152, 199, 200, 202, 211, 213, 224, 272, 273, 274, 368, 369
Newman, John Henry 40
New South Wales 34, 37, 38, 39, 60, 62, 168, 291, 379, 381
New South Wales Magazine, The 38
Nightingale, Florence 59
Norfolk Island 34

O

Oakum 26, 147, 148, 200
Observer, The 147, 195, 252, 272, 381
Old Bailey 9, 10, 84, 87, 151, 209, 285, 290, 373
Oliver, Augusta 201
Oliver Twist 52
Onslow, Richard 43, 44, 74, 77, 142, 162, 184, 185, 216, 219, 220, 228, 269, 326, 358

Oppidans 32
Osborne House 273
Oxford 11, 37, 40, 193, 349, 379, 380
Oxford Movement 40

P

Paddington 67, 154, 180, 246, 248, 250, 252
Page, Lewis 43
Paglesham 351, 352, 353, 380
Palmerston, Viscount 17, 199, 273
Paris 37
Parsons, William H 152
Peel, Lawrence 33
Peel, Sir Robert 33, 199
Peel, Sir Robert, 3rd Baronet 199
Pennington 348
Penrhyn, Captain Sylvester 144
Pentonville Prison 20, 21, 26, 27, 28
Perceval, Spencer 56
Persian Gulf 30
Peter Green 342, 380
Pharaoh 354
Philanthropist, The 59, 60, 61, 62, 63, 64, 165, 167, 206, 353, 368, 381
Phillips, Mr Commissioner 49
Phrenology 38
Pisa 37
Plato 38
Plummer, Caroline 10, 17, 66, 68, 69, 70, 71, 72, 76, 130, 131, 132, 133, 134, 135, 136, 137, 138, 139, 140, 141, 143, 148, 153, 154, 155, 157, 158, 159, 160, 161, 170, 175, 176, 189, 215, 221, 223, 225, 235, 242, 243, 244, 245, 246, 247, 248, 249, 250, 252, 253, 255, 263, 284, 285, 293, 325, 358, 359, 361, 362, 363, 371, 372

Plummer, Mary Eugenia  9, 10, 12, 13, 15, 16, 17, 66, 67, 68, 69, 74, 79, 80, 81, 83, 84, 87, 88, 89, 90, 91, 92, 93, 94, 95, 96, 97, 98, 99, 100, 101, 102, 103, 104, 105, 106, 107, 108, 109, 110, 111, 112, 113, 114, 115, 116, 117, 118, 119, 120, 121, 130, 131, 132, 133, 138, 141, 143, 144, 148, 149, 153, 154, 155, 156, 157, 158, 159, 160, 161, 168, 169, 170, 171, 172, 173, 174, 176, 177, 179, 183, 193, 194, 199, 202, 209, 210, 211, 212, 213, 215, 216, 217, 218, 220, 221, 222, 223, 224, 225, 226, 227, 228, 229, 230, 232, 233, 234, 235, 236, 237, 238, 240, 241, 242, 243, 244, 245, 246, 247, 248, 249, 250, 251, 253, 254, 255, 256, 257, 261, 262, 263, 265, 267, 268, 269, 270, 272, 273, 274, 275, 276, 277, 278, 279, 280, 281, 282, 285, 290, 291, 292, 293, 298, 300, 301, 302, 303, 308, 309, 311, 312, 313, 316, 321, 325, 327, 330, 351, 357, 358, 359, 361, 362, 363, 364, 365, 366, 370, 371, 372

Plummer, Stephana Augusta  9, 13, 17, 67, 69, 84, 87, 101, 115, 116, 118, 122, 123, 124, 125, 126, 127, 128, 129, 130, 135, 139, 141, 148, 158, 160, 161, 169, 171, 183, 209, 212, 216, 217, 218, 222, 225, 229, 238, 239, 240, 241, 242, 243, 244, 245, 248, 249, 251, 260, 270, 293, 308, 325, 357, 366, 371, 372

Plummer, Thomas  12, 17, 66, 74, 75, 90, 151, 174, 191, 249, 252, 253, 292, 362, 371

Plunkett, John Hubert  40
Plutarch  38
Pollock, Mr Charles  298
Pollock, Sir Frederick  16, 297, 318, 321, 364
Poplar  75, 162, 219, 220, 225, 226, 228, 274, 336, 358
Port Jackson  34
Port Phillip  34, 35
Pratt, James  254
Pratt, Walters Freake  12, 15, 16, 17, 77, 78, 142, 163, 164, 180, 181, 182, 183, 184, 185, 186, 187, 188, 189, 190, 191, 192, 193, 194, 200, 202, 209, 212, 220, 222, 240, 244, 250, 254, 255, 256, 257, 290, 358, 359, 360, 361, 370
Prince Albert  273
Prince of Wales  86, 296

Q
Queen's Bench  182, 183, 191, 212, 255, 298, 374

R
Raffiel, Leonie  66, 230, 231, 235
Raffiel, Valerie  66, 231, 235
Reed, Mary Ann  210, 229, 231, 232, 235, 362
Reformatory and Refuge Union  51
Riddell, D  37
Rider, Frances Jane  30
Rider, William  30
Ridler's Hotel  77, 78, 184, 222, 255
Roach, River  350, 351
Robinson, Mr  17, 85, 87, 308, 326, 338
Rochford  352, 353
Rome  31, 37, 281, 354

Rouen 37
Rowe, W S 43
Royal Pardon 9, 196, 197, 199, 273, 288, 292, 360, 366, 370
Ryde 144
Ryegate 53

**S**

Saul, Charles 152
Scutari 59
Separate System 19, 20, 22, 23, 24, 28, 51, 146, 358, 369
Serjeant-at-Law 85, 182
Shaftsbury, Earl of 201
Shakespeare 38
Shee, Serjeant 17, 212, 213, 214, 216, 217, 218, 219, 220, 227, 229, 230, 232, 233, 234, 235, 236, 237, 238, 242, 259, 261, 298, 304, 305, 307, 309, 332
Silent System 19
Simpson, Isabella 40
Smethurst, Thomas 17, 166, 195, 196, 197, 198, 199, 283, 287, 361
Southampton 37, 239, 246, 247
Southend 37, 353
Spiller, Susan 176
Sri Lanka 64
St Andrew's Church 40
Stead, William 53
Stephen, Sir Alfred 37, 40
Stepney 51
St James' Palace 273
St John's College 64
St Leonard's 356
St Mary's 31, 351
Stocks, James Staniland 350
St Paul 354
St Peter's 348
Strachey, Litton 33
Strand 348
Strong, Joseph B 152

St Thomas's College, Colombo 64
Suez 37
Sumner, Dr Charles 17, 85
Sutton 9, 10, 30, 31, 34, 39, 41, 42, 44, 45, 46, 47, 48, 49, 52, 53, 54, 55, 56, 57, 58, 64, 201, 298, 348, 349, 350, 368, 375, 379
Swindon 66, 67, 68, 250
Sydney 34, 35, 36, 37, 38, 39, 40, 41, 42, 62, 218, 220, 353, 379, 380
Sydney Morning Herald, The 37

**T**

Talke 41
Taylor, Constable, William 17, 77, 78, 141, 164, 188, 256, 369
Taylor, Mr Pitt 289
Thackeray 85
The Iron Chest 262
The Paglesham Oyster 353
Times, The 9, 17, 20, 42, 47, 49, 65, 86, 167, 180, 195, 197, 198, 199, 204, 209, 252, 272, 275, 277, 278, 279, 281, 288, 289, 290, 295, 301, 337, 338, 339, 340, 341, 342, 348, 349, 353, 360, 361, 381
Townshend, Thomas 34
Tranby Croft scandal, The 296
Treadwheel 24, 26
Trelawney, Sir John 198
Trollope 85
Tulkinghorn, Mr 87

**U**

University Life Assurance Society 352
USA 34

**V**

Van Diemen's Land 34
Venice 38

Vernon, Reverend  48
Victoria, Queen  48, 274, 331, 345
Virgil  38

**W**

Walker, Thomas  37, 38
Walton on Thames  29, 31, 60, 220
Wandsworth Prison  9, 13, 22, 23,
        24, 26, 27, 28, 29, 42, 43, 44,
        49, 50, 51, 59, 63, 64, 67, 69,
        73, 74, 84, 142, 144, 147, 152,
        158, 161, 164, 168, 169, 171,
        180, 183, 184, 188, 194, 214,
        215, 219, 221, 229, 238, 243,
        244, 250, 252, 256, 269, 274,
        306, 326, 358, 379
Wasbrough, Frances  371
Wasbrough, Rice  371, 372
Weatherhead, Mr  277
Webb, Mr  47
Westbury on Trym  371
Weston Super Mare  371
Wexford, Samuel  46
Whittington, Richard  146
Wightman, Sir William  17, 187, 190,
        360
Wilde, Oscar  296
Wilkinson, Charles  144
Wilkinson, Mr C N  180
Williams, Captain  25
Winchester, Bishop of  12, 17, 46, 49,
        69, 85, 142, 161, 216, 218,
        235, 291, 297, 306
Windsor  30
Wise, Edward  37, 62, 144, 180, 203,
        274, 291
Wise, George, JP  37
Wiseman, James  353
Wooley, Matilda  201